Information Technology Management

Information Technology Management

Edited by
Hamza Lowe

Larsen & Keller
www.larsen-keller.com

Information Technology Management
Edited by Hamza Lowe
ISBN: 978-1-63549-152-4 (Hardback)

© 2017 Larsen & Keller

☰ Larsen & Keller

Published by Larsen and Keller Education,
5 Penn Plaza,
19th Floor,
New York, NY 10001, USA

Cataloging-in-Publication Data

Information technology management / edited by Hamza Lowe.
    p. cm.
Includes bibliographical references and index.
ISBN 978-1-63549-152-4
1. Information technology--Management. 2. Information Technology.
3. Information resources management. I. Lowe, Hamza.
T58.64 .I54 2017
658.403 8--dc23

The publisher's policy is to use permanent paper from mills that operate a sustainable forestry policy. Furthermore, the publisher ensures that the text paper and cover boards used have met acceptable environmental accreditation standards.

Printed and bound in the United States of America.

For more information regarding Larsen and Keller Education and its products, please visit the publisher's website www.larsen-keller.com

Table of Contents

Preface   **VII**

Chapter 1   **An Overview of Information Technology**   **1**
            i. Information Technology   1
            ii. Computer Science   7
            iii. Information and Communications Technology   19

Chapter 2   **Tools and Techniques in Information Technology**   **27**
            i. Information Retrieval   27
            ii. Information Retrieval Facility   39
            iii. Data Mining   54
            iv. Information Extraction   65
            v. Data Storage Device   70
            vi. Data Transmission   79

Chapter 3   **Information Management and its Methods**   **86**
            i. Information Management   86
            ii. IBM Information Management System   93
            iii. Data Modeling   97
            iv. Computer Data Storage   105
            v. Ontology (Information Science)   116
            vi. Knowledge Organization   129
            vii. Strategic Management   133
            viii. Content Management   162
            ix. Information Society   165
            x. Data Processing   176

Chapter 4   **General Aspects of Information Technology**   **179**
            i. Information Access   179
            ii. Information Architecture   180
            iii. Philosophy of Information   202
            iv. Cluster Analysis   205
            v. Software   221
            vi. Internet   229

Chapter 5   **Information System: An Overview**   **255**
            i. Information System   255
            ii. Management Information System   264

Permissions

Index

Preface

As a part of information and communications technology, information technology refers to the science of using Internet and computers to store, transmit and manipulate data. Though the term predominantly deals with computers and networking devices, development of compatible technology has expanded the subject to include television, telephones, tablets, smart watches, etc. This book attempts to understand the multiple branches that fall under the discipline of information technology and management and how such concepts have practical applications. It is a valuable compilation of topics, ranging from the basic to the most complex theories and principles in this field. For someone with an interest and eye for detail, this text covers the most significant ideas and technologies about this subject matter.

To facilitate a deeper understanding of the contents of this book a short introduction of every chapter is written below:

Chapter 1- The application of computers and the Internet to transmit and control data is known as information technology. The industries related with information management are computer hardware, semiconductors, telecom equipment and e-commerce. This chapter will provide an integrated understanding of information technology.

Chapter 2- Tools and techniques are important components in any field of study. The main techniques used in the field of information technology are information retrieval, information retrieval facility, data mining, data storage device, data transmission etc. The following section elucidates the various tools and techniques that are related to information technology.

Chapter 3- The following section discusses information management, IBM information management system, data modeling, computer data storage and data processing. It gives an overview of the theories andtechniques related to information management. The chapter strategically encompasses and incorporates the methods associated with this field.

Chapter 4- The general aspects of information technology are information access, information architecture, cluster analysis, software etc. Information access covers topics such as informatics, information science, language technology and library science. Information architecture is the structure of the information shared between communities of software. This chapter has bee carefully written to provide an easy understanding of the varied facets of information technology.

Chapter 5- An information system is an organized system that is mainly used in collecting and storing information. The management of this information is done by the processes laid out by management information systems. The section on information system is an overview of the subject matter incorporating all the major aspects of information system.

Finally, I would like to thank the entire team involved in the inception of this book for their valuable time and contribution. This book would not have been possible without their efforts. I would also like to thank my friends and family for their constant support.

Editor

An Overview of Information Technology

The application of computers and the Internet to transmit and control data is known as information technology. The industries related with information management are computer hardware, semiconductors, telecom equipment and e-commerce. This chapter will provide an integrated understanding of information technology.

Information Technology

Information technology (IT) is the application of computers to store, retrieve, transmit and manipulate data, often in the context of a business or other enterprise. IT is considered a subset of information and communications technology (ICT). In 2012, Zuppo proposed an ICT hierarchy where each hierarchy level "contain some degree of commonality in that they are related to technologies that facilitate the transfer of information and various types of electronically mediated communications." Business/IT was one level of the ICT hierarchy.

The term is commonly used as a synonym for computers and computer networks, but it also encompasses other information distribution technologies such as television and telephones. Several industries are associated with information technology, including computer hardware, software, electronics, semiconductors, internet, telecom equipment, engineering, healthcare, e-commerce and computer services.

Humans have been storing, retrieving, manipulating and communicating information since the Sumerians in Mesopotamia developed writing in about 3000 BC, but the term information technology in its modern sense first appeared in a 1958 article published in the Harvard Business Review; authors Harold J. Leavitt and Thomas L. Whisler commented that "the new technology does not yet have a single established name. We shall call it information technology (IT)." Their definition consists of three categories: techniques for processing, the application of statistical and mathematical methods to decision-making, and the simulation of higher-order thinking through computer programs.

Based on the storage and processing technologies employed, it is possible to distinguish four distinct phases of IT development: pre-mechanical (3000 BC – 1450 AD), mechanical (1450–1840), electromechanical (1840–1940) electronic (1940–present), and moreover, IT as a service. This article focuses on the most recent period (electronic), which began in about 1940.

History of Computer Technology

Zuse Z3 replica on display at Deutsches Museum in Munich. The Zuse Z3 is the first programmable computer.

Devices have been used to aid computation for thousands of years, probably initially in the form of a tally stick. The Antikythera mechanism, dating from about the beginning of the first century BC, is generally considered to be the earliest known mechanical analog computer, and the earliest known geared mechanism. Comparable geared devices did not emerge in Europe until the 16th century, and it was not until 1645 that the first mechanical calculator capable of performing the four basic arithmetical operations was developed.

Electronic computers, using either relays or valves, began to appear in the early 1940s. The electromechanical Zuse Z3, completed in 1941, was the world's first programmable computer, and by modern standards one of the first machines that could be considered a complete computing machine. Colossus, developed during the Second World War to decrypt German messages was the first electronic digital computer. Although it was programmable, it was not general-purpose, being designed to perform only a single task. It also lacked the ability to store its program in memory; programming was carried out using plugs and switches to alter the internal wiring. The first recognisably modern electronic digital stored-program computer was the Manchester Small-Scale Experimental Machine (SSEM), which ran its first program on 21 June 1948.

The development of transistors in the late 1940s at Bell Laboratories allowed a new generation of computers to be designed with greatly reduced power consumption. The first commercially available stored-program computer, the Ferranti Mark I, contained 4050 valves and had a power consumption of 25 kilowatts. By comparison the first transistorised computer, developed at the University of Manchester and operational by November 1953, consumed only 150 watts in its final version.

Data Processing

Data storage

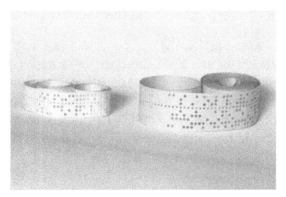

Punched tapes that were used in early computers to represent data.

Early electronic computers such as Colossus made use of punched tape, a long strip of paper on which data was represented by a series of holes, a technology now obsolete. Electronic data storage, which is used in modern computers, dates from World War II, when a form of delay line memory was developed to remove the clutter from radar signals, the first practical application of which was the mercury delay line. The first random-access digital storage device was the Williams tube, based on a standard cathode ray tube, but the information stored in it and delay line memory was volatile in that it had to be continuously refreshed, and thus was lost once power was removed. The earliest form of non-volatile computer storage was the magnetic drum, invented in 1932 and used in the Ferranti Mark 1, the world's first commercially available general-purpose electronic computer.

IBM introduced the first hard disk drive in 1956, as a component of their 305 RAMAC computer system. Most digital data today is still stored magnetically on hard disks, or optically on media such as CD-ROMs. Until 2002 most information was stored on analog devices, but that year digital storage capacity exceeded analog for the first time. As of 2007 almost 94% of the data stored worldwide was held digitally: 52% on hard disks, 28% on optical devices and 11% on digital magnetic tape. It has been estimated that the worldwide capacity to store information on electronic devices grew from less than 3 exabytes in 1986 to 295 exabytes in 2007, doubling roughly every 3 years.

Databases

Database management systems emerged in the 1960s to address the problem of storing and retrieving large amounts of data accurately and quickly. One of the earliest such systems was IBM's Information Management System (IMS), which is still widely deployed more than 40 years later. IMS stores data hierarchically, but in the 1970s Ted Codd proposed an alternative relational storage model based on set theory and predicate logic and the familiar concepts of tables, rows and columns. The first commercially available relational database management system (RDBMS) was available from Oracle in 1980.

All database management systems consist of a number of components that together allow the data they store to be accessed simultaneously by many users while maintaining its integrity. A characteristic of all databases is that the structure of the data they contain is defined and stored separately from the data itself, in a database schema.

The extensible markup language (XML) has become a popular format for data representation in recent years. Although XML data can be stored in normal file systems, it is commonly held in relational databases to take advantage of their "robust implementation verified by years of both theoretical and practical effort". As an evolution of the Standard Generalized Markup Language (SGML), XML's text-based structure offers the advantage of being both machine and human-readable.

Data Retrieval

The relational database model introduced a programming-language independent Structured Query Language (SQL), based on relational algebra.

The terms "data" and "information" are not synonymous. Anything stored is data, but it only becomes information when it is organized and presented meaningfully. Most of the world's digital data is unstructured, and stored in a variety of different physical formats[b] even within a single organization. Data warehouses began to be developed in the 1980s to integrate these disparate stores. They typically contain data extracted from various sources, including external sources such as the Internet, organized in such a way as to facilitate decision support systems (DSS).

Data Transmission

Data transmission has three aspects: transmission, propagation, and reception. It can be broadly categorized as broadcasting, in which information is transmitted unidirectionally downstream, or telecommunications, with bidirectional upstream and downstream channels.

XML has been increasingly employed as a means of data interchange since the early 2000s, particularly for machine-oriented interactions such as those involved in web-oriented protocols such as SOAP, describing "data-in-transit rather than ... data-at-rest". One of the challenges of such usage is converting data from relational databases into XML Document Object Model (DOM) structures.

Data Manipulation

Hilbert and Lopez identify the exponential pace of technological change (a kind of Moore's law): machines' application-specific capacity to compute information per capita roughly doubled every 14 months between 1986 and 2007; the per capita capacity of the world's general-purpose computers doubled every 18 months during the same two decades; the global telecommunication capacity per capita doubled every 34 months;

the world's storage capacity per capita required roughly 40 months to double (every 3 years); and per capita broadcast information has doubled every 12.3 years.

Massive amounts of data are stored worldwide every day, but unless it can be analysed and presented effectively it essentially resides in what have been called data tombs: "data archives that are seldom visited". To address that issue, the field of data mining – «the process of discovering interesting patterns and knowledge from large amounts of data» – emerged in the late 1980s.

Perspective

Academic Perspective

In an academic context, the Association for Computing Machinery defines IT as "undergraduate degree programs that prepare students to meet the computer technology needs of business, government, healthcare, schools, and other kinds of organizations .... IT specialists assume responsibility for selecting hardware and software products appropriate for an organization, integrating those products with organizational needs and infrastructure, and installing, customizing, and maintaining those applications for the organization's computer users."

Commercial and Employment Perspective

In a business context, the Information Technology Association of America has defined information technology as "the study, design, development, application, implementation, support or management of computer-based information systems". The responsibilities of those working in the field include network administration, software development and installation, and the planning and management of an organization's technology life cycle, by which hardware and software are maintained, upgraded and replaced.

The business value of information technology lies in the automation of business processes, provision of information for decision making, connecting businesses with their customers, and the provision of productivity tools to increase efficiency.

Worldwide IT spending forecast (billions of U.S. dollars)		
Category	2014 spending	2015 spending
Devices	685	725
Data center systems	140	144
	321	344
	967	1,007
Telecom services	1,635	1,668
Total	3,748	3,888

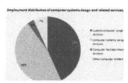

Employment distribution of computer systems design and related services, 2011

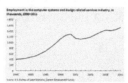

Employment in the computer systems and design related services industry, in thousands, 1990-2011

Occupational growth and wages in computer systems design and related services, 2010-2020

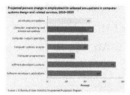

Projected percent change in employment in selected occupations in computer systems design and related services, 2010-2020

Projected average annual percent change in output and employment in selected industries, 2010-2020

Ethical Perspective

The field of information ethics was established by mathematician Norbert Wiener in the 1940s. Some of the ethical issues associated with the use of information technology include:

- Breaches of copyright by those downloading files stored without the permission of the copyright holders

- Employers monitoring their employees' emails and other Internet usage

- Unsolicited emails

- Hackers accessing online databases

- Web sites installing cookies or spyware to monitor a user's online activities

Computer Science

Computer science is the scientific and practical approach to computation and its applications. It is the systematic study of the feasibility, structure, expression, and mechanization of the methodical procedures (or algorithms) that underlie the acquisition, representation, processing, storage, communication of, and access to information. An alternate, more succinct definition of computer science is the study of automating algorithmic processes that scale. A computer scientist specializes in the theory of computation and the design of computational systems.

Its fields can be divided into a variety of theoretical and practical disciplines. Some fields, such as computational complexity theory (which explores the fundamental properties of computational and intractable problems), are highly abstract, while fields such as computer graphics emphasize real-world visual applications. Still other fields focus on challenges in implementing computation. For example, programming language theory considers various approaches to the description of computation, while the study of computer programming itself investigates various aspects of the use of programming language and complex systems. Human–computer interaction considers the challenges in making computers and computations useful, usable, and universally accessible to humans.

History

Charles Babbage is credited with inventing the first mechanical computer.

The earliest foundations of what would become computer science predate the invention of the modern digital computer. Machines for calculating fixed numerical tasks such as the abacus have existed since antiquity, aiding in computations such as multiplication and division. Further, algorithms for performing computations have existed since antiquity, even before the development of sophisticated computing equipment. The ancient Sanskrit treatise Shulba Sutras, or "Rules of the Chord", is a book of algorithms written in 800 BC for constructing geometric objects like altars using a peg and chord, an early precursor of the modern field of computational geometry.

Ada Lovelace is credited with writing the first algorithm intended for processing on a computer.

Blaise Pascal designed and constructed the first working mechanical calculator, Pascal's calculator, in 1642. In 1673, Gottfried Leibniz demonstrated a digital mechanical calculator, called the Stepped Reckoner. He may be considered the first computer scientist and information theorist, for, among other reasons, documenting the binary number system. In 1820, Thomas de Colmar launched the mechanical calculator industry[note 1] when he released his simplified arithmometer, which was the first calculating machine strong enough and reliable enough to be used daily in an office environment. Charles Babbage started the design of the first automatic mechanical calculator, his Difference Engine, in 1822, which eventually gave him the idea of the first programmable mechanical calculator, his Analytical Engine. He started developing this machine in 1834 and "in less than two years he had sketched out many of the salient features of the modern computer". "A crucial step was the adoption of a punched card system derived from the Jacquard loom" making it infinitely programmable.[note 2] In 1843, during the translation of a French article on the Analytical Engine, Ada Lovelace wrote, in one of the many notes she included, an algorithm to compute the Bernoulli numbers, which is considered to be the first computer program. Around 1885, Herman Hollerith invented the tabulator, which used punched cards to process statistical information; eventually his company became part of IBM. In 1937, one hundred years after Babbage's impossible dream, Howard Aiken convinced IBM, which was making all kinds of punched card equipment and was also in the calculator business to develop his giant programmable calculator, the ASCC/Harvard Mark I, based on Babbage's Analytical Engine, which itself used cards and a central computing unit. When the machine was finished, some hailed it as "Babbage's dream come true".

During the 1940s, as new and more powerful computing machines were developed, the term computer came to refer to the machines rather than their human predecessors. As it became clear that computers could be used for more than just mathematical calculations, the field of computer science broadened to study computation in general. Computer science began to be established as a distinct academic discipline in the 1950s and early 1960s. The world's first computer science degree program, the Cambridge Diploma in Computer Science, began at the University of Cambridge Computer Laboratory in 1953. The first computer science degree program in the United States was formed at Purdue University in 1962. Since practical computers became available, many applications of computing have become distinct areas of study in their own rights.

Although many initially believed it was impossible that computers themselves could actually be a scientific field of study, in the late fifties it gradually became accepted among the greater academic population. It is the now well-known IBM brand that formed part of the computer science revolution during this time. IBM (short for International Business Machines) released the IBM 704 and later the IBM 709 computers, which were widely used during the exploration period of such devices. "Still, working with the IBM [computer] was frustrating [...] if you had misplaced as much as one letter in one instruction, the program would crash, and you would have to start the whole process over again". During the late 1950s, the computer science discipline was very much in its developmental stages, and such issues were commonplace.

Time has seen significant improvements in the usability and effectiveness of computing technology. Modern society has seen a significant shift in the users of computer technology, from usage only by experts and professionals, to a near-ubiquitous user base. Initially, computers were quite costly, and some degree of human aid was needed for efficient use—in part from professional computer operators. As computer adoption became more widespread and affordable, less human assistance was needed for common usage.

Contributions

The German military used the Enigma machine (shown here) during World War II for communications they wanted kept secret. The large-scale decryption of Enigma traffic at Bletchley Park was an important factor that contributed to Allied victory in WWII.

Despite its short history as a formal academic discipline, computer science has made a number of fundamental contributions to science and society—in fact, along with electronics, it is a founding science of the current epoch of human history called the Information Age and a driver of the Information Revolution, seen as the third major leap in human technological progress after the Industrial Revolution (1750–1850 CE) and the Agricultural Revolution (8000–5000 BC).

These contributions include:

- The start of the "digital revolution", which includes the current Information Age and the Internet.

- A formal definition of computation and computability, and proof that there are computationally unsolvable and intractable problems.

- The concept of a programming language, a tool for the precise expression of methodological information at various levels of abstraction.

- In cryptography, breaking the Enigma code was an important factor contributing to the Allied victory in World War II.

- Scientific computing enabled practical evaluation of processes and situations of great complexity, as well as experimentation entirely by software. It also enabled advanced study of the mind, and mapping of the human genome became possible with the Human Genome Project. Distributed computing projects such as Folding@home explore protein folding.

- Algorithmic trading has increased the efficiency and liquidity of financial markets by using artificial intelligence, machine learning, and other statistical and numerical techniques on a large scale. High frequency algorithmic trading can also exacerbate volatility.

- Computer graphics and computer-generated imagery have become ubiquitous in modern entertainment, particularly in television, cinema, advertising, animation and video games. Even films that feature no explicit CGI are usually "filmed" now on digital cameras, or edited or post-processed using a digital video editor.

- Simulation of various processes, including computational fluid dynamics, physical, electrical, and electronic systems and circuits, as well as societies and social situations (notably war games) along with their habitats, among many others. Modern computers enable optimization of such designs as complete aircraft. Notable in electrical and electronic circuit design are SPICE, as well as software for physical realization of new (or modified) designs. The latter includes essential design software for integrated circuits.

- Artificial intelligence is becoming increasingly important as it gets more efficient and complex. There are many applications of AI, some of which can be seen at home, such as robotic vacuum cleaners. It is also present in video games and on the modern battlefield in drones, anti-missile systems, and squad support robots.

Etymology

Although first proposed in 1956, the term "computer science" appears in a 1959 article in Communications of the ACM, in which Louis Fein argues for the creation of a Graduate School in Computer Sciences analogous to the creation of Harvard Business School in 1921, justifying the name by arguing that, like management science, the subject is applied and interdisciplinary in nature, while having the characteristics typical of an academic discipline. His efforts, and those of others such as numerical analyst George Forsythe, were rewarded: universities went on to create such programs, starting with Purdue in 1962. Despite its name, a significant amount of computer science does not involve the study of computers themselves. Because of this, several alternative names have been proposed. Certain departments of major universities prefer the term computing science, to emphasize precisely that difference. Danish scientist Peter Naur suggested the term datalogy, to reflect the fact that the scientific discipline revolves around data and data treatment, while not necessarily involving computers. The first scientific institution to use the term was the Department of Datalogy at the University of Copenhagen, founded in 1969, with Peter Naur being the first professor in datalogy. The term is used mainly in the Scandinavian countries. An alternative term, also proposed by Naur, is data science; this is now used for a distinct field of data analysis, including statistics and databases.

Also, in the early days of computing, a number of terms for the practitioners of the field of computing were suggested in the Communications of the ACM—turingineer, turologist, flow-charts-man, applied meta-mathematician, and applied epistemologist. Three months later in the same journal, comptologist was suggested, followed next year by hypologist. The term computics has also been suggested. In Europe, terms derived from contracted translations of the expression "automatic information" (e.g. "informazione automatica" in Italian) or "information and mathematics" are often used, e.g. informatique (French), Informatik (German), informatica (Italian, Dutch), informática (Spanish, Portuguese), informatika (Slavic languages and Hungarian) or pliroforiki (which means informatics) in Greek. Similar words have also been adopted in the UK (as in the School of Informatics of the University of Edinburgh). "In the U.S., however, informatics is linked with applied computing, or computing in the context of another domain."

A folkloric quotation, often attributed to—but almost certainly not first formulated by—Edsger Dijkstra, states that "computer science is no more about computers than astronomy is about telescopes." The design and deployment of computers and computer systems is generally considered the province of disciplines other than computer science. For example, the study of computer hardware is usually considered part of computer engineering, while the study of commercial computer systems and their deployment is often called information technology or information systems. However, there has been much cross-fertilization of ideas between the various computer-related disciplines. Computer science research also often intersects other disciplines, such as philosophy, cognitive science, linguistics, mathematics, physics, biology, statistics, and logic.

Computer science is considered by some to have a much closer relationship with mathematics than many scientific disciplines, with some observers saying that computing is a mathematical science. Early computer science was strongly influenced by the work of mathematicians such as Kurt Gödel and Alan Turing, and there continues to be a useful interchange of ideas between the two fields in areas such as mathematical logic, category theory, domain theory, and algebra.

The relationship between computer science and software engineering is a contentious issue, which is further muddied by disputes over what the term "software engineering" means, and how computer science is defined. David Parnas, taking a cue from the relationship between other engineering and science disciplines, has claimed that the principal focus of computer science is studying the properties of computation in general, while the principal focus of software engineering is the design of specific computations to achieve practical goals, making the two separate but complementary disciplines.

The academic, political, and funding aspects of computer science tend to depend on whether a department formed with a mathematical emphasis or with an engineering emphasis. Computer science departments with a mathematics emphasis and with a numerical orientation consider alignment with computational science. Both types of departments tend to make efforts to bridge the field educationally if not across all research.

Philosophy

A number of computer scientists have argued for the distinction of three separate paradigms in computer science. Peter Wegner argued that those paradigms are science, technology, and mathematics. Peter Denning's working group argued that they are theory, abstraction (modeling), and design. Amnon H. Eden described them as the "rationalist paradigm" (which treats computer science as a branch of mathematics, which is prevalent in theoretical computer science, and mainly employs deductive reasoning), the "technocratic paradigm" (which might be found in engineering approaches, most prominently in software engineering), and the "scientific paradigm" (which approaches computer-related artifacts from the empirical perspective of natural sciences, identifiable in some branches of artificial intelligence).

Areas of Computer Science

As a discipline, computer science spans a range of topics from theoretical studies of algorithms and the limits of computation to the practical issues of implementing computing systems in hardware and software. CSAB, formerly called Computing Sciences Accreditation Board—which is made up of representatives of the Association for Computing Machinery (ACM), and the IEEE Computer Society (IEEE CS)—identifies four areas that it considers crucial to the discipline of computer science: theory of computation, algorithms and data structures, programming methodology and languages, and computer elements and architecture. In addition to these four areas, CSAB also identifies fields such as software engineering, artificial intelligence, computer networking and communication, database systems, parallel computation, distributed computation, human–computer interaction, computer graphics, operating systems, and numerical and symbolic computation as being important areas of computer science.

Theoretical Computer Science

Theoretical Computer Science is mathematical and abstract in spirit, but it derives its motivation from practical and everyday computation. Its aim is to understand the nature of computation and, as a consequence of this understanding, provide more efficient methodologies. All papers introducing or studying mathematical, logic and formal concepts and methods are welcome, provided that their motivation is clearly drawn from the field of computing.

Theory of Computation

According to Peter Denning, the fundamental question underlying computer science is, "What can be (efficiently) automated?" Theory of computation is focused on answering fundamental questions about what can be computed and what amount of resources are required to perform those computations. In an effort to answer the first question, computability theory examines which computational problems are solvable on various theoretical models of computation. The second question is addressed by computational complexity theory, which studies the time and space costs associated with different approaches to solving a multitude of computational problems.

The famous P = NP? problem, one of the Millennium Prize Problems, is an open problem in the theory of computation.

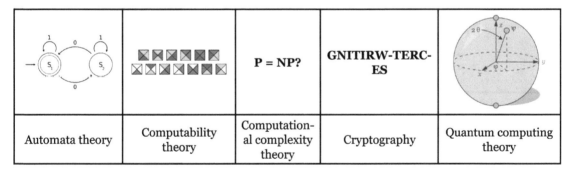

Automata theory	Computability theory	Computational complexity theory	Cryptography	Quantum computing theory

Information and Coding Theory

Information theory is related to the quantification of information. This was developed by Claude Shannon to find fundamental limits on signal processing operations such as compressing data and on reliably storing and communicating data. Coding theory is the study of the properties of codes (systems for converting information from one form to another) and their fitness for a specific application. Codes are used for data compression, cryptography, error detection and correction, and more recently also for network coding. Codes are studied for the purpose of designing efficient and reliable data transmission methods.

Algorithms and Data Structures

Algorithms and data structures is the study of commonly used computational methods and their computational efficiency.

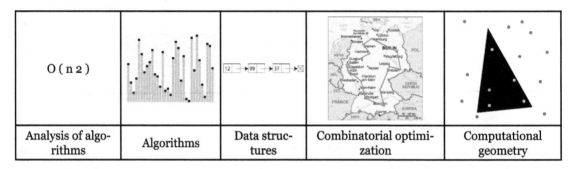

$O(n2)$	Algorithms	Data structures	Combinatorial optimization	Computational geometry
Analysis of algorithms				

Programming language Theory

Programming language theory is a branch of computer science that deals with the design, implementation, analysis, characterization, and classification of programming languages and their individual features. It falls within the discipline of computer science, both depending on and affecting mathematics, software engineering, and linguistics. It is an active research area, with numerous dedicated academic journals.

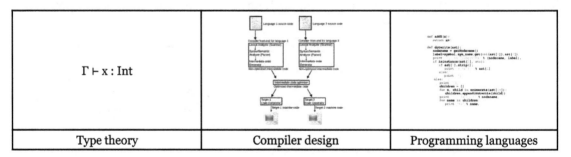

$\Gamma \vdash x : Int$		
Type theory	Compiler design	Programming languages

Formal methods

Formal methods are a particular kind of mathematically based technique for the specification, development and verification of software and hardware systems. The use of formal methods for software and hardware design is motivated by the expectation that, as in other engineering disciplines, performing appropriate mathematical analysis can contribute to the reliability and robustness of a design. They form an important theoretical underpinning for software engineering, especially where safety or security is involved. Formal methods are a useful adjunct to software testing since they help avoid errors and can also give a framework for testing. For industrial use, tool support is required. However, the high cost of using formal methods means that they are usually only used in the development of high-integrity and life-critical systems, where safety or security is of utmost importance. Formal methods are best described as the application of a fairly broad variety of theoretical computer science fundamentals, in particular logic calculi, formal languages, automata theory, and program semantics, but also type systems and algebraic data types to problems in software and hardware specification and verification.

Applied Computer Science

Applied computer science aims at identifying certain computer science concepts that can be used directly in solving real world problems.

Artificial Intelligence

Artificial intelligence (AI) aims to or is required to synthesise goal-orientated processes such as problem-solving, decision-making, environmental adaptation, learning and communication found in humans and animals. From its origins in cybernetics and in the Dartmouth Conference (1956), artificial intelligence research has been necessarily cross-disciplinary, drawing on areas of expertise such as applied mathematics, symbolic logic, semiotics, electrical engineering, philosophy of mind, neurophysiology, and social intelligence. AI is associated in the popular mind with robotic development, but the main field of practical application has been as an embedded component in areas of software development, which require computational understanding. The starting-point in the late 1940s was Alan Turing's question "Can computers think?", and the question remains effectively unanswered although the Turing test is still used to assess computer output on the scale of human intelligence. But the automation of evaluative and predictive tasks has been increasingly successful as a substitute for human monitoring and intervention in domains of computer application involving complex real-world data.

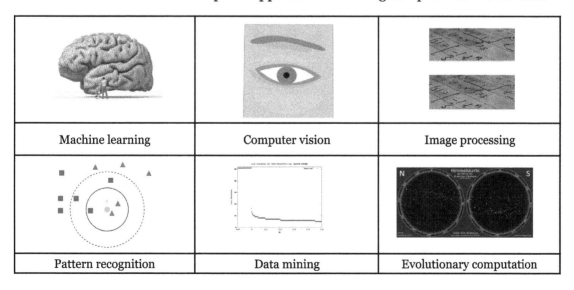

Machine learning	Computer vision	Image processing
Pattern recognition	Data mining	Evolutionary computation

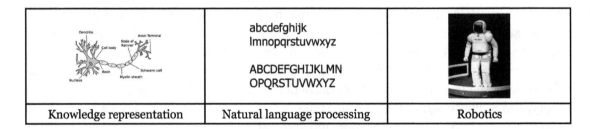

| Knowledge representation | Natural language processing | Robotics |

Computer Architecture and Engineering

Computer architecture, or digital computer organization, is the conceptual design and fundamental operational structure of a computer system. It focuses largely on the way by which the central processing unit performs internally and accesses addresses in memory. The field often involves disciplines of computer engineering and electrical engineering, selecting and interconnecting hardware components to create computers that meet functional, performance, and cost goals.

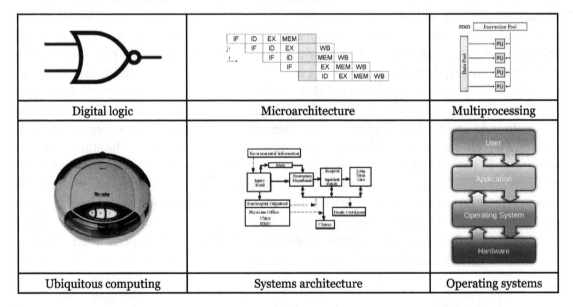

| Digital logic | Microarchitecture | Multiprocessing |
| Ubiquitous computing | Systems architecture | Operating systems |

Computer Performance Analysis

Computer performance analysis is the study of work flowing through computers with the general goals of improving throughput, controlling response time, using resources efficiently, eliminating bottlenecks, and predicting performance under anticipated peak loads.

Computer Graphics and Visualization

Computer graphics is the study of digital visual contents, and involves synthesis and manipulation of image data. The study is connected to many other fields in computer science, including computer vision, image processing, and computational geometry, and is heavily applied in the fields of special effects and video games.

Computer Security and Cryptography

Computer security is a branch of computer technology, whose objective includes protection of information from unauthorized access, disruption, or modification while maintaining the accessibility and usability of the system for its intended users. Cryptography is the practice and study of hiding (encryption) and therefore deciphering (decryption) information. Modern cryptography is largely related to computer science, for many encryption and decryption algorithms are based on their computational complexity.

Computational Science

Computational science (or scientific computing) is the field of study concerned with constructing mathematical models and quantitative analysis techniques and using computers to analyze and solve scientific problems. In practical use, it is typically the application of computer simulation and other forms of computation to problems in various scientific disciplines.

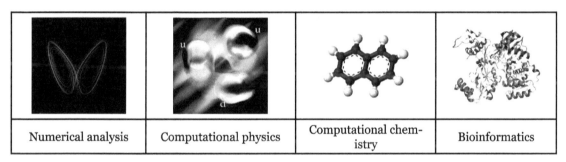

Numerical analysis	Computational physics	Computational chemistry	Bioinformatics

Computer Networks

This branch of computer science aims to manage networks between computers worldwide.

Concurrent, Parallel and Distributed Systems

Concurrency is a property of systems in which several computations are executing simultaneously, and potentially interacting with each other. A number of mathematical models have been developed for general concurrent computation including Petri nets, process calculi and the Parallel Random Access Machine model. A distributed system extends the idea of concurrency onto multiple computers connected through a network. Computers within the same distributed system have their own private memory, and information is often exchanged among themselves to achieve a common goal.

Databases

A database is intended to organize, store, and retrieve large amounts of data easily. Digital databases are managed using database management systems to store, create, maintain, and search data, through database models and query languages.

Software Engineering

Software engineering is the study of designing, implementing, and modifying software in order to ensure it is of high quality, affordable, maintainable, and fast to build. It is a systematic approach to software design, involving the application of engineering practices to software. Software engineering deals with the organizing and analyzing of software—it doesn't just deal with the creation or manufacture of new software, but its internal maintenance and arrangement. Both computer applications software engineers and computer systems software engineers are projected to be among the fastest growing occupations from 2008 to 2018.

The Great Insights of Computer Science

The philosopher of computing Bill Rapaport noted three Great Insights of Computer Science:

- Gottfried Wilhelm Leibniz's, George Boole's, Alan Turing's, Claude Shannon's, and Samuel Morse's insight: there are only two objects that a computer has to deal with in order to represent "anything".

  All the information about any computable problem can be represented using only 0 and 1 (or any other bistable pair that can flip-flop between two easily distinguishable states, such as "on/off", "magnetized/de-magnetized", "high-voltage/low-voltage", etc.).

- Alan Turing's insight: there are only five actions that a computer has to perform in order to do "anything".

  Every algorithm can be expressed in a language for a computer consisting of only five basic instructions:

    - move left one location;

    - move right one location;

    - read symbol at current location;

    - print 0 at current location;

    - print 1 at current location.

- Corrado Böhm and Giuseppe Jacopini's insight: there are only three ways of combining these actions (into more complex ones) that are needed in order for a computer to do "anything".

  Only three rules are needed to combine any set of basic instructions into more complex ones:

    - sequence: first do this, then do that;

- selection: IF such-and-such is the case, THEN do this, ELSE do that;

- repetition: WHILE such-and-such is the case DO this.

Note that the three rules of Boehm's and Jacopini's insight can be further simplified with the use of goto (which means it is more elementary than structured programming).

Academia

Conferences are important events for computer science research. During these conferences, researchers from the public and private sectors present their recent work and meet. Unlike in most other academic fields, in computer science, the prestige of conference papers is greater than that of journal publications. One proposed explanation for this is the quick development of this relatively new field requires rapid review and distribution of results, a task better handled by conferences than by journals.

Education

Since computer science is a relatively new field, it is not as widely taught in schools and universities as other academic subjects. For example, in 2014, Code.org estimated that only 10 percent of high schools in the United States offered computer science education. A 2010 report by Association for Computing Machinery (ACM) and Computer Science Teachers Association (CSTA) revealed that only 14 out of 50 states have adopted significant education standards for high school computer science. However, computer science education is growing. Some countries, such as Israel, New Zealand and South Korea, have already included computer science in their respective national secondary education curriculum. Several countries are following suit.

In most countries, there is a significant gender gap in computer science education. For example, in the US about 20% of computer science degrees in 2012 were conferred to women. This gender gap also exists in other Western countries. However, in some parts of the world, the gap is small or nonexistent. In 2011, approximately half of all computer science degrees in Malaysia were conferred to women. In 2001, women made up 54.5% of computer science graduates in Guyana.

Information and Communications Technology

Information and communications technology (ICT) is an extended term for information technology (IT) which stresses the role of unified communications and the integration of telecommunications (telephone lines and wireless signals), computers as well as necessary enterprise software, middleware, storage, and audio-visual systems, which enable users to access, store, transmit, and manipulate information.

The term ICT is also used to refer to the convergence of audio-visual and telephone networks with computer networks through a single cabling or link system. There are large economic incentives (huge cost savings due to elimination of the telephone network) to merge the telephone network with the computer network system using a single unified system of cabling, signal distribution and management.

However, ICT has no universal definition, as "the concepts, methods and applications involved in ICT are constantly evolving on an almost daily basis." The broadness of ICT covers any product that will store, retrieve, manipulate, transmit or receive information electronically in a digital form, e.g. personal computers, digital television, email, robots. For clarity, Zuppo provided an ICT hierarchy where all levels of the hierarchy "contain some degree of commonality in that they are related to technologies that facilitate the transfer of information and various types of electronically mediated communications.". Skills Framework for the Information Age is one of many models for describing and managing competencies for ICT professionals for the 21st century.

Etymology

The phrase information and communication technology has been used by academic researchers since the 1980s, and the abbreviation ICT became popular after it was used in a report to the UK government by Dennis Stevenson in 1997, and in the revised National Curriculum for England, Wales and Northern Ireland in 2000. But in 2012, the Royal Society recommended that ICT should no longer be used in British schools "as it has attracted too many negative connotations", and with effect from 2014 the National Curriculum uses the word computing, which reflects the addition of computer programming into the curriculum.

Variations of the phrase have spread worldwide, with the United Nations creating a "United Nations Information and Communication Technologies Task Force" and an internal "Office of Information and Communications Technology".

Monetization of ICT

The money spent on IT worldwide has been most recently estimated as US $3.5 trillion and is currently growing at 6% per year – doubling every 15 years. The 2014 IT budget of US federal government is nearly $82 billion. IT costs, as a percentage of corporate revenue, have grown 50% since 2002, putting a strain on IT budgets. When looking at current companies' IT budgets, 75% are recurrent costs, used to "keep the lights on" in the IT department, and 25% are cost of new initiatives for technology development.

The average IT budget has the following breakdown:

- 31% personnel costs (internal)

- 29% software costs (external/purchasing category)

- 26% hardware costs (external/purchasing category)

- 14% costs of external service providers (external/services).

Technological Capacity

The world's technological capacity to store information grew from 2.6 (optimally compressed) exabytes in 1986 to 15.8 in 1993, over 54.5 in 2000, and to 295 (optimally compressed) exabytes in 2007, and some 5 zettabytes in 2014. This is the informational equivalent to 1.25 stacks of CD-ROM from the earth to the moon in 2007, and the equivalent of 4,500 stacks of printed books from the earth to the sun in 2014. The world's technological capacity to receive information through one-way broadcast networks was 432 exabytes of (optimally compressed) information in 1986, 715 (optimally compressed) exabytes in 1993, 1.2 (optimally compressed) zettabytes in 2000, and 1.9 zettabytes in 2007. The world's effective capacity to exchange information through two-way telecommunication networks was 281 petabytes of (optimally compressed) information in 1986, 471 petabytes in 1993, 2.2 (optimally compressed) exabytes in 2000, 65 (optimally compressed) exabytes in 2007, The world's technological capacity to compute information with humanly guided general-purpose computers grew from 3.0×10^{8} MIPS in 1986, to 6.4×10^{12} MIPS in 2007. and some 100 exabytes in 2014.

ICT Sector in the OECD

The following is a list of OECD countries by share of ICT sector in total value added in 2013.

Rank	Country	ICT sector in %	Relative size
1	Korea	10.7	10.7
2	Japan	7.02	7.02
3	Ireland	6.99	6.99
4	Sweden	6.82	6.82
5	Hungary	6.09	6.09

6	United States	5.89	5.89
7	Czech Republic	5.74	5.74
8	Finland	5.60	5.6
9	United Kingdom	5.53	5.53
10	Estonia	5.33	5.33
11	Slovakia	4.87	4.87
12	Germany	4.84	4.84
13	Luxembourg	4.54	4.54
14	Netherlands	4.44	4.44
15	Switzerland	4.63	4.63
16	France	4.33	4.33
17	Slovenia	4.26	4.26
18	Denmark	4.06	4.06
19	Spain	4.00	4
20	Canada	3.86	3.86
21	Italy	3.72	3.72
22	Belgium	3.72	3.72

23	Austria	3.56	3.56
24	Portugal	3.43	3.43
25	Poland	3.33	3.33
26	Norway	3.32	3.32
27	Greece	3.31	3.31
28	Iceland	2.87	2.87
29	Mexico	2.77	2.77
30	Mongolia	2.75	2.75

ICT Development Index

The ICT Development Index ranks and compares the level of ICT use and access across the various countries around the world. In 2014 ITU (International Communications Union) released the latest rankings of the IDI, with Denmark attaining the top spot, followed by South Korea. The top 30 countries in the rankings include most high-income countries where quality of life is higher than average, which includes countries from Europe and other regions such as "Australia, Bahrain, Canada, Japan, Macao (China), New Zealand, Singapore and the United States; almost all countries surveyed improved their IDI ranking this year."

The WSIS Process and ICT Development Goals

On 21 December 2001, the United Nations General Assembly approved Resolution 56/183, endorsing the holding of the World Summit on the Information Society (WSIS) to discuss the opportunities and challenges facing today's information society. According to this resolution, the General Assembly related the Summit to the United Nations Millennium Declaration's goal of implementing ICT to achieve Millennium Development Goals. It also emphasized a multi-stakeholder approach to achieve these goals, using all stakeholders including civil society and the private sector, in addition to governments.

To help anchor and expand ICT to every habitable part of the world, "2015 is the dead-line for achievements of the UN Millennium Development Goals (MDGs), which global leaders agreed upon in the year 2000."

ICT in Education

Today's society shows the ever-growing computer-centric lifestyle, which includes the rapid influx of computers in the modern classroom.

Information and Communication Technology can contribute to universal access to education, equity in education, the delivery of quality learning and teaching, teachers' professional development and more efficient education management, governance and administration. UNESCO takes a holistic and comprehensive approach to promoting ICT in education. Access, inclusion and quality are among the main challenges they can address. The Organization's Intersectral Platform for ICT in education focuses on these issues through the joint work of three of its sectors: Communication & Information, Education and Science.

ICT Today

In modern society ICT is ever-present, with over three billion people having access to the Internet. With approximately 8 out of 10 Internet users owning a smartphone, information and data are increasing by leaps and bounds. This rapid growth, especially in developing countries, has led ICT to become a keystone of everyday life, in which life without some facet of technology renders most of clerical, work and routine tasks dysfunctional. The most recent authoritative data, released in 2014, shows "that Internet use continues to grow steadily, at 6.6% globally in 2014 (3.3% in developed countries, 8.7% in the developing world); the number of Internet users in developing countries has doubled in five years (2009-2014), with two thirds of all people online now living in the developing world."

However, hurdles are still at large. "Of the 4.3 billion people not yet using the Internet, 90% live in developing countries. In the world's 42 Least Connected Countries (LCCs), which are home to 2.5 billion people, access to ICTs remains largely out of reach, particularly for these countries' large rural populations." ICT has yet to penetrate the remote areas of some countries, with many developing countries dearth of any type of Internet. This also includes the availability of telephone lines, particularly the availability of cellular coverage, and other forms of electronic transmission of data. The latest "Measuring the Information Society Report" cautiously stated that the increase in the aforementioned cellular data coverage is ostensible, as "many users have multiple subscriptions, with global growth figures sometimes translating into little real improvement in the level of connectivity of those at the very bottom of the pyramid; an estimated 450 million people worldwide live in places which are still out of reach of mobile cellular service."

Favorably, the gap between the access to the Internet and mobile coverage has decreased substantially in the last fifteen years, in which "2015 is the deadline for achievements of the UN Millennium Development Goals (MDGs), which global leaders agreed upon in the year 2000, and the new data show ICT progress and highlight remaining gaps." ICT continues to take on new form, with nanotechnology set to usher in a new wave of ICT electronics and gadgets. ICT newest editions into the modern electronic world include smart watches, such as the Apple Watch, smart wristbands such as the Nike+ FuelBand, and smart TVs such as Google TV. With desktops soon becoming part of a bygone era, and laptops becoming the preferred method of computing, ICT continues to insinuate and alter itself in the ever-changing globe.

Information communication technologies play a role in facilitating accelerated pluralism in new social movements today. The internet according to Bruce Bimber is "accelerating the process of issue group formation and action" and coined the term accelerated pluralism to explain this new phenomena. ICTs are tools for "enabling social movement leaders and empowering dictators" in effect promoting societal change. ICTs can be used to garner grassroots support for a cause due to the internet allowing for political discourse and direct interventions with state policy as well as change the way complaints from the populace are handled by governments.

References

* Committee on the Fundamentals of Computer Science: Challenges and Opportunities, National Research Council (2004). Computer Science: Reflections on the Field, Reflections from the Field. National Academies Press. ISBN 978-0-309-09301-9.

* Zuppo, Colrain M. "Defining ICT in a Boundaryless World: The Development of a Working Hierarchy" (PDF). International Journal of Managing Information Technology (IJMIT). p. 19. Retrieved 2016-02-13.

* Zuppo, Colrain M. "Defining ICT in a Boundaryless World: The Development of a Working Hierarchy" (PDF). International Journal of Managing Information Technology (IJMIT). p. 19. Retrieved 2016-02-13.

* Maly, Timy. "How Digital Filmmakers Produced a Gorgeous Sci-Fi Movie on a Kickstarter Budget". Wired. Retrieved November 24, 2015.

* Matthau, Charles. "How Tech Has Shaped Film Making: The Film vs. Digital Debate Is Put to

Rest". Wired. Retrieved November 24, 2015.

- "ITU releases annual global ICT data and ICT Development Index country rankings - librarylearn-ingspace.com". Retrieved 2015-09-01.

- "ITU releases annual global ICT data and ICT Development Index country rankings". www.itu.int. Retrieved 2015-09-01.

- "ITU releases annual global ICT data and ICT Development Index country rankings". www.itu.int. Retrieved 2015-09-01.

- Matti Tedre (2006). "The Development of Computer Science: A Sociocultural Perspective" (PDF). p. 260. Retrieved December 12, 2014.

- P. Collins, Graham (October 14, 2002). "Claude E. Shannon: Founder of Information Theory". Scientific American. Retrieved December 12, 2014.

- "IBM 709: a powerful new data processing system" (PDF). Computer History Museum. Retrieved December 12, 2014.

- "Computer science pioneer Samuel D. Conte dies at 85". Purdue Computer Science. July 1, 2002. Retrieved December 12, 2014.

- Donald Knuth (1972). "George Forsythe and the Development of Computer Science". Comms. ACM. Archived October 20, 2013, at the Wayback Machine.

- Murray, James (2011-12-18). "Cloud network architecture and ICT - Modern Network Architecture". ITKnowledgeExchange. TechTarget. Retrieved 2013-08-18.

- "Measuring the Information Society" (PDF). International Telecommunication Union. 2011. Retrieved 25 July 2013.

Tools and Techniques in Information Technology

Tools and techniques are important components in any field of study. The main techniques used in the field of information technology are information retrieval, information retrieval facility, data mining, data storage device, data transmission etc. The following section elucidates the various tools and techniques that are related to information technology.

Information Retrieval

Information retrieval (IR) is the activity of obtaining information resources relevant to an information need from a collection of information resources. Searches can be based on or on full-text (or other content-based) indexing.

Automated information retrieval systems are used to reduce what has been called "information overload". Many universities and public libraries use IR systems to provide access to books, journals and other documents. Web search engines are the most visible IR applications.

Overview

An information retrieval process begins when a user enters a query into the system. Queries are formal statements of information needs, for example search strings in web search engines. In information retrieval a query does not uniquely identify a single object in the collection. Instead, several objects may match the query, perhaps with different degrees of relevancy.

An object is an entity that is represented by information in a content collection or database. User queries are matched against the database information. However, as opposed to classical SQL queries of a database, in information retrieval the results returned may or may not match the query, so results are typically ranked. This ranking of results is a key difference of information retrieval searching compared to database searching.

Depending on the application the data objects may be, for example, text documents, images, audio, mind maps or videos. Often the documents themselves are not kept or stored directly in the IR system, but are instead represented in the system by document surrogates or metadata.

Most IR systems compute a numeric score on how well each object in the database matches the query, and rank the objects according to this value. The top ranking objects are then shown to the user. The process may then be iterated if the user wishes to refine the query.

History

> **"** there is ... a machine called the Univac ... whereby letters and figures are coded as a pattern of magnetic spots on a long steel tape. By this means the text of a document, preceded by its subject code symbol, can be recorded ... the machine ... automatically selects and types out those references which have been coded in any desired way at a rate of 120 words a minute
>
> — *J. E. Holmstrom, 1948* **"**

The idea of using computers to search for relevant pieces of information was popularized in the article As We May Think by Vannevar Bush in 1945. It would appear that Bush was inspired by patents for a 'statistical machine' - filed by Emanuel Goldberg in the 1920s and '30s - that searched for documents stored on film. The first description of a computer searching for information was described by Holmstrom in 1948, detailing an early mention of the Univac computer. Automated information retrieval systems were introduced in the 1950s: one even featured in the 1957 romantic comedy, Desk Set. In the 1960s, the first large information retrieval research group was formed by Gerard Salton at Cornell. By the 1970s several different retrieval techniques had been shown to perform well on small text corpora such as the Cranfield collection (several thousand documents). Large-scale retrieval systems, such as the Lockheed Dialog system, came into use early in the 1970s.

In 1992, the US Department of Defense along with the National Institute of Standards and Technology (NIST), cosponsored the Text Retrieval Conference (TREC) as part of the TIPSTER text program. The aim of this was to look into the information retrieval community by supplying the infrastructure that was needed for evaluation of text retrieval methodologies on a very large text collection. This catalyzed research on methods that scale to huge corpora. The introduction of web search engines has boosted the need for very large scale retrieval systems even further.

Model Types

For effectively retrieving relevant documents by IR strategies, the documents are typically transformed into a suitable representation. Each retrieval strategy incorporates a specific model for its document representation purposes. The picture on the right illustrates the relationship of some common models. In the picture, the models are categorized according to two dimensions: the mathematical basis and the properties of the model.

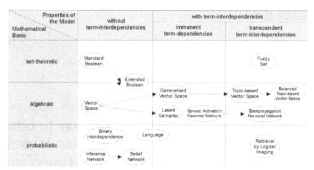

Categorization of IR-models (translated from German entry, original source Dominik Kuropka).

First Dimension: Mathematical Basis

- Set-theoretic models represent documents as sets of words or phrases. Similarities are usually derived from set-theoretic operations on those sets. Common models are:

    o   Standard Boolean model

    o   Extended Boolean model

    o   Fuzzy retrieval

- Algebraic models represent documents and queries usually as vectors, matrices, or tuples. The similarity of the query vector and document vector is represented as a scalar value.

    o   Vector space model

    o   Generalized vector space model

    o   (Enhanced) Topic-based Vector Space Model

    o   Extended Boolean model

    o   Latent semantic indexing a.k.a. latent semantic analysis

- Probabilistic models treat the process of document retrieval as a probabilistic inference. Similarities are computed as probabilities that a document is relevant for a given query. Probabilistic theorems like the Bayes' theorem are often used in these models.

    o   Binary Independence Model

    o   Probabilistic relevance model on which is based the okapi (BM25) relevance function

    o   Uncertain inference

    o   Language models

    o   Divergence-from-randomness model

    o   Latent Dirichlet allocation

- Feature-based retrieval models view documents as vectors of values of feature functions (or just features) and seek the best way to combine these features into a single relevance score, typically by learning to rank methods. Feature functions are arbitrary functions of document and query, and as such can easily incorporate almost any other retrieval model as just another feature.

Second Dimension: Properties of the Model

- Models without term-interdependencies treat different terms/words as independent. This fact is usually represented in vector space models by the orthogonality assumption of term vectors or in probabilistic models by an independency assumption for term variables.

- Models with immanent term interdependencies allow a representation of interdependencies between terms. However the degree of the interdependency between two terms is defined by the model itself. It is usually directly or indirectly derived (e.g. by dimensional reduction) from the co-occurrence of those terms in the whole set of documents.

- Models with transcendent term interdependencies allow a representation of interdependencies between terms, but they do not allege how the interdependency between two terms is defined. They rely an external source for the degree of interdependency between two terms. (For example, a human or sophisticated algorithms.)

Performance and Correctness Measures

The evaluation of an information retrieval system is the process of assessing how well a system meets the information needs of its users. Traditional evaluation metrics, designed for Boolean retrieval or top-k retrieval, include precision and recall. Many more measures for evaluating the performance of information retrieval systems have also been proposed. In general, measurement considers a collection of documents to be searched and a search query. All common measures described here assume a ground truth notion of relevancy: every document is known to be either relevant or non-relevant to a particular query. In practice, queries may be ill-posed and there may be different shades of relevancy.

Virtually all modern evaluation metrics (e.g., mean average precision, discounted cumulative gain) are designed for ranked retrieval without any explicit rank cutoff, taking into account the relative order of the documents retrieved by the search engines and giving more weight to documents returned at higher ranks.

The mathematical symbols used in the formulas below mean:

- $X \cap Y$ Intersection - in this case, specifying the documents in both sets X and Y

- $|X|$ Cardinality - in this case, the number of documents in set X

- $\int$ Integral

- $\sum$ Summation

- Δ Symmetric difference

Precision

Precision is the fraction of the documents retrieved that are relevant to the user's information need.

$$\text{precision} = \frac{|\{\text{relevant documents}\} \cap \{\text{retrieved document}\}|}{|\{\text{retrieved documents}\}|}$$

In binary classification, precision is analogous to positive predictive value. Precision takes all retrieved documents into account. It can also be evaluated at a given cut-off rank, considering only the topmost results returned by the system. This measure is called precision at n or P@n.

Note that the meaning and usage of "precision" in the field of information retrieval differs from the definition of accuracy and precision within other branches of science and statistics.

Recall

Recall is the fraction of the documents that are relevant to the query that are successfully retrieved.

$$\text{recall} = \frac{|\{\text{relevant documents}\} \cap \{\text{retrieved documents}\}|}{|\{\text{relevant documents}\}|}$$

In binary classification, recall is often called sensitivity. So it can be looked at as the probability that a relevant document is retrieved by the query.

It is trivial to achieve recall of 100% by returning all documents in response to any query. Therefore, recall alone is not enough but one needs to measure the number of non-relevant documents also, for example by computing the precision.

Fall-out

The proportion of non-relevant documents that are retrieved, out of all non-relevant documents available:

$$\text{fall-out} = \frac{|\{\text{non-relevant documents}\} \cap \{\text{retrieved documents}\}|}{|\{\text{non-relevant documents}\}|}$$

In binary classification, fall-out is closely related to specificity and is equal to $(1-\text{specificity})$ (1−specificity). It can be looked at as the probability that a non-relevant document is retrieved by the query.

It is trivial to achieve fall-out of 0% by returning zero documents in response to any query.

F-score / F-measure

The weighted harmonic mean of precision and recall, the traditional F-measure or balanced F-score is:

$$F = \frac{2 \cdot \text{precision} \cdot \text{recall}}{(\text{precision} + \text{recall})}$$

This is also known as the F_1 measure, because recall and precision are evenly weighted.

The general formula for non-negative real β is:

$$F_\beta = \frac{(1+\beta^2) \cdot (\text{precision} \cdot \text{recall}}{(\beta^2 \cdot \text{precision} + \text{recall})}$$

Two other commonly used F measures are the F_2 F 2 measure, which weights recall twice as much as precision, and the $F_{0.5}$ F 0.5 measure, which weights precision twice as much as recall.

The F-measure was derived by van Rijsbergen (1979) so that F_β F β "measures the effectiveness of retrieval with respect to a user who attaches β times as much importance

to recall as precision". It is based on van Rijsbergen's effectiveness measure $E = 1 - \dfrac{1}{\dfrac{\alpha}{P} + \dfrac{1-\alpha}{R}}$ Their relationship is:

$$F_\beta = 1 - E \text{ where } \alpha = \frac{1}{1+\beta^2}$$

F-measure can be a better single metric when compared to precision and recall; both precision and recall give different information that can complement each other when combined. If one of them excels more than the other, F-measure will reflect it.

Average Precision

Precision and recall are single-value metrics based on the whole list of documents returned by the system. For systems that return a ranked sequence of documents, it is desirable to also consider the order in which the returned documents are presented. By computing a precision and recall at every position in the ranked sequence of documents, one can plot a precision-recall curve, plotting precision $p(r)$ as a function of recall r. r Average precision computes the average value of $p(r)$ over the interval from $r = 0$ $r = 0$ to $r = 1$

$$AveP = \int_0^1 p(r)dr$$

That is the area under the precision-recall curve. This integral is in practice replaced with a finite sum over every position in the ranked sequence of documents:

$$AveP = \sum_{k=1}^{n} P(k)\Delta r(k)$$

Where k is the number of retrieved documents, $P(k)$ is the precision $\Delta r(k)$ $\Delta r (k)$ is the change in recall from items $k-1$ to k

This finite sum is equivale nt to:

$$AveP = \frac{\sum_{k=1}^{n}(P(k)\times rel(k))}{number\ of\ relevant\ documents}$$

where $rel(k)$ is an indicator function equaling 1 if the item at rank k is a relevant document, zero otherwise. Note that the average is over all relevant documents and the relevant documents not retrieved get a precision score of zero.

Some authors choose to interpolate the $p(r)$ function to reduce the impact of "wiggles" in the curve. For example, the PASCAL Visual Object Classes challenge (a benchmark for computer vision object detection) computes average precision by averaging the precision over a set of evenly spaced recall levels {0, 0.1, 0.2, ... 1.0}:

$$AveP = \frac{1}{11} \sum_{r\in\{0,0.1,...,1.0\}} P_{interp}(r)$$

where $P_{interp}(r)$ is an interpolated precision that takes the maximum precision over all recalls greater than r r

$$P_{interp}(r) = \max_{\tilde{r}:\tilde{r}\geq r} p(\tilde{r}).$$

An alternative is to derive an analytical p(r) p (r) function by assuming a particular parametric distribution for the underlying decision values. For example, a binormal precision-recall curve can be obtained by assuming decision values in both classes to follow a Gaussian distribution.

Precision at K

For modern (Web-scale) information retrieval, recall is no longer a meaningful metric, as many queries have thousands of relevant documents, and few users will be interested in reading all of them. Precision at k documents (P@k) is still a useful metric (e.g., P@10 or "Precision at 10" corresponds to the number of relevant results on the first search results page), but fails to take into account the positions of the relevant documents among the top k. Another shortcoming is that on a query with fewer relevant results than k, even a perfect system will have a score less than 1. It is easier to score manually since only the top k results need to be examined to determine if they are relevant or not.

R-Precision

R-precision requires knowing all documents that are relevant to a query. The number of relevant documents, R, is used as the cutoff for calculation, and this varies from query to query. For example, if there are 15 documents relevant to "red" in a corpus (R=15), R-precision for "red" looks at the top 15 documents returned, counts the number that are relevant r turns that into a relevancy fraction $r / R = r / 15$:

Precision is equal to recall at the R-th position.

Empirically, this measure is often highly correlated to mean average precision.

Mean Average Precision

Mean average precision for a set of queries is the mean of the average precision scores for each query.

$$MAP = \frac{\sum_{q=1}^{Q} AveP(q)}{Q}$$

where Q is the number of queries.

Discounted Cumulative Gain

DCG uses a graded relevance scale of documents from the result set to evaluate the usefulness, or gain, of a document based on its position in the result list. The premise of DCG is that highly relevant documents appearing lower in a search result list should be penalized as the graded relevance value is reduced logarithmically proportional to the position of the result.

The DCG accumulated at a particular rank position p is defined as:

$$DCG_p = rel_1 + \sum_{i=2}^{p} \frac{rel_i}{\log_2 i}.$$

Since result set may vary in size among different queries or systems, to compare performances the normalised version of DCG uses an ideal DCG. To this end, it sorts documents of a result list by relevance, producing an ideal DCG at position p ($IDCG_p$), which normalizes the score:

$$nDCG_p = \frac{DCG_p}{IDCGp}.$$

The nDCG values for all queries can be averaged to obtain a measure of the average performance of a ranking algorithm. Note that in a perfect ranking algorithm, the DCG_p will be the same as the $IDCG_p$ of 1.0. All nDCG calculations are then relative values on the interval 0.0 to 1.0 and so are cross-query comparable.

Other Measures

- Mean reciprocal rank

- Spearman's rank correlation coefficient

- bpref - a summation-based measure of how many relevant documents are ranked before irrelevant documents

- GMAP - geometric mean of (per-topic) average precision

- Measures based on marginal relevance and document diversity

Visualization

Visualizations of information retrieval performance include:

- Graphs which chart precision on one axis and recall on the other

- Histograms of average precision over various topics

- Receiver operating characteristic (ROC curve)

- Confusion matrix

Timeline

- Before the 1900s

  1801: Joseph Marie Jacquard invents the Jacquard loom, the first machine to use punched cards to control a sequence of operations.

  1880s: Herman Hollerith invents an electro-mechanical data tabulator using punch cards as a machine readable medium.

  1890 Hollerith cards, keypunches and tabulators used to process the 1890 US Census data.

- 1920s-1930s

Emanuel Goldberg submits patents for his "Statistical Machine" a document search engine that used photoelectric cells and pattern recognition to search the metadata on rolls of microfilmed documents.

- 1940s–1950s

late 1940s: The US military confronted problems of indexing and retrieval of wartime scientific research documents captured from Germans.

1945: Vannevar Bush's As We May Think appeared in Atlantic Monthly.

1947: Hans Peter Luhn (research engineer at IBM since 1941) began work on a mechanized punch card-based system for searching chemical compounds.

1950s: Growing concern in the US for a "science gap" with the USSR motivated, encouraged funding and provided a backdrop for mechanized literature searching systems (Allen Kent et al.) and the invention of citation indexing (Eugene Garfield).

1950: The term "information retrieval" was coined by Calvin Mooers.

1951: Philip Bagley conducted the earliest experiment in computerized document retrieval in a master thesis at MIT.

1955: Allen Kent joined Case Western Reserve University, and eventually became associate director of the Center for Documentation and Communications Research. That same year, Kent and colleagues published a paper in American Documentation describing the precision and recall measures as well as detailing a proposed "framework" for evaluating an IR system which included statistical sampling methods for determining the number of relevant documents not retrieved.

1958: International Conference on Scientific Information Washington DC included consideration of IR systems as a solution to problems identified.

1959: Hans Peter Luhn published "Auto-encoding of documents for information retrieval."

- 1960s:

early 1960s: Gerard Salton began work on IR at Harvard, later moved to Cornell.

1960: Melvin Earl Maron and John Lary Kuhns published "On relevance, probabilistic indexing, and information retrieval" in the Journal of the ACM 7(3):216–244, July 1960.

1962:

- Cyril W. Cleverdon published early findings of the Cranfield studies, developing a model for IR system evaluation. "Report on the Testing and Analysis of an Investigation into the Comparative Efficiency of Indexing Systems". Cranfield Collection of Aeronautics, Cranfield, England, 1962.

- Kent published Information Analysis and Retrieval.

1963:

- Weinberg report "Science, Government and Information" gave a full articulation of the idea of a "crisis of scientific information." The report was named after Dr. Alvin Weinberg.

- Joseph Becker and Robert M. Hayes published text on information retrieval. Becker, Joseph; Hayes, Robert Mayo. Information storage and retrieval: tools, elements, theories. New York, Wiley (1963).

1964:

- Karen Spärck Jones finished her thesis at Cambridge, Synonymy and Semantic Classification, and continued work on computational linguistics as it applies to IR.

- The National Bureau of Standards sponsored a symposium titled "Statistical Association Methods for Mechanized Documentation." Several highly significant papers, including G. Salton's first published reference (we believe) to the SMART system.

mid-1960s:

- National Library of Medicine developed MEDLARS Medical Literature Analysis and Retrieval System, the first major machine-readable database and batch-retrieval system.

- Project Intrex at MIT.

1965: J. C. R. Licklider published Libraries of the Future.

1966: Don Swanson was involved in studies at University of Chicago on Requirements for Future Catalogs.

late 1960s: F. Wilfrid Lancaster completed evaluation studies of the MEDLARS system and published the first edition of his text on information retrieval.

1968:

- o   Gerard Salton published Automatic Information Organization and Retrieval.

- o   John W. Sammon, Jr.'s RADC Tech report "Some Mathematics of Information Storage and Retrieval..." outlined the vector model.

1969: Sammon's "A nonlinear mapping for data structure analysis" (IEEE Transactions on Computers) was the first proposal for visualization interface to an IR system.

- • 1970s

early 1970s:

- o   First online systems—NLM's AIM-TWX, MEDLINE; Lockheed's Dialog; SDC's ORBIT.

- o   Theodor Nelson promoting concept of hypertext, published Computer Lib/Dream Machines.

1971: Nicholas Jardine and Cornelis J. van Rijsbergen published "The use of hierarchic clustering in information retrieval", which articulated the "cluster hypothesis."

1975: Three highly influential publications by Salton fully articulated his vector processing framework and term discrimination model:

- o   A Theory of Indexing (Society for Industrial and Applied Mathematics)

- o   A Theory of Term Importance in Automatic Text Analysis (JASIS v. 26)

- o   A Vector Space Model for Automatic Indexing (CACM 18:11)

1978: The First ACM SIGIR conference.

1979: C. J. van Rijsbergen published Information Retrieval (Butterworths). Heavy emphasis on probabilistic models.

1979: Tamas Doszkocs implemented the CITE natural language user interface for MEDLINE at the National Library of Medicine. The CITE system supported free form query input, ranked output and relevance feedback.

- • 1980s

1980: First international ACM SIGIR conference, joint with British Computer Society IR group in Cambridge.

1982: Nicholas J. Belkin, Robert N. Oddy, and Helen M. Brooks proposed the ASK (Anomalous State of Knowledge) viewpoint for information retrieval. This was an important concept, though their automated analysis tool proved ultimately disappointing.

1983: Salton (and Michael J. McGill) published Introduction to Modern Information Retrieval (McGraw-Hill), with heavy emphasis on vector models.

1985: David Blair and Bill Maron publish: An Evaluation of Retrieval Effectiveness for a Full-Text Document-Retrieval System

mid-1980s: Efforts to develop end-user versions of commercial IR systems.

1985–1993: Key papers on and experimental systems for visualization interfaces.

Work by Donald B. Crouch, Robert R. Korfhage, Matthew Chalmers, Anselm Spoerri and others.

1989: First World Wide Web proposals by Tim Berners-Lee at CERN.

- 1990s

1992: First TREC conference.

1997: Publication of Korfhage's Information Storage and Retrieval with emphasis on visualization and multi-reference point systems.

late 1990s: Web search engines implementation of many features formerly found only in experimental IR systems. Search engines become the most common and maybe best instantiation of IR models.

Awards in the Field

- Tony Kent Strix award

- Gerard Salton Award

Information Retrieval Facility

IRF logo

The Information Retrieval Facility (IRF), founded 2006 and located in Vienna, Austria, was a research platform for networking and collaboration for professionals in the field of information retrieval. It ceased operations in 2012.

The IRF had members in the following categories:

- Researchers in information retrieval (IR) or related scientific areas

- Industrial/corporate information management professionals

- Patent authorities and governmental institutions

- Students of one of the above

The Scientific Board

Maristella Agosti, Professor, Department of Information Engineering, University of Padova

Gerhard Budin, Director of the Center of Translation Studies at the University of Vienna, Director of the Department of Corpuslinguistics and Text Technology, Austrian Academy of Sciences

Jamie Callan, Professor, Language Technologies Institute, CMU, Carnegie Mellon University

Yves Chiaramella, Professor Emeritus, Department of Computer Science and Applied Mathematics, Joseph Fourier University

Kilnam Chon, Professor, Computer Science Department, Korea Advanced Institute of Science and Technology (KAIST)

W. Bruce Croft, Distinguished Professor, Department of Computer Science and Director Center for Intelligent IR University of Massachusetts Amherst

Hamish Cunningham, Research Professor, Computer Science Department University Sheffield

Norbert Fuhr, Chairman of the Scientific Board, Professor, Institute of Informatics and Interactive Systems University Duisburg-Essen

David Hawking, Science Leader, Project Leader, CSIRO ICT Centre

Noriko Kando, Professor, Software Engineering Research, Software Research Division, National Institute of Informatics (NII)

Arcot Desai Narasimhalu, Associate Dean, School of Information Systems Singapore Management University

John Tait, Chief Scientific Officer of the IRF, Until July 2007 Professor of Intelligent Information Systems and Associate Dean of the School of Computing and Technology

Benjamin T'sou, Director, Language Information Sciences Research Centre, City University of Hong Kong

C.J. van Rijsbergen, Dept. Computer Science at the University of Glasgow

Scientific Goals

- Modelling innovative and specialised information retrieval systems for global patent document collections.

- Investigating and developing an adequate technical infrastructure that allows interactive experimentation with formal, mathematical retrieval concepts for very large-scale document collections.<

- Studying the usability of multi modal user-interfaces to very large-scale information retrieval systems.

- Integrating real users with actual information needs into the research process of modelling information retrieval systems to allow accurate performance evaluation.

- Ability to create different views of patent data depending on the focus of the information need.

- Defining standardised methods for benchmarking the information retrieval process in patent document collections.

- Ability to handle text and non-text parts of a patent in a coherent manner.

- Designing, experimenting and evaluating search engines able to retrieve structured and semi-structured documents in very large-scale patent collections.

- Integrating the temporal dimension of patent documents in retrieval strategies.

- Improving effectiveness and precision of patent retrieval, based on ontologies and natural-language understanding techniques.

- Refining IR methods that allow unstructured querying by exploiting available structure within the patent documents.

- Formal (mathematical) identification and specification of relevant business information needs in the field of intellectual property information.

- Investigating efficient scaling mechanisms for information retrieval taking into account the characteristics of patent data.

- Investigating and experimenting with computing architectures for very high-capacity information management.

- Establishing an open eScience platform that enables a standardised and easy way of creating and performing IR experiments on a common research infrastructure.

- Discovering and investigating novel use cases and business applications deriving from intellectual property information.

- Enabling the formal information retrieval, natural language and semantic processing research to grow into the field of applied sciences in the global, industrial context.

- Development and integration of different information access methods.

- Research on effective methods for interactive information retrieval.

Semantic Supercomputing

Current technologies to extract concepts from unstructured documents are extremely computational intensive. To allow interactive experimentation with rich and huge text corpora, the IRF has built a high performance computing environment, into which the latest technological advances have been implemented:

- multi-node clusters (currently 80 cores, up to 1024)

- highest speed interconnect technology

- single system image with large compound memory (currently 320 GB, up to 4 TB)

- fully integrated configurable computing (currently 4 FPGA cores, up to 256)

The combination of these HPC features to accelerate text mining represents the IRF implementation of semantic supercomputing.

The World Patent Corpus

The IRF aims to bring state-of-the-art information retrieval technology to the community of patent information professionals. We expect information retrieval (IR) technology to become the focus of information technology very soon. All industry sectors can profit from applying modern and future text mining processes to the special requirements of patent research. Although all ideas and concepts are universally applicable to all sorts of intellectual property information, patents require the most sophistication, and confront us with challenging technical and organisational problems. The entire body of patent-related documents possibly constitutes the largest corpus of compound documents, making it a rewarding target for text mining scientists and end-users alike. What's more, patents have become a crucial issue, in particular for large global corporations and universities. The industrial users of patent data are among the most demanding and important information professionals. As a consequence, they could benefit the most from technology that relieves the burden of researching the large body of patent information.

Research Collections

The IRF provides a number of test data collections that have either been developed by the IRF, by one of its members or by third parties. These data collections can be used freely for scientific experimentations.

The MAtrixware REsearch Collection (MAREC) is the first standardised patent data corpus for research purposes. It consists of 19 million patent documents in different languages, normalised to a highly specific XML format. The collection has been developed by Matrixware for the IRF.

The ClueWeb09 collection is a 25 terabyte dataset of about 1 billion web pages crawled in January and February, 2009. It has been created by the Language Technologies Institute at Carnegie Mellon University to support research on information retrieval and related human language technologies.

Information Seeking and its Type

Information Seeking

Information seeking is the process or activity of attempting to obtain information in both human and technological contexts. Information seeking is related to, but different from, information retrieval (IR).

Information Retrieval

Traditionally, IR tools have been designed for IR professionals to enable them to effectively and efficiently retrieve information from a source. It is assumed that the information exists in the source and that a well-formed query will retrieve it (and nothing else). It has been argued that laypersons' information seeking on the internet is very different from information retrieval as performed within the IR discourse. Yet, internet search engines are built on IR principles. Since the late 1990s a body of research on how casual users interact with internet search engines has been forming, but the topic is far from fully understood. IR can be said to be technology-oriented, focusing on algorithms and issues such as precision and recall. Information seeking may be understood as a more human-oriented and open-ended process than information retrieval. In information seeking, one does not know whether there exists an answer to one's query, so the process of seeking may provide the learning required to satisfy one's information need.

In Different Contexts

Much library and information science (LIS) research has focused on the information-seeking practices of practitioners within various fields of professional work. Studies have been carried out into the information-seeking behaviors of librarians, academics, medical professionals, engineers and lawyers (among others). Much of this research has drawn on the work done by Leckie, Pettigrew (now Fisher) and Sylvain, who in 1996 conducted an extensive review of the LIS literature (as well as the literature of other academic fields) on professionals' information seeking. The authors proposed an analytic model of professionals' information seeking behaviour, intended to be generalizable across the professions, thus providing a platform for future research in the area. The model was intended to "prompt new insights... and give rise to more refined and applicable theories of information seeking" (1996, p. 188). The model has been adapted by Wilkinson (2001) who proposes a model of the information seeking of lawyers.

Theories of Information-seeking Behavior

A variety of theories of information behavior – e.g. Zipf's Principle of Least Effort, Brenda Dervin's Sense Making, Elfreda Chatman's Life in the Round – seek to understand the processes that surround information seeking.

A review of the literature on information seeking behavior shows that information seeking has generally been accepted as dynamic and non-linear (Foster, 2005; Kuhlthau 2006). People experience the information search process as an interplay of thoughts, feelings and actions (Kuhlthau, 2006). Donald O. Case (2007) also wrote a good book that is a review of the literature.

Information seeking has been found to be linked to a variety of interpersonal communication behaviors beyond question-asking, to include strategies such as candidate answers.

Robinson's (2010) research suggests that when seeking information at work, people rely on both other people and information repositories (e.g., documents and databases), and spend similar amounts of time consulting each (7.8% and 6.4% of work time, respectively; 14.2% in total). However, the distribution of time among the constituent information seeking stages differs depending on the source. When consulting other people, people spend less time locating the information source and information within that source, similar time understanding the information, and more time problem solving and decision making, than when consulting information repositories. Furthermore, the research found that people spend substantially more time receiving information passively (i.e., information that they have not requested) than actively (i.e., information that they have requested), and this pattern is also reflected when they provide others with information.

Wilson's Nested Model of Conceptual Areas

The concepts of information seeking, information retrieval, and information behaviour are objects of investigation of information science. Within this scientific discipline a variety of studies has been undertaken analyzing the interaction of an individual with information sources in case of a specific information need, task, and context. The research models developed in these studies vary in their level of scope. Wilson (1999) therefore developed a nested model of conceptual areas, which visualizes the interrelation of the here mentioned central concepts.

Wilson's Nested Model of Conceptual Areas (Wilson 1999)

Wilson's Nested Model of Conceptual Areas

Wilson defines models of information behavior to be "statements, often in the form of diagrams, that attempt to describe an information-seeking activity, the causes and consequences of that activity, or the relationships among stages in information-seeking behaviour" (1999: 250).

Collaborative Information Seeking

Collaborative information seeking (CIS) is a field of research that involves studying situations, motivations, and methods for people working in collaborative groups for information seeking projects, as well as building systems for supporting such activities. Such projects often involve information searching or information retrieval (IR), information gathering, and information sharing. Beyond that, CIS can extend to collaborative information synthesis and collaborative sense-making.

Background

Seeking for information is often considered a solo activity, but there are many situations that call for people working together for information seeking. Such situations are typically complex in nature, and involve working through several sessions exploring, evaluating, and gathering relevant information. Take for example, a couple going on a trip. They have the same goal, and in order to accomplish their goal, they need to seek out several kinds of information, including flights, hotels, and sightseeing. This may involve them working together over multiple sessions, exploring and collecting useful information, and collectively making decisions that help them move toward their common goal.

It is a common knowledge that collaboration is either necessary or highly desired in many activities that are complex or difficult to deal with for an individual. Despite its natural appeal and situational necessity, collaboration in information seeking is an understudied domain. The nature of the available information and its role in our lives have changed significantly, but the methods and tools that are used to access and share that information in collaboration have remained largely unaltered. People still use general-purpose systems such as email and IM for doing CIS projects, and there is a lack of specialized tools and techniques to support CIS explicitly.

There are also several models to explain information seeking and information behavior, but the areas of collaborative information seeking and collaborative information behavior remain understudied. A few specialized systems for supporting CIS have emerged in the recent past, but their usage and evaluations have underwhelmed. Despite such limitations, the field of CIS has been getting a lot of attention lately, and several promising theories and tools have come forth. A recent review of CIS related literature is written by Shah. Shah provides a comprehensive review of this field, including theories, models, systems, evaluation, and future research directions. Other books in this area include one by Morris and Teevan, as well as Foster's book on collaborative information behavior.

Theories

Depending upon what one includes or excludes while talking about CIS, we have many or hardly any theories. If we consider the past work on the groupware systems, many interesting insights can be obtained about people working on collaborative projects, the issues they face, and the guidelines for system designers. One of the notable works is by Grudin, who laid out eight design principles for developers of groupware systems.

The discussion below is primarily based on some of the recent works in the field of computer supported cooperative work CSCW, collaborative IR, and CIS.

Definitions and Terminology

The literature is filled with works that use terms such as collaborative information retrieval, social searching, concurrent search, collaborative exploratory search, co-browsing, collaborative information behavior, collaborative information synthesis, and collaborative information seeking, which are often used interchangeably.

There are several definitions of such related or similar terms in the literature. For instance, Foster defined collaborative IR as "the study of the systems and practices that enable individuals to collaborate during the seeking, searching, and retrieval of information." Shah defined CIS as a process of collaboratively seeking information that is "defined explicitly among the participants, interactive, and mutually beneficial." While there is still a lack of a definition or a terminology that is universally accepted, but most agree that CIS is an active process, as opposed to collaborative filtering, where a system connects the users based on their passive involvement (e.g., buying similar products on Amazon).

Models of Collaboration

Foley and Smeaton defined two key aspects of collaborative information seeking as division of labor and the sharing of knowledge. Division of labor allows collaborating searchers to tackle larger problems by reducing the duplication of effort (e.g., finding documents that one's collaborator has already discovered). The sharing of knowledge allows searchers to influence each other's activities as they interact with the retrieval system in pursuit of their (often evolving) information need. This influence can occur in real time if the collaborative search system supports it, or it can occur in a turn-taking, asynchronous manner if that is how interaction is structured.

Teevan et al. characterized two classes of collaboration, task-based vs. trait-based. Task-based collaboration corresponds to intentional collaboration; trait-based collaboration facilitates the sharing of knowledge through inferred similarity of information need.

Situations, Motivations, and Methods for CIS

One of the important issues to study in CIS is the instance, reason, and the methods behind a collaboration. For instance, Morris, using a survey with 204 knowledge workers at a large technology company found that people often like and want to collaborate, but they do not find specialized tools to help them in such endeavors. Some of the situations for doing collaborative information seeking in this survey were travel planning, shopping, and literature search. Shah, similarly, using personal interviews, identified three main reasons why people collaborate.

1. Requirement/setup. Sometimes a group of people are "forced" to collaborate. Example includes a merger between two companies.

2. Division of labor. Working together may help the participants to distribute the workload. Example includes a group of students working on a class project.

3. Diversity of skills. Often people get together because they could not individually possess the required set of skills. Example includes co-authorship, where different authors bring different set of skills to the table.

As far as the tools and/or methods for CIS are concerned, both Morris and Shah found that email is still the most used tool. Other popular methods are face-to-face meetings, IM, and phone or conference calls. In general, the choice of the method or tool for our respondents depended on their situation (co-located or remote), and objective (brainstorming or working on independent parts).

Space-time Organization of CIS Systems and Methods

The classical way of organizing collaborative activities is based on two factors: location and time. Recently Hansen & Jarvelin and Golovchinsky, Pickens, & Back also classified approaches to collaborative IR using these two dimensions of space and time.

The majority of collaborative activities in conventional libraries are co-located and synchronous, whereas collaborative activities relating to digital libraries are more remote and synchronous. Social information filtering, or collaborative filtering, as we saw earlier, is a process benefitting from other users' actions in the past; thus, it falls under asynchronous and mostly remote domain. These days email also serves as a tool for doing asynchronous collaboration among users who are not co-located. Chat or IM (represented as 'internet' in the figure) helps to carry out synchronous and remote collaboration.

Rodden, similarly, presented a classification of CSCW systems using the form of inter-action and the geographical nature of cooperative systems. Further, Rodden & Blair presented an important characteristic to all CSCW systems - control. According to the authors, two predominant control mechanisms have emerged within CSCW systems: speech act theory systems, and procedure based systems. These mechanisms are tightly coupled with the kind of control the system can support in a collaborative environment.

Often researchers also talk about other dimensions, such as intentionality and depth of mediation (system mediated or user mediated), while classifying various CIS systems.

Control, Communication, and Awareness

Three components specific to group-work or collaboration that are highly predom-inant in the CIS or CSCW literature are control, communication, and awareness. In this section key definitions and related works for these components will be highlight-ed. Understanding their roles can also help us address various design issues with CIS systems.

Control

Rodden identified the value of control in CSCW systems and listed a number of proj-ects with their corresponding schemes for implementing for control. For instance, the COSMOS project had a formal structure to represent control in the system. They used roles to represent people or automatons, and rules to represent the flow and processes. Roles of the people could be supervisor, processor, or analyst. Rules could be a condi-tion that a process needs to satisfy in order to start or finish. Due to such a structure seen in projects like COSMOS, Rodden classified these control systems as procedural based systems.

Communication

This is one of the most critical components of any collaboration. In fact, Rodden (1991) identified message or communication systems as the class of systems in CSCW that is most mature and most widely used.

Since the focus here is on CIS systems that allow its participants to engage in an intentional and interactive collaboration, there must be a way for the participants to communicate with each other. What is interesting to note is that often, collaboration could begin by letting a group of users communicate with each other. For instance, Donath & Robertson presented a system that allows a user to know that others were currently viewing the same webpage and communicate with those people to initiate a possible collaboration or at least a co-browsing experience. Providing communication capabilities even in an environment that was not originally designed for carrying out collaboration is an interesting way of encouraging collaboration.

Awareness

Awareness, in the context of CSCW, has been defined as "an understanding of the activities of others, which provides a context for your own activity". The following four kinds of awareness are often discussed and addressed in the CSCW literature:

1. Group awareness. This kind of awareness includes providing information to each group member about the status and activities of the other collaborators at a given time.

2. Workspace awareness. This refers to a common workspace that the group has where they can bring and discuss their findings, and create a common product.

3. Contextual awareness. This type of awareness relates to the application domain, rather than the users. Here, we want to identify what content is useful for the group, and what the goals are for the current project.

4. Peripheral awareness. This relates to the kind of information that has resulted from personal and the group's collective history, and should be kept separate from what a participant is currently viewing or doing.

Shah and Marchionini studied awareness as provided by interface in collaborative information seeking. They found that one needs to provide "right" (not too little, not too much, and appropriate for the task at hand) kind of awareness to reduce the cost of coordination and maximize the benefits of collaboration.

Systems

A number of specialized systems have been developed back from the days of the groupware systems to today's Web 2.0 interfaces. A few such examples, in chronological order, are given below.

Ariadne

Twidale et al. developed Ariadne to support the collaborative learning of database browsing skills. In addition to enhancing the opportunities and effectiveness of the collaborative learning that already occurred, Ariadne was designed to provide the facilities that would allow collaborations to persist as people increasingly searched information remotely and had less opportunity for spontaneous face-to-face collaboration.

Ariadne was developed in the days when Telnet-based access to library catalogs was a common practice. Building on top of this command-line interface, Ariadne could capture the users' input and the database's output, and form them into a search history that consisted of a series of command-output pairs. Such a separation of capture and display allowed Ariadne to work with various forms of data capture methods.

To support complex browsing processes in collaboration, Ariadne presented a visualization of the search process. This visualization consisted of thumbnails of screens, looking like playing cards, which represented command-output pairs. Any such card can be expanded to reveal its details. The horizontal axis on Ariadne's display represented time, and the vertical axis showed information on the semantics of the action it represented: the top row for the top level menus, the middle row for specifying a search, and the bottom row for looking at particular book details.

This visualization of the search process in Ariadne makes it possible to annotate, discuss with colleagues around the screen, and distribute to remote collaborators for asynchronous commenting easily and effectively. As we saw in the previous section, having access to one's history as well as the history of one's collaborators are very crucial to effective collaboration. Ariadne implements these requirements with the features that let one visualize, save, and share a search process. In fact, the authors found one of the advantages of search visualization was the ability to recap previous searching sessions easily in a multi-session exploratory searching.

SearchTogether

More recently, one of the collaborative information seeking tools that have caught a lot of attention is SearchTogether, developed by Morris and Horvitz. The design of this tool was motivated by a survey that the researchers did with 204 knowledge workers, in which they discovered the following.

- A majority of respondents wanted to collaborate while searching on the Web.

- The most common ways of collaborating in information seeking tasks are sending emails back and forth, using IM to exchange links and query terms, and using phone calls while looking at a Web browser.

- Some of the most popular Web searching tasks on which people like to collaborate are planning travels or social events, making expensive purchases, researching medical conditions, and looking for information related to a common project.

Based on the survey responses, and the current and desired practices for collaborative search, the authors of SearchTogether identified three key features for supporting people's collaborative information behavior while searching on the Web: awareness, division of labor, and persistence. Let us look at how these three features are implemented.

SearchTogether instantiates awareness in several ways, one of which is per-user query histories. This is done by showing each group member's screen name, his/her photo and queries in the "Query Awareness" region. The access to the query histories is immediate and interactive, as clicking on a query brings back the results of that query from when it was executed. The authors identified query awareness as a very important feature in collaborative searching, which allows group members to not only share their query terms, but also learn better query formulation techniques from one another.

Another component of SearchTogether that facilitates awareness is the display of page-specific metadata. This region includes several pieces of information about the displayed page, including group members who viewed the given page, and their comments and ratings. The authors claim that such visitation information can help one either choose to avoid a page already visited by someone in the group to reduce the duplication of efforts, or perhaps choose to visit such pages, as they provide a sign of promising leads as indicated by the presence of comments and/or ratings.

Division of labor in SearchTogether is implemented in three ways: (1) "Split Search" allows one to split the search results among all online group members in a round-robin fashion, (2) "Multi-Engine Search" takes a query and runs it on n different search engines, where n is the number of online group members, (3) manual division of labor can be facilitated using integrated IM.

Finally, the persistence feature in SearchTogether is instantiated by storing all the objects and actions, including IM conversations, query histories, recommendation queues, and page-specific metadata. Such data about all the group members are available to each member when he/she logs in. This allows one to easily carry a multi-session collaborative project.

Cerchiamo

Cerchiamo is a collaborative information seeking tool that explores issues related to algorithmic mediation of information seeking activities and how collaborators' roles can be used to structure the user interface. Cerchiamo introduced the notion of algorithmic mediation, that is, the ability of the system to collect input asynchronously from multiple collaborating searchers, and to use these multiple streams of input to affect the information that is being retrieved and displayed to the searchers.

Cerchiamo collected judgments of relevance from multiple collaborating searchers and used those judgments to create a ranked list of items that were potentially relevant to the information need. This algorithm prioritized items that were retrieved by multiple queries and that were retrieved by queries that also retrieved many other relevant documents. This rank fusion is just one way in which a search system that manages activities of multiple collaborating searchers can combine their inputs to generate results that are better than those produced by individuals working independently.

Cerchiamo implemented two roles—Prospector and Miner—that searchers could assume. Each role had an associated interface. The Prospector role/interface focused on running many queries and making a few judgments of relevance for each query to explore the information space. The Miner role/interface focused on making relevance judgments on a ranked list of items selected from items retrieved by all queries in the current session. This combination of roles allowed searchers to explore and exploit the information space, and led teams to discover more unique relevant documents than pairs of individuals working separately.

Coagmento

Coagmento (Latin for "working together") is a new and unique system that allows a group of people work together for their information seeking tasks without leaving their browsers. Coagmento has been developed with a client-server architecture, where the client is implemented as a Firefox plug-in that helps multiple people working in collaboration to communicate, and search, share and organize information. The server component stores and provides all the objects and actions collected from the client. Due to this decoupling, Coagmento provides a flexible architecture that allows its users to be co-located or remote, working synchronously or asynchronously, and use different platforms.

Coagmento includes a toolbar and a sidebar. The toolbar has several buttons that helps one collect information and be aware of the progress in a given collaboration. The toolbar has three major parts:

- Buttons for collecting information and making annotations. These buttons help one save or remove a webpage, make annotations on a webpage, and highlight and collect text snippets.

- Page-specific statistics. The middle portion of the toolbar shows various statistics, such as the number of views, annotations, and snippets, for the displayed page. A user can click on a given statistic and obtain more information. For instance, clicking on the number of snippets will bring up a window that shows all the snippets collected by the collaborators from the displayed page.

- Project-specific statistics. The last portion of the toolbar displays task/project name and various statistics, including number of pages visited and saved, about the current project. Clicking on that portion brings up the workspace where one can view all the collected objects (pages and snippets) brought in by the collaborators for that project.

The sidebar features a chat window, under which there are three tabs with the history of search engine queries, saved pages and snippets. With each of these objects, the user who created or collected that object is shown. Anyone in the group can access an object by clicking on it. For instance, one can click on a query issued by anyone in the group to re-run that query and bring up the results in the main browser window.

An Android (operating system) app for Coagmento can be found in the Android Market.

Cosme

Fernandez-Luna et al. introduce Cosme (COde Search MEeting) as a NetBeans IDE plug-in that enables remote team of software developers to collaborate in real time during source-code search sessions. The COSME design was motivated by early stadies of C. Foley, M. R. Morris, C. Shah, among others researchers, and by habits of software developers identified in a survey of 117 universities students and professors related with projects of software development, as well as to computer programmers of some companies. The five more commons collaborative search habits (or related to it) of the interviewees was:

- Revision of problems by the team in the workstation of one of them.

- Suggest addresses of Web pages that they have already visited previously, digital books stored in some FTP, or source files of a version control system.

- Send emails with algorithms or explanatory text.

- Division of search tasks among each member of the team for sharing the final result.

- Store relevant information in individual workstation.

COSME is designed to enable either synchronous or asynchronous, but explicit remote collaboration among team developers with shared technical information needs. Its client user interface include a search panel that lets developers to specify queries, division of labor principle (possible combination include the use of different search engines, ranking fusion, and split algorithms), searching field (comments, source-code, class or methods declaration), and the collection type (source-code files or digital documentation). The sessions panel wraps the principal options to management the collaborative search sessions, which consists in a team of developers working together to satisfy their shared technical information needs. For example, a developer can use the embedded chat room to negotiate the creation of a collaborative search session, and show comments of the current and historical search results. The implementation of Cosme was based on CIRLab (Collaborative Information Retrieval Laboratory) instantiation, a groupware framework for CIS research and experimentation, Java as programming language, NetBeans IDE Platform as plug-in base, and Amenities (A MEthodology for aNalysis and desIgn of cooperaTIve systEmS) as software engineering methodology.

Open-source Application Frameworks and Toolkits

CIS systems development is a complex task, which involves software technologies and Know-how in different areas such as distributed programming, information search and retrieval, collaboration among people, task coordination and many others according to the context. This situation is not ideal because it requires great programming efforts. Fortunately, some CIS application frameworks and toolkits are increasing their popularity since they have a high reusability impact for both developers and researchers, like Coagmento Collaboratory and DrakkarKeel.

Many interesting and important questions remain to be addressed in the field of CIS, including

1. Why do people collaborate? Identifying their motivations can help us design better support for their specific needs.

2. What additional tools are required to enhance existing methods of collaboration, given a specific domain?

3. How to evaluate various aspects of collaborative information seeking, including system and user performance?

4. How to measure the costs and benefits of collaboration?

5. What are the information seeking situations in which collaboration is beneficial? When does it not pay off?

6. How can we measure the performance of a collaborative group?

7. How can we measure the contribution of an individual in a collaborative group?

8. What sorts of retrieval algorithms can be used to combine input from multiple searchers?

9. What kinds of algorithmic mediation can improve team performance?

Data Mining

Data mining is an interdisciplinary subfield of computer science. It is the computational process of discovering patterns in large data sets involving methods at the intersection of artificial intelligence, machine learning, statistics, and database systems. The overall goal of the data mining process is to extract information from a data set and transform it into an understandable structure for further use. Aside from the raw analysis step, it involves database and data management aspects, data pre-processing, model and inference considerations, interestingness metrics, complexity considerations, post-processing of discovered structures, visualization, and online updating. Data mining is the analysis step of the "knowledge discovery in databases" process, or KDD.

The term is a misnomer, because the goal is the extraction of patterns and knowledge from large amounts of data, not the extraction (mining) of data itself. It also is a buzzword and is frequently applied to any form of large-scale data or information processing (collection, extraction, warehousing, analysis, and statistics) as well as any application of computer decision support system, including artificial intelligence, machine learning, and business intelligence. The book Data mining: Practical machine learning tools and techniques with Java (which covers mostly machine learning material) was originally to be named just Practical machine learning, and the term data mining was only added for marketing reasons. Often the more general terms (large scale) data analysis and analytics – or, when referring to actual methods, artificial intelligence and machine learning – are more appropriate.

The actual data mining task is the automatic or semi-automatic analysis of large quantities of data to extract previously unknown, interesting patterns such as groups of data records (cluster analysis), unusual records (anomaly detection), and dependencies (association rule mining). This usually involves using database techniques such as spatial indices. These patterns can then be seen as a kind of summary of the input data, and may be used in further analysis or, for example, in machine learning and predictive analytics. For example, the data mining step might identify multiple groups in the data, which can then be used to obtain more accurate prediction results by a decision support system. Neither the data collection, data preparation, nor result interpretation and reporting is part of the data mining step, but do belong to the overall KDD process as additional steps.

The related terms data dredging, data fishing, and data snooping refer to the use of data mining methods to sample parts of a larger population data set that are (or may be) too small for reliable statistical inferences to be made about the validity of any patterns discovered. These methods can, however, be used in creating new hypotheses to test against the larger data populations.

Etymology

In the 1960s, statisticians used terms like "Data Fishing" or "Data Dredging" to refer to what they considered the bad practice of analyzing data without an a-priori hypothesis. The term "Data Mining" appeared around 1990 in the database community. For a short time in 1980s, a phrase "database mining"™, was used, but since it was trademarked by HNC, a San Diego-based company, to pitch their Database Mining Workstation; researchers consequently turned to "data mining". Other terms used include Data Archaeology, Information Harvesting, Information Discovery, Knowledge Extraction, etc. Gregory Piatetsky-Shapiro coined the term "Knowledge Discovery in Databases" for the first workshop on the same topic (KDD-1989) and this term became more popular in AI and Machine Learning Community. However, the term data mining became more popular in the business and press communities. Currently, Data Mining and Knowledge Discovery are used interchangeably. Since about 2007, "Predictive Analytics" and since 2011, "Data Science" terms were also used to describe this field.

In the Academic community, the major forums for research started in 1995 when the First International Conference on Data Mining and Knowledge Discovery (KDD-95) was started in Montreal under AAAI sponsorship. It was co-chaired by Usama Fayyad and Ramasamy Uthurusamy. A year later, in 1996, Usama Fayyad launched the journal by Kluwer called Data Mining and Knowledge Discovery as its founding Editor-in-Chief. Later he started the SIGKDDD Newsletter SIGKDD Explorations. The KDD International conference became the primary highest quality conference in Data Mining with an acceptance rate of research paper submissions below 18%. The Journal Data Mining and Knowledge Discovery is the primary research journal of the field.

Background

The manual extraction of patterns from data has occurred for centuries. Early methods of identifying patterns in data include Bayes' theorem (1700s) and regression analysis (1800s). The proliferation, ubiquity and increasing power of computer technology has dramatically increased data collection, storage, and manipulation ability. As data sets have grown in size and complexity, direct "hands-on" data analysis has increasingly been augmented with indirect, automated data processing, aided by other discoveries in computer science, such as neural networks, cluster analysis, genetic algorithms (1950s), decision trees and decision rules (1960s), and support vector machines (1990s). Data mining is the process of applying these methods with the intention of uncovering hidden patterns in large data sets. It bridges the gap from applied statistics and artificial intelligence (which usually provide the mathematical background) to database management by exploiting the way data is stored and indexed in databases to execute the actual learning and discovery algorithms more efficiently, allowing such methods to be applied to ever larger data sets.

Process

The Knowledge Discovery in Databases (KDD) process is commonly defined with the stages:

   (1) Selection

   (2) Pre-processing

   (3) Transformation

   (4) Data Mining

   (5) Interpretation/Evaluation.

It exists, however, in many variations on this theme, such as the Cross Industry Standard Process for Data Mining (CRISP-DM) which defines six phases:

(1) Business Understanding

(2) Data Understanding

(3) Data Preparation

(4) Modeling

(5) Evaluation

(6) Deployment

or a simplified process such as (1) pre-processing, (2) data mining, and (3) results validation.

Polls conducted in 2002, 2004, 2007 and 2014 show that the CRISP-DM methodology is the leading methodology used by data miners. The only other data mining standard named in these polls was SEMMA. However, 3–4 times as many people reported using CRISP-DM. Several teams of researchers have published reviews of data mining process models, and Azevedo and Santos conducted a comparison of CRISP-DM and SEMMA in 2008.

Pre-processing

Before data mining algorithms can be used, a target data set must be assembled. As data mining can only uncover patterns actually present in the data, the target data set must be large enough to contain these patterns while remaining concise enough to be mined within an acceptable time limit. A common source for data is a data mart or data warehouse. Pre-processing is essential to analyze the multivariate data sets before data mining. The target set is then cleaned. Data cleaning removes the observations containing noise and those with missing data.

Data mining

Data mining involves six common classes of tasks:

- Anomaly detection (Outlier/change/deviation detection) – The identification of unusual data records, that might be interesting or data errors that require further investigation.

- Association rule learning (Dependency modelling) – Searches for relationships between variables. For example, a supermarket might gather data on customer purchasing habits. Using association rule learning, the supermarket can determine which products are frequently bought together and use this information for marketing purposes. This is sometimes referred to as market basket analysis.

- Clustering – is the task of discovering groups and structures in the data that are in some way or another "similar", without using known structures in the data.

- Classification – is the task of generalizing known structure to apply to new data. For example, an e-mail program might attempt to classify an e-mail as "legitimate" or as "spam".

- Regression – attempts to find a function which models the data with the least error.

- Summarization – providing a more compact representation of the data set, including visualization and report generation.

Results Validation

Data mining can unintentionally be misused, and can then produce results which appear to be significant; but which do not actually predict future behaviour and cannot be reproduced on a new sample of data and bear little use. Often this results from investigating too many hypotheses and not performing proper statistical hypothesis testing. A simple version of this problem in machine learning is known as overfitting, but the same problem can arise at different phases of the process and thus a train/test split - when applicable at all - may not be sufficient to prevent this from happening.

The final step of knowledge discovery from data is to verify that the patterns produced by the data mining algorithms occur in the wider data set. Not all patterns found by the data mining algorithms are necessarily valid. It is common for the data mining algorithms to find patterns in the training set which are not present in the general data set. This is called overfitting. To overcome this, the evaluation uses a test set of data on which the data mining algorithm was not trained. The learned patterns are applied to this test set, and the resulting output is compared to the desired output. For example, a data mining algorithm trying to distinguish "spam" from "legitimate" emails would be trained on a training set of sample e-mails. Once trained, the learned patterns would be applied to the test set of e-mails on which it had not been trained. The accuracy of the patterns can then be measured from how many e-mails they correctly classify. A number of statistical methods may be used to evaluate the algorithm, such as ROC curves.

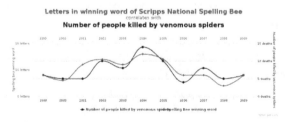

An example of data produced by data dredging through a bot operated by statistician Tyler Viglen, apparently showing a close link between the best word winning a spelling bee competition and the number of people in the United States killed by venomous spiders. The similarity in trends is obviously a coincidence.

If the learned patterns do not meet the desired standards, subsequently it is necessary to re-evaluate and change the pre-processing and data mining steps. If the learned patterns do meet the desired standards, then the final step is to interpret the learned patterns and turn them into knowledge.

Research

The premier professional body in the field is the Association for Computing Machinery's (ACM) Special Interest Group (SIG) on Knowledge Discovery and Data Mining (SIGKDD). Since 1989 this ACM SIG has hosted an annual international conference and published its proceedings, and since 1999 it has published a biannual academic journal titled "SIGKDD Explorations".

Computer science conferences on data mining include:

- CIKM Conference – ACM Conference on Information and Knowledge Management

- DMIN Conference – International Conference on Data Mining

- DMKD Conference – Research Issues on Data Mining and Knowledge Discovery

- DSAA Conference – IEEE International Conference on Data Science and Advanced Analytics

- ECDM Conference – European Conference on Data Mining

- ECML-PKDD Conference – European Conference on Machine Learning and Principles and Practice of Knowledge Discovery in Databases

- EDM Conference – International Conference on Educational Data Mining

- INFOCOM Conference – IEEE INFOCOM

- ICDM Conference – IEEE International Conference on Data Mining

- KDD Conference – ACM SIGKDD Conference on Knowledge Discovery and Data Mining

- MLDM Conference – Machine Learning and Data Mining in Pattern Recognition

- PAKDD Conference – The annual Pacific-Asia Conference on Knowledge Discovery and Data Mining

- PAW Conference – Predictive Analytics World

- SDM Conference – SIAM International Conference on Data Mining (SIAM)

- SSTD Symposium – Symposium on Spatial and Temporal Databases

- WSDM Conference – ACM Conference on Web Search and Data Mining

Data mining topics are also present on many data management/database conferences such as the ICDE Conference, SIGMOD Conference and International Conference on Very Large Data Bases

Standards

There have been some efforts to define standards for the data mining process, for example the 1999 European Cross Industry Standard Process for Data Mining (CRISP-DM 1.0) and the 2004 Java Data Mining standard (JDM 1.0). Development on successors to these processes (CRISP-DM 2.0 and JDM 2.0) was active in 2006, but has stalled since. JDM 2.0 was withdrawn without reaching a final draft.

For exchanging the extracted models – in particular for use in predictive analytics – the key standard is the Predictive Model Markup Language (PMML), which is an XML-based language developed by the Data Mining Group (DMG) and supported as exchange format by many data mining applications. As the name suggests, it only covers prediction models, a particular data mining task of high importance to business applications. However, extensions to cover (for example) subspace clustering have been proposed independently of the DMG.

Notable Uses

Data mining is used wherever there is digital data available today. Notable examples of data mining can be found throughout business, medicine, science, and surveillance.

Privacy Concerns and Ethics

While the term "data mining" itself has no ethical implications, it is often associated with the mining of information in relation to peoples' behavior (ethical and otherwise).

The ways in which data mining can be used can in some cases and contexts raise questions regarding privacy, legality, and ethics. In particular, data mining government or commercial data sets for national security or law enforcement purposes, such as in the Total Information Awareness Program or in ADVISE, has raised privacy concerns.

Data mining requires data preparation which can uncover information or patterns which may compromise confidentiality and privacy obligations. A common way for this to occur is through data aggregation. Data aggregation involves combining data together (possibly from various sources) in a way that facilitates analysis (but that also might make identification of private, individual-level data deducible or otherwise apparent). This is not data mining per se, but a result of the preparation of data before – and for the purposes of – the analysis. The threat to an individual's privacy comes into play when the data, once compiled, cause the data miner, or anyone who has access to the newly compiled data set, to be able to identify specific individuals, especially when the data were originally anonymous.

It is recommended that an individual is made aware of the following before data are collected:

- the purpose of the data collection and any (known) data mining projects;

- how the data will be used;

- who will be able to mine the data and use the data and their derivatives;

- the status of security surrounding access to the data;

- how collected data can be updated.

Data may also be modified so as to become anonymous, so that individuals may not readily be identified. However, even "de-identified"/"anonymized" data sets can potentially contain enough information to allow identification of individuals, as occurred when journalists were able to find several individuals based on a set of search histories that were inadvertently released by AOL.

The inadvertent revelation of personally identifiable information leading to the provider violates Fair Information Practices. This indiscretion can cause financial, emotional, or bodily harm to the indicated individual. In one instance of privacy violation, the patrons of Walgreens filed a lawsuit against the company in 2011 for selling prescription information to data mining companies who in turn provided the data to pharmaceutical companies.

Situation in Europe

Europe has rather strong privacy laws, and efforts are underway to further strengthen the rights of the consumers. However, the U.S.-E.U. Safe Harbor Principles currently effectively expose European users to privacy exploitation by U.S. companies. As a consequence of Edward Snowden's Global surveillance disclosure, there has been increased discussion to revoke this agreement, as in particular the data will be fully exposed to the National Security Agency, and attempts to reach an agreement have failed.

Situation in the United States

In the United States, privacy concerns have been addressed by the US Congress via the passage of regulatory controls such as the Health Insurance Portability and Accountability Act (HIPAA). The HIPAA requires individuals to give their "informed consent" regarding information they provide and its intended present and future uses. According to an article in Biotech Business Week', "'[i]n practice, HIPAA may not offer any greater protection than the longstanding regulations in the research arena,' says the AAHC. More importantly, the rule's goal of protection through informed consent is undermined by the complexity of consent forms that are required of patients and participants, which approach a level of incomprehensibility to average individuals." This underscores the necessity for data anonymity in data aggregation and mining practices.

U.S. information privacy legislation such as HIPAA and the Family Educational Rights and Privacy Act (FERPA) applies only to the specific areas that each such law addresses. Use of data mining by the majority of businesses in the U.S. is not controlled by any legislation.

Copyright Law

Situation in Europe

Due to a lack of flexibilities in European copyright and database law, the mining of in-copyright works such as web mining without the permission of the copyright owner is not legal. Where a database is pure data in Europe there is likely to be no copyright, but database rights may exist so data mining becomes subject to regulations by the Database Directive. On the recommendation of the Hargreaves review this led to the UK government to amend its copyright law in 2014 to allow content mining as a limitation and exception. Only the second country in the world to do so after Japan, which introduced an exception in 2009 for data mining. However, due to the restriction of the Copyright Directive, the UK exception only allows content mining for non-commercial purposes. UK copyright law also does not allow this provision to be overridden by contractual terms and conditions. The European Commission facilitated stakeholder discussion on text and data mining in 2013, under the title of Licences for Europe. The focus on the solution to this legal issue being licences and not limitations and exceptions led to representatives of universities, researchers, libraries, civil society groups and open access publishers to leave the stakeholder dialogue in May 2013.

Situation in the United States

By contrast to Europe, the flexible nature of US copyright law, and in particular fair use means that content mining in America, as well as other fair use countries such as Israel, Taiwan and South Korea is viewed as being legal. As content mining is transformative, that is it does not supplant the original work, it is viewed as being lawful under fair use. For example, as part of the Google Book settlement the presiding judge on the case ruled that Google's digitisation project of in-copyright books was lawful, in part because of the transformative uses that the digitisation project displayed - one being text and data mining.

Software

Free open-source data mining software and applications

The following applications are available under free/open source licenses. Public access to application sourcecode is also available.

- Carrot2: Text and search results clustering framework.

- Chemicalize.org: A chemical structure miner and web search engine.

- ELKI: A university research project with advanced cluster analysis and outlier detection methods written in the Java language.

- GATE: a natural language processing and language engineering tool.

- KNIME: The Konstanz Information Miner, a user friendly and comprehensive data analytics framework.

- Massive Online Analysis (MOA): a real-time big data stream mining with concept drift tool in the Java programming language.

- ML-Flex: A software package that enables users to integrate with third-party machine-learning packages written in any programming language, execute classification analyses in parallel across multiple computing nodes, and produce HTML reports of classification results.

- MLPACK library: a collection of ready-to-use machine learning algorithms written in the C++ language.

- NLTK (Natural Language Toolkit): A suite of libraries and programs for symbolic and statistical natural language processing (NLP) for the Python language.

- OpenNN: Open neural networks library.

- Orange: A component-based data mining and machine learning software suite written in the Python language.

- R: A programming language and software environment for statistical computing, data mining, and graphics. It is part of the GNU Project.

- SCaViS: Java cross-platform data analysis framework developed at Argonne National Laboratory.

- scikit-learn is an open source machine learning library for the Python programming language

- SenticNet API: A semantic and affective resource for opinion mining and sentiment analysis.

- Torch: An open source deep learning library for the Lua programming language and scientific computing framework with wide support for machine learning algorithms.

- UIMA: The UIMA (Unstructured Information Management Architecture) is a component framework for analyzing unstructured content such as text, audio and video – originally developed by IBM.

- Weka: A suite of machine learning software applications written in the Java programming language.

Proprietary Data-mining Software and Applications

The following applications are available under proprietary licenses.

- Angoss KnowledgeSTUDIO: data mining tool provided by Angoss.

- Clarabridge: enterprise class text analytics solution.

- HP Vertica Analytics Platform: data mining software provided by HP.

- IBM SPSS Modeler: data mining software provided by IBM.

- KXEN Modeler: data mining tool provided by KXEN.

- LIONsolver: an integrated software application for data mining, business intelligence, and modeling that implements the Learning and Intelligent OptimizatioN (LION) approach.

- Megaputer Intelligence: data and text mining software is called PolyAnalyst.

- Microsoft Analysis Services: data mining software provided by Microsoft.

- NetOwl: suite of multilingual text and entity analytics products that enable data mining.

- OpenText™ Big Data Analytics: Visual Data Mining & Predictive Analysis by Open Text Corporation

- Oracle Data Mining: data mining software by Oracle.

- PSeven: platform for automation of engineering simulation and analysis, multidisciplinary optimization and data mining provided by DATADVANCE.

- Qlucore Omics Explorer: data mining software provided by Qlucore.

- RapidMiner: An environment for machine learning and data mining experiments.

- SAS Enterprise Miner: data mining software provided by the SAS Institute.

- STATISTICA Data Miner: data mining software provided by StatSoft.

- Tanagra: A visualisation-oriented data mining software, also for teaching.

Marketplace Surveys

Several researchers and organizations have conducted reviews of data mining tools and surveys of data miners. These identify some of the strengths and weaknesses of the software packages. They also provide an overview of the behaviors, preferences and views of data miners. Some of these reports include:

- Hurwitz Victory Index: Report for Advanced Analytics as a market research assessment tool, it highlights both the diverse uses for advanced analytics technology and the vendors who make those applications possible.Recent-research

- 2011 Wiley Interdisciplinary Reviews: Data Mining and Knowledge Discovery

- Rexer Analytics Data Miner Surveys (2007–2013)

- Forrester Research 2010 Predictive Analytics and Data Mining Solutions report

- Gartner 2008 "Magic Quadrant" report

- Robert A. Nisbet's 2006 Three Part Series of articles "Data Mining Tools: Which One is Best For CRM?"

- Haughton et al.'s 2003 Review of Data Mining Software Packages in The American Statistician

- Goebel & Gruenwald 1999 "A Survey of Data Mining a Knowledge Discovery Software Tools" in SIGKDD Explorations

Information Extraction

Information extraction (IE) is the task of automatically extracting structured information from unstructured and/or semi-structured machine-readable documents. In most of the cases this activity concerns processing human language texts by means of natural language processing (NLP). Recent activities in multimedia document processing like automatic annotation and content extraction out of images/audio/video could be seen as information extraction.

Due to the difficulty of the problem, current approaches to IE focus on narrowly restricted domains. An example is the extraction from news wire reports of corporate mergers, such as denoted by the formal relation:

$$\text{MergerBetween}(company_1, company_2, date),$$

from an online news sentence such as:

"Yesterday, New York based Foo Inc. announced their acquisition of Bar Corp."

A broad goal of IE is to allow computation to be done on the previously unstructured data. A more specific goal is to allow logical reasoning to draw inferences based on the logical content of the input data. Structured data is semantically well-defined data from a chosen target domain, interpreted with respect to category and context.

Information Extraction is the part of a greater puzzle which deals with the problem of devising automatic methods for text management, beyond its transmission, storage and display. The discipline of information retrieval (IR) has developed automatic methods, typically of a statistical flavor, for indexing large document collections and classifying documents. Another complementary approach is that of natural language processing (NLP) which has solved the problem of modelling human language processing with considerable success when taking into account the magnitude of the task. In terms of both difficulty and emphasis, IE deals with tasks in between both IR and NLP. In terms of input, IE assumes the existence of a set of documents in which each document follows a template, i.e. describes one or more entities or events in a manner that is similar to those in other documents but differing in the details. An example, consider a group of newswire articles on Latin American terrorism with each article is presumed to be based upon one or more terroristic acts. We also define for any given IE task a template, which is a(or a set of) case frame(s) to hold the information contained in a single document. For the terrorism example, a template would have slots corresponding to the perpetrator, victim, and weapon of the terroristic act, and the date on which the event happened. An IE system for this problem is required to "understand" an attack article only enough to find data corresponding to the slots in this template.

History

Information extraction dates back to the late 1970s in the early days of NLP. An early commercial system from the mid-1980s was JASPER built for Reuters by the Carnegie Group with the aim of providing real-time financial news to financial traders.

Beginning in 1987, IE was spurred by a series of Message Understanding Conferences. MUC is a competition-based conference that focused on the following domains:

- MUC-1 (1987), MUC-2 (1989): Naval operations messages.

- MUC-3 (1991), MUC-4 (1992): Terrorism in Latin American countries.

- MUC-5 (1993): Joint ventures and microelectronics domain.

- MUC-6 (1995): News articles on management changes.

- MUC-7 (1998): Satellite launch reports.

Considerable support came from the U.S. Defense Advanced Research Projects Agency (DARPA), who wished to automate mundane tasks performed by government analysts, such as scanning newspapers for possible links to terrorism.

Present Significance

The present significance of IE pertains to the growing amount of information available in unstructured form. Tim Berners-Lee, inventor of the world wide web, refers to the existing Internet as the web of documents and advocates that more of the content be made available as a web of data. Until this transpires, the web largely consists of unstructured documents lacking semantic metadata. Knowledge contained within these documents can be made more accessible for machine processing by means of transformation into relational form, or by marking-up with XML tags. An intelligent agent monitoring a news data feed requires IE to transform unstructured data into something that can be reasoned with. A typical application of IE is to scan a set of documents written in a natural language and populate a database with the information extracted.

Tasks and Subtasks

Applying information extraction on text, is linked to the problem of text simplification in order to create a structured view of the information present in free text. The overall goal being to create a more easily machine-readable text to process the sentences. Typical subtasks of IE include:

- Named entity extraction which could include:

  o Named entity recognition: recognition of known entity names (for people and organizations), place names, temporal expressions, and certain types of numerical expressions, employing existing knowledge of the domain or information extracted from other sentences. Typically the recognition task involves assigning a unique identifier to the extracted entity. A simpler task is named entity detection, which aims to detect entities without having any existing knowledge about the entity instances. For example, in processing the sentence "M. Smith likes fishing", named entity detection would denote detecting that the phrase "M. Smith" does refer to a person, but without necessarily having (or using) any knowledge about a certain M. Smith who is (or, "might be") the specific person whom that sentence is talking about.

  o Coreference resolution: detection of coreference and anaphoric links between text entities. In IE tasks, this is typically restricted to finding links between previously-extracted named entities. For example, "International Business Machines" and "IBM" refer to the same real-world entity. If we take the two sentences "M. Smith likes fishing. But he doesn't like biking", it would be beneficial to detect that "he" is referring to the previously detected person "M. Smith".

  o Relationship extraction: identification of relations between entities, such as:

- PERSON works for ORGANIZATION (extracted from the sentence "Bill works for IBM.")

- PERSON located in LOCATION (extracted from the sentence "Bill is in France.")

- Semi-structured information extraction which may refer to any IE that tries to restore some kind information structure that has been lost through publication such as:

  o Table extraction: finding and extracting tables from documents.

  o Comments extraction : extracting comments from actual content of article in order to restore the link between author of each sentence

- Language and vocabulary analysis

  o Terminology extraction: finding the relevant terms for a given corpus

- Audio extraction

  o Template-based music extraction: finding relevant characteristic in an audio signal taken from a given repertoire; for instance time indexes of occurrences of percussive sounds can be extracted in order to represent the essential rhythmic component of a music piece.

Note this list is not exhaustive and that the exact meaning of IE activities is not commonly accepted and that many approaches combine multiple sub-tasks of IE in order to achieve a wider goal. Machine learning, statistical analysis and/or natural language processing are often used in IE.

IE on non-text documents is becoming an increasing topic in research and information extracted from multimedia documents can now be expressed in a high level structure as it is done on text. This naturally lead to the fusion of extracted information from multiple kind of documents and sources.

World Wide Web Applications

IE has been the focus of the MUC conferences. The proliferation of the Web, however, intensified the need for developing IE systems that help people to cope with the enormous amount of data that is available online. Systems that perform IE from online text should meet the requirements of low cost, flexibility in development and easy adaptation to new domains. MUC systems fail to meet those criteria. Moreover, linguistic analysis performed for unstructured text does not exploit the HTML/XML tags and layout format that are available in online text. As a result, less linguistically intensive approaches have been developed for IE on the Web using wrappers, which are sets of highly accurate rules that extract a particular page's content. Manually developing wrappers has proved to be a time-consuming task, requiring a high level of expertise. Machine learning techniques, either supervised or unsupervised, have been used to induce such rules automatically.

Wrappers typically handle highly structured collections of web pages, such as product catalogs and telephone directories. They fail, however, when the text type is less structured, which is also common on the Web. Recent effort on adaptive information extraction motivates the development of IE systems that can handle different types of text, from well-structured to almost free text -where common wrappers fail- including mixed types. Such systems can exploit shallow natural language knowledge and thus can be also applied to less structured text.

A recent development is Visual Information Extraction, that relies on rendering a webpage in a browser and creating rules based on the proximity of regions in the rendered web page. This helps in extracting entities from complex web pages that may exhibit a visual pattern, but lack a discernible pattern in the HTML source code.

Approaches

Three standard approaches are now widely accepted

- Hand-written regular expressions (perhaps stacked
- Using classifiers
    - Generative: naïve Bayes classifier
    - Discriminative: maximum entropy models such as Multinomial logistic regression
- Sequence models
    - Hidden Markov model
    - Conditional Markov model (CMM) / Maximum-entropy Markov model (MEMM)
    - Conditional random fields (CRF) are commonly used in conjunction with IE for tasks as varied as extracting information from research papers to extracting navigation instructions.

Numerous other approaches exist for IE including hybrid approaches that combine some of the standard approaches previously listed.

Free or Open Source Software and Services

- General Architecture for Text Engineering "General Architecture for Text Engineering", which is bundled with a free Information Extraction system

- OpenNLP Apache OpenNLP is a Java machine learning toolkit for natural language processing

- OpenCalais Automated information extraction web service from Thomson Reuters (Free limited version)

- Machine Learning for Language Toolkit (Mallet) is a Java-based package for a variety of natural language processing tasks, including information extraction.

- DBpedia Spotlight is an open source tool in Java/Scala (and free web service) that can be used for named entity recognition and name resolution.

- Natural Language Toolkit is a suite of libraries and programs for symbolic and statistical natural language processing (NLP) for the Python programming language

Commercial Software and Services

- IBM Watson

- Wolfram Language

Data Storage Device

Many different consumer electronic devices can store data.

A data storage device is a device for recording (storing) information (data). Recording can be done using virtually any form of energy, spanning from manual muscle power in handwriting, to acoustic vibrations in phonographic recording, to electromagnetic energy modulating magnetic tape and optical discs.

A storage device may hold information, process information, or both. A device that only holds information is a recording medium. Devices that process information (data storage equipment) may either access a separate portable (removable) recording medium or a permanent component to store and retrieve data.

Edison cylinder phonograph ca. 1899. The phonograph cylinder is a storage medium. The phonograph may be considered a storage device.

Electronic data storage requires electrical power to store and retrieve that data. Most storage devices that do not require vision and a brain to read data fall into this category. Electromagnetic data may be stored in either an analog data or digital data format on a variety of media. This type of data is considered to be electronically encoded data, whether it is electronically stored in a semiconductor device, for it is certain that a semiconductor device was used to record it on its medium. Most electronically processed data storage media (including some forms of computer data storage) are considered permanent (non-volatile) storage, that is, the data will remain stored when power is removed from the device. In contrast, most electronically stored information within most types of semiconductor (computer chips) microcircuits are volatile memory, for it vanishes if power is removed.

A reel-to-reel tape recorder (Sony TC-630). The magnetic tape is a data storage medium. The recorder is data storage equipment using a portable medium (tape reel) to store the data.

Crafting tools such as paint brushes can be used as data storage equipment. The paint and canvas can be used as data storage media.

Except for barcodes, optical character recognition (OCR), and magnetic ink character recognition (MICR) data, electronic data storage is easier to revise and may be more cost effective than alternative methods due to smaller physical space requirements and the ease of replacing (rewriting) data on the same medium. However, the durability of methods such as printed data is still superior to that of most electronic storage media. The durability limitations may be overcome with the ease of duplicating (backing-up) electronic data.

Terminology

Devices that are not used exclusively for recording such as hands, mouths, musical instruments, and devices that are intermediate in the storing/retrieving process, like eyes, ears, cameras, scanners, microphones, speakers, monitors, or video projectors, are generally not considered storage devices. Devices that are exclusively for recording such as printers, exclusively for reading, like barcode readers, or devices that process only one form of information, like phonographs may or may not be considered storage devices. In computing these are known as input/output devices.

All information is data. However, not all data is information.

Many data storage devices are also media players. Any device that can store and play-back multimedia may also be considered a media player such as in the case with the HD media player. Designated hard drives are used to play saved or streaming media on home cinemas or home theater PCs.

Global Capacity, Digitization, and Trends

In a recent study in Science it was estimated that the world's technological capacity to store information in analog and digital devices grew from less than 3 (optimally compressed) exabytes in 1986, to 295 (optimally compressed) exabytes in 2007, and doubles roughly every 3 years.

It is estimated that the year 2002 marked the beginning of the digital age for information storage, the year that marked the date when human kind started to store more information on digital than on analog storage devices. In 1986 only 1% of the world's capacity to store information was in digital format, which grew to 3% by 1993, 25% in the year 2000, and exploded to 97% of the world's storage capacity by 2007.

Equipment

Any input/output equipment may be considered data storage equipment if it writes to and reads from a data storage medium.

Data storage equipment uses either:

- portable methods (easily replaced),

- semi-portable methods, requiring mechanical disassembly tools and/or opening a chassis, or

- Volatile methods, meaning loss of memory if disconnected from the unit.

The following are examples of those methods:

Portable Methods

- Hand crafting

- Flat surface

  - Printmaking

  - Photographic

- Fabrication

  - Automated assembly

  - Textile

  - Molding

  - Solid freeform fabrication

- Cylindrical accessing

- Memory card reader/drive

- Tape drive

  - Mono reel or reel-to-reel

  - Compact Cassette player/recorder

  - Data cartridge (tape)

- Disk accessing

  - Disk drive

  - Disk pack

  - Disk enclosure

- ROM cartridge

- Peripheral networking

- Flash memory devices

Semi-portable Methods

- Hard disk drive

- non-volatile RAM

Volatile Methods

- Volatile RAM

- Neurons

Recording Medium

A recording medium is a physical material that holds data expressed in any of the existing recording formats. With electronic media, the data and the recording medium is sometimes part of the surface of the medium.

Some recording media may be temporary either by design or by nature. Volatile organic compounds may be used to preserve the environment or to purposely make data expire over time. Data such as smoke signals or skywriting are temporary by nature.

Ancient Examples

The Gutenberg Bible displayed by the United States Library of Congress, demonstrating printed pages as a storage medium

A set of index cards in a file box are a nonlinear storage medium.

- Optical

    o Any object visible to the eye, used to mark a location such as a stone, flag, or skull.

    o Any crafting material used to form shapes such as clay, wood, metal, glass, wax, or quipu.

    o Any hard surface that could hold carvings.

    o Any branding surface that would scar under intense heat (chiefly for livestock or humans).

    o Any marking substance such as paint, ink, or chalk.

    o Any surface that would hold a marking substance such as, papyrus, paper, or skin.

- Chemical

    o RNA

    o DNA – for uses of DNA by people for storing information,

    o Pheromone

Modern Examples by Energy Used

Graffiti on a public wall. Public surfaces are being used as unconventional data storage media, often without permission.

Photographic film is a photochemical data storage medium

A floppy disk is a magnetic data storage medium

- Chemical

  o Dipstick

- Thermodynamic

  o Thermometer

- Photochemical

  o Photographic film

- Mechanical

  o Pins and holes

    ▪ Paper

A 3.5" PATA hard drive is both storage equipment and a storage medium.

    ▪ Punched card

    ▪ Paper tape

      ▪ Music roll

    ▪ Music box cylinder or disk

- o   Grooves

  - Phonograph cylinder

  - Gramophone record

  - Dictabelt (groove on plastic belt)

  - Capacitance Electronic Disc

- Magnetic storage

  - o   Wire recording (stainless steel wire)

  - o   Magnetic tape

  - o   Drum memory (magnetic drum)

  - o   Floppy disk

- Optical storage

  - o   Optical jukebox

  - o   Photographic paper

  - o   X-ray

  - o   Microform

  - o   Hologram

  - o   Projected foil

  - o   Optical disc

  - o   Magneto-optical drive

  - o   Holographic data storage

  - o   3D optical data storage

- Electrical

  - o   Semiconductor used in volatile random-access memory

  - o   Floating-gate transistor used in non-volatile memory cards

Modern Examples by Shape

A typical way to classify data storage media is to consider its shape and type of movement (or non-movement) relative to the read/write device(s) of the storage apparatus as listed:

- Paper card storage

    o Punched card (mechanical)

- Cams and tracers (pipe organ combination-action memory memorizing stop selections)

- Tape storage (long, thin, flexible, linearly moving bands)

    o Paper tape (mechanical)

    o Magnetic tape (a tape passing one or more read/write/erase heads)

- Disk storage (flat, round, rotating object)

    o Gramophone record (used for distributing some 1980s home computer programs) (mechanical)

    o Carousel memory (magnetic rolls)

    o Floppy disk, ZIP disk (removable) (magnetic)

    o Holographic

    o Optical disc such as CD, DVD, Blu-ray Disc

    o Minidisc

    o Hard disk drive (magnetic)

- Magnetic bubble memory

- Flash memory/memory card (solid state semiconductor memory)

    o xD-Picture Card

    o MultiMediaCard

    o USB flash drive (also known as a "thumb drive" or "keydrive")

    o SmartMedia

    o CompactFlash I and II

    o Secure Digital

    o Sony Memory Stick (Std/Duo/PRO/MagicGate versions)

    o Solid-state drive

Bekenstein (2003) foresees that miniaturization might lead to the invention of devices that store bits on a single atom.

Weight and Volume

Especially for carrying around data, the weight and volume per MB are relevant. They are quite large for written and printed paper compared with modern electronic media. On the other hand, written and printer paper do not require (the weight and volume of) reading equipment, and handwritten edits only require simple writing equipment, such as a pen.

With mobile data connections the data need not be carried around to be available.

Data Transmission

Data transmission, digital transmission or digital communications is the physical transfer of data (a digital bit stream or a digitized analog signal) over a point-to-point or point-to-multipoint communication channel. Examples of such channels are copper wires, optical fibers, wireless communication channels, storage media and computer buses. The data are represented as an electromagnetic signal, such as an electrical voltage, radiowave, microwave, or infrared signal.

Analog or analogue transmission is a transmission method of conveying voice, data, image, signal or video information using a continuous signal which varies in amplitude, phase, or some other property in proportion to that of a variable. The messages are either represented by a sequence of pulses by means of a line code (baseband transmission), or by a limited set of continuously varying wave forms (passband transmission), using a digital modulation method. The passband modulation and corresponding demodulation (also known as detection) is carried out by modem equipment. According to the most common definition of digital signal, both baseband and passband signals representing bit-streams are considered as digital transmission, while an alternative definition only considers the baseband signal as digital, and passband transmission of digital data as a form of digital-to-analog conversion.

Data transmitted may be digital messages originating from a data source, for example a computer or a keyboard. It may also be an analog signal such as a phone call or a video signal, digitized into a bit-stream for example using pulse-code modulation (PCM) or more advanced source coding (analog-to-digital conversion and data compression) schemes. This source coding and decoding is carried out by codec equipment.

Distinction Between Related Subjects

Courses and textbooks in the field of data transmission as well as digital transmission and digital communications have similar content.

Digital transmission or data transmission traditionally belongs to telecommunications and electrical engineering. Basic principles of data transmission may also be covered within the computer science/computer engineering topic of data communications, which also includes computer networking or computer communication applications and networking protocols, for example routing, switching and inter-process communication. Although the Transmission control protocol (TCP) involves the term "transmission", TCP and other transport layer protocols are typically not discussed in a textbook or course about data transmission, but in computer networking.

The term tele transmission involves the analog as well as digital communication. In most textbooks, the term analog transmission only refers to the transmission of an analog message signal (without digitization) by means of an analog signal, either as a non-modulated baseband signal, or as a passband signal using an analog modulation method such as AM or FM. It may also include analog-over-analog pulse modulatated baseband signals such as pulse-width modulation. In a few books within the computer networking tradition, "analog transmission" also refers to passband transmission of bit-streams using digital modulation methods such as FSK, PSK and ASK. Note that these methods are covered in textbooks named digital transmission or data transmission, for example.

The theoretical aspects of data transmission are covered by information theory and coding theory.

Protocol Layers and Sub-topics

Courses and textbooks in the field of data transmission typically deal with the following OSI model protocol layers and topics:

- Layer 1, the physical layer:
    - Channel coding including
        - Digital modulation schemes
        - Line coding schemes
        - Forward error correction (FEC) codes
    - Bit synchronization
    - Multiplexing
    - Equalization
    - Channel models
- Layer 2, the data link layer:
    - Channel access schemes, media access control (MAC)

- o Packet mode communication and Frame synchronization

- o Error detection and automatic repeat request (ARQ)

- o Flow control

- Layer 6, the presentation layer:

  - o Source coding (digitization and data compression), and information theory.

  - o Cryptography (may occur at any layer)

Applications and History

Data (mainly but not exclusively informational) has been sent via non-electronic (e.g. optical, acoustic, mechanical) means since the advent of communication. Analog signal data has been sent electronically since the advent of the telephone. However, the first data electromagnetic transmission applications in modern time were telegraphy (1809) and teletypewriters (1906), which are both digital signals. The fundamental theoretical work in data transmission and information theory by Harry Nyquist, Ralph Hartley, Claude Shannon and others during the early 20th century, was done with these applications in mind.

Data transmission is utilized in computers in computer buses and for communication with peripheral equipment via parallel ports and serial ports such as RS-232 (1969), Firewire (1995) and USB (1996). The principles of data transmission are also utilized in storage media for Error detection and correction since 1951.

Data transmission is utilized in computer networking equipment such as modems (1940), local area networks (LAN) adapters (1964), repeaters, hubs, microwave links, wireless network access points (1997), etc.

In telephone networks, digital communication is utilized for transferring many phone calls over the same copper cable or fiber cable by means of Pulse code modulation (PCM), i.e. sampling and digitization, in combination with Time division multiplexing (TDM) (1962). Telephone exchanges have become digital and software controlled, facilitating many value added services. For example, the first AXE telephone exchange was presented in 1976. Since the late 1980s, digital communication to the end user has been possible using Integrated Services Digital Network (ISDN) services. Since the end of the 1990s, broadband access techniques such as ADSL, Cable modems, fiber-to-the-building (FTTB) and fiber-to-the-home (FTTH) have become widespread to small offices and homes. The current tendency is to replace traditional telecommunication services by packet mode communication such as IP telephony and IPTV.

Transmitting analog signals digitally allows for greater signal processing capability. The ability to process a communications signal means that errors caused by random processes can be detected and corrected. Digital signals can also be sampled instead of continuously monitored. The multiplexing of multiple digital signals is much simpler to the multiplexing of analog signals.

Because of all these advantages, and because recent advances in wideband communication channels and solid-state electronics have allowed scientists to fully realize these advantages, digital communications has grown quickly. Digital communications is quickly edging out analog communication because of the vast demand to transmit computer data and the ability of digital communications to do so.

The digital revolution has also resulted in many digital telecommunication applications where the principles of data transmission are applied. Examples are second-generation (1991) and later cellular telephony, video conferencing, digital TV (1998), digital radio (1999), telemetry, etc.

Data transmission, digital transmission or digital communications is the physical transfer of data (a digital bit stream or a digitized analog signal) over a point-to-point or point-to-multipoint communication channel. Examples of such channels are copper wires, optical fibers, wireless communication channels, storage media and computer buses. The data are represented as an electromagnetic signal, such as an electrical voltage, radiowave, microwave, or infrared signal.

While analog transmission is the transfer of a continuously varying analog signal over an analog channel, digital communications is the transfer of discrete messages over a digital or an analog channel. The messages are either represented by a sequence of pulses by means of a line code (baseband transmission), or by a limited set of continuously varying wave forms (passband transmission), using a digital modulation method. The passband modulation and corresponding demodulation (also known as detection) is carried out by modem equipment. According to the most common definition of digital signal, both baseband and passband signals representing bit-streams are considered as digital transmission, while an alternative definition only considers the baseband signal as digital, and passband transmission of digital data as a form of digital-to-analog conversion.

Data transmitted may be digital messages originating from a data source, for example a computer or a keyboard. It may also be an analog signal such as a phone call or a video signal, digitized into a bit-stream for example using pulse-code modulation (PCM) or more advanced source coding (analog-to-digital conversion and data compression) schemes. This source coding and decoding is carried out by codec equipment.

Serial and Parallel Transmission

In telecommunications, serial transmission is the sequential transmission of signal elements of a group representing a character or other entity of data. Digital serial transmissions are bits sent over a single wire, frequency or optical path sequentially. Because it requires less signal processing and less chances for error than parallel transmission, the transfer rate of each individual path may be faster. This can be used over longer distances as a check digit or parity bit can be sent along it easily.

In telecommunications, parallel transmission is the simultaneous transmission of the signal elements of a character or other entity of data. In digital communications, parallel transmission is the simultaneous transmission of related signal elements over two or more separate paths. Multiple electrical wires are used which can transmit multiple bits simultaneously, which allows for higher data transfer rates than can be achieved with serial transmission. This method is used internally within the computer, for example the internal buses, and sometimes externally for such things as printers, The major issue with this is "skewing" because the wires in parallel data transmission have slightly different properties (not intentionally) so some bits may arrive before others, which may corrupt the message. A parity bit can help to reduce this. However, electrical wire parallel data transmission is therefore less reliable for long distances because corrupt transmissions are far more likely.

Types of communication Channels

There are many types of communication are there some are -

- Data transmission circuit

- Full-duplex

- Half-duplex

- Multi-drop:

    o   Bus network

    o   Mesh network

    o   Ring network

    o   Star network

    o   Wireless network

- Point-to-point

- Simplex

Asynchronous and Synchronous Data Transmission

Asynchronous start-stop transmission uses start and stop bits to signify the beginning bit ASCII character would actually be transmitted using 10 bits. For example, "0100 0001" would become "1 0100 0001 0". The extra one (or zero, depending on parity bit) at the start and end of the transmission tells the receiver first that a character is coming and secondly that the character has ended. This method of transmission is used when data are sent intermittently as opposed to in a solid stream. In the previous example the start and stop bits are in bold. The start and stop bits must be of opposite polarity. This allows the receiver to recognize when the second packet of information is being sent.

Synchronous transmission uses no start and stop bits, but instead synchronizes transmission speeds at both the receiving and sending end of the transmission using clock signal(s) built into each component.A continual stream of data is then sent between the two nodes. Due to there being no start and stop bits the data transfer rate is quicker although more errors will occur, as the clocks will eventually get out of sync, and the receiving device would have the wrong time that had been agreed in the protocol for sending/receiving data, so some bytes could become corrupted (by losing bits). Ways to get around this problem include re-synchronization of the clocks and use of check digits to ensure the byte is correctly interpreted and received

References

- Frakes, William B. (1992). Information Retrieval Data Structures & Algorithms. Prentice-Hall, Inc. ISBN 0-13-463837-9.

- Doyle, Lauren; Becker, Joseph (1975). Information Retrieval and Processing. Melville. pp. 410 pp. ISBN 0-471-22151-1.

- Korfhage, Robert R. (1997). Information Storage and Retrieval. Wiley. pp. 368 pp. ISBN 978-0-471-14338-3.

- Shah, C (2012). Collaborative Information Seeking: The Art and Science of Making the Whole Greater than the Sum of All. The Information Retrieval Series, Vol. 34. Springer. ISBN 978-3-642-28812-8.

- Witten, Ian H.; Frank, Eibe; Hall, Mark A. (30 January 2011). Data Mining: Practical Machine Learning Tools and Techniques (3 ed.). Elsevier. ISBN 978-0-12-374856-0.

- Mena, Jesús (2011). Machine Learning Forensics for Law Enforcement, Security, and Intelligence. Boca Raton, FL: CRC Press (Taylor & Francis Group). ISBN 978-1-4398-6069-4.

- Kantardzic, Mehmed (2003). Data Mining: Concepts, Models, Methods, and Algorithms. John Wiley & Sons. ISBN 0-471-22852-4. OCLC 50055336.

- David R. Smith, "Digital Transmission Systems", Kluwer International Publishers, 2003, ISBN 1-4020-7587-1.

- Sergio Benedetto, Ezio Biglieri, "Principles of Digital Transmission: With Wireless Applications", Springer 2008, ISBN 0-306-45753-9, ISBN 978-0-306-45753-1.

- Simon Haykin, "Digital Communications", John Wiley & Sons, 1988. ISBN 978-0-471-62947-4.

- John Proakis, "Digital Communications", 4th edition, McGraw-Hill, 2000. ISBN 0-07-232111-3.

- Jiang, Jing (2012). "Information Extraction from Text" (PDF). Ohio State University Department of Statistics. Retrieved July 13, 2016.

- Rotenstreich, Shmuel. "The Difference between Electronic and Paper Documents" (PDF). The George Washington University. Retrieved 12 April 2016.

- Mark Sanderson & W. Bruce Croft (2012). "The History of Information Retrieval Research". Proceedings of the IEEE 100: 1444–1451. doi:10.1109/jproc.2012.2189916.

Information Management and its Methods

The following section discusses information management, IBM information management system, data modeling, computer data storage and data processing. It gives an overview of the theories and techniques related to information management. The chapter strategically encompasses and incorporates the methods associated with this field.

Information Management

Information management (IM) concerns a cycle of organisational activity: the acquisition of information from one or more sources, the custodianship and the distribution of that information to those who need it, and its ultimate disposition through archiving or deletion.

This cycle of organisational involvement with information involves a variety of stakeholders: for example those who are responsible for assuring the quality, accessibility and utility of acquired information, those who are responsible for its safe storage and disposal, and those who need it for decision making. Stakeholders might have rights to originate, change, distribute or delete information according to organisational information management policies.

Information management embraces all the generic concepts of management, including: planning, organizing, structuring, processing, controlling, evaluation and reporting of information activities, all of which is needed in order to meet the needs of those with organisational roles or functions that depend on information.

Information management is closely related to, and overlaps with, the management of data, systems, technology, processes and – where the availability of information is critical to organisational success – strategy. This broad view of the realm of information management contrasts with the earlier, more traditional view, that the life cycle of managing information is an operational matter that requires specific procedures, organisational capabilities and standards that deal with information as a product or a service.

History

Emergent Ideas Out of Data Management

In the 1970s the management of information largely concerned matters closer to what would now be called data management: punched cards, magnetic tapes and other record-keeping media, involving a life cycle of such formats requiring origination, distribution, backup, maintenance and disposal. At this time the huge potential of information technology began to be recognised: for example a single chip storing a whole book, or electronic mail moving messages instantly around the world, remarkable ideas at the time. With the proliferation of information technology and the extending reach of information systems in the 1980s and 1990s, information management took on a new form. Progressive businesses such as British Petroleum transformed the vocabulary of what was then "IT management", so that "systems analysts" became "business analysts", "monopoly supply" became a mixture of "insourcing" and "outsourcing", and the large IT function was transformed into "lean teams" that began to allow some agility in the processes that harness information for business benefit. The scope of senior management interest in information at British Petroleum extended from the creation of value through improved business processes, based upon the effective management of information, permitting the implementation of appropriate information systems (or "applications") that were operated on IT infrastructure that was outsourced. In this way, information management was no longer a simple job that could be performed by anyone who had nothing else to do, it became highly strategic and a matter for senior management attention. An understanding of the technologies involved, an ability to manage information systems projects and business change well, and a willingness to align technology and business strategies all became necessary.

Positioning Information Management in the Bigger Picture

In the transitional period leading up to the strategic view of information management, Venkatraman (a strong advocate of this process of transition and transformation, proffered a simple arrangement of ideas that succinctly brought data management, information management and knowledge management together) argued that:

- Data that is maintained in IT infrastructure has to be interpreted in order to render information.

- The information in our information systems has to be understood in order to emerge as knowledge.

- Knowledge allows managers to take effective decisions.

- Effective decisions have to lead to appropriate actions.

- Appropriate actions are expected to deliver meaningful results.

This simple model summarises a presentation by Venkatraman in 1996, as reported by Ward and Peppard (2002, page 207).

This is often referred to as the DIKAR model: Data, Information, Knowledge, Action and Result, it gives a strong clue as to the layers involved in aligning technology and organisational strategies, and it can be seen as a pivotal moment in changing attitudes to information management. The recognition that information management is an investment that must deliver meaningful results is important to all modern organisations that depend on information and good decision making for their success.

Some Theoretical Background

Behavioural and Organisational Theories

Clearly, good information management is crucial to the smooth working of organisations, and although there is no commonly accepted theory of information management per se, behavioural and organisational theories help. Following the behavioural science theory of management, mainly developed at Carnegie Mellon University and prominently supported by March and Simon, most of what goes on in modern organizations is actually information handling and decision making. One crucial factor in information handling and decision making is an individuals' ability to process information and to make decisions under limitations that might derive from the context: a person's age, the situational complexity, or a lack of requisite quality in the information that is at hand – all of which is exacerbated by the rapid advance of technology and the new kinds of system that it enables, especially as the social web emerges as a phenomenon that business cannot ignore. And yet, well before there was any general recognition of the importance of information management in organisations, March and Simon argued that organizations have to be considered as cooperative systems, with a high level of information processing and a vast need for decision making at various levels. Instead of using the model of the "economic man", as advocated in classical theory they proposed "administrative man" as an alternative, based on their argumentation about the cognitive limits of rationality. Additionally they proposed the notion of satisficing, which entails searching through the available alternatives until an acceptability threshold is met - another idea that still has currency.

Economic Theory

In addition to the organisational factors mentioned by March and Simon, there are other issues that stem from economic and environmental dynamics. There is the cost of collecting and evaluating the information needed to take a decision, including the time and effort required. The transaction cost associated with information processes can be high. In particular, established organizational rules and procedures can prevent the taking of the most appropriate decision, leading to sub-optimum outcomes . This is an issue that has been presented as a major problem with bureaucratic organizations that lose the economies of strategic change because of entrenched attitudes.

Strategic Information Management

Background

According to the Carnegie Mellon School an organization's ability to process information is at the core of organizational and managerial competency, and an organization's strategies must be designed to improve information processing capability and as information systems that provide that capability became formalised and automated, competencies were severely tested at many levels. It was recognised that organisations needed to be able to learn and adapt in ways that were never so evident before and academics began to organise and publish definitive works concerning the strategic management of information, and information systems. Concurrently, the ideas of business process management and knowledge management although much of the optimistic early thinking about business process redesign has since been discredited in the information management literature.

Aligning Technology and Business Strategy with Information Management

Venkatraman has provided a simple view of the requisite capabilities of an organisation that wants to manage information well – the DIKAR model. He also worked with others to understand how technology and business strategies could be appropriately aligned in order to identify specific capabilities that are needed. This work was paralleled by other writers in the world of consulting, practice and academia.

A contemporary Portfolio Model for Information

Bytheway has collected and organised basic tools and techniques for information management in a single volume. At the heart of his view of information management is a portfolio model that takes account of the surging interest in external sources of information and the need to organise un-structured information external so as to make it useful.

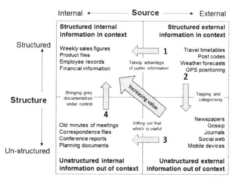

This portfolio model organizes issues of internal and external sourcing and management of information, that may be either structured or unstructured.

Such an information portfolio as this shows how information can be gathered and usefully organised, in four stages:

Stage 1: Taking advantage of public information: recognise and adopt well-structured external schemes of reference data, such as post codes, weather data, GPS positioning data and travel timetables, exemplified in the personal computing press.

Stage 2: Tagging the noise on the world wide web: use existing schemes such as post codes and GPS data or more typically by adding "tags", or construct a formal ontology that provides structure. Shirky provides an overview of these two approaches.

Stage 3: Sifting and analysing: in the wider world the generalised ontologies that are under development extend to hundreds of entities and hundreds of relations between them and provide the means to elicit meaning from large volumes of data. Structured data in databases works best when that structure reflects a higher-level information model – an ontology, or an entity-relationship model.

Stage 4: Structuring and archiving: with the large volume of data available from sources such as the social web and from the miniature telemetry systems used in personal health management, new ways to archive and then trawl data for meaningful information. Map-reduce methods, originating from functional programming, are a more recent way of eliciting information from large archival datasets that is becoming interesting to regular businesses that have very large data resources to work with, but it requires advanced multi-processor resources.

Competencies to Manage Information Well

The Information Management Body of Knowledge was made available on the world wide web in 2004 and sets out to show that the required management competencies to derive real benefits from an investment in information are complex and multi-layered. The framework model that is the basis for understanding competencies comprises six "knowledge" areas and four "process" areas:

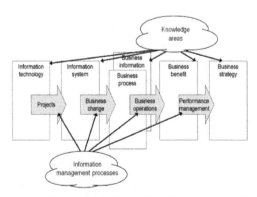

This framework is the basis of organising the "Information Management Body of Knowledge" first made available in 2004. This version is adapted by the addition of "Business information" in 2014.

The Information Management Knowledge Areas:

The IMBOK is based on the argument that there are six areas of required management competency, two of which ("business process management" and "business information management") are very closely related.

- Information technology: The pace of change of technology and the pressure to constantly acquire the newest technological products can undermine the stability of the infrastructure that supports systems, and thereby optimises business processes and delivers benefits. It is necessary to manage the "supply side" and recognise that technology is, increasingly, becoming a commodity.

- Information system: While historically information systems were developed in-house, over the years it has become possible to acquire most of the software systems that an organisation needs from the software package industry. However, there is still the potential for competitive advantage from the implementation of new systems ideas that deliver to the strategic intentions of organisations.

- Business processes and Business information: Information systems are applied to business processes in order to improve them, and they bring data to the business that becomes useful as business information. Business process management is still seen as a relatively new idea because it is not universally adopted, and it has been difficult in many cases; business information management is even more of a challenge.

- Business benefit: What are the benefits that we are seeking? It is necessary not only to be brutally honest about what can be achieved, but also to ensure the active management and assessment of benefit delivery. Since the emergence and popularisation of the Balanced scorecard there has been huge interest in business performance management but not much serious effort has been made to relate business performance management to the benefits of information technology investments and the introduction of new information systems until the turn of the millennium.

- Business strategy: Although a long way from the workaday issues of managing information in organisations, strategy in most organisations simply has to be informed by information technology and information systems opportunities, whether to address poor performance or to improve differentiation and competitiveness. Strategic analysis tools such as the value chain and critical success factor analysis are directly dependent on proper attention to the information that is (or could be) managed

The Information Management Processes:

Even with full capability and competency within the six knowledge areas, it is argued that things can still go wrong. The problem lies in the migration of ideas and information management value from one area of competency to another. Summarising what

Bytheway explains in some detail (and supported by selected secondary references):

- Projects: Information technology is without value until it is engineered into information systems that meet the needs of the business by means of good project management.

- Business change: The best information systems succeed in delivering benefits through the achievement of change within the business systems, but people do not appreciate change that makes new demands upon their skills in the ways that new information systems often do. Contrary to common expectations, there is some evidence that the public sector has succeeded with information technology induced business change.

- Business operations: With new systems in place, with business processes and business information improved, and with staff finally ready and able to work with new processes, then the business can get to work, even when new systems extend far beyond the boundaries of a single business.

- Performance management: Investments are no longer solely about financial results, financial success must be balanced with internal efficiency, customer satisfaction, and with organisational learning and development.

Summary

There are always many ways to see a business, and the information management viewpoint is only one way. It is important to remember that other areas of business activity will also contribute to strategy – it is not only good information management that moves a business forwards. Corporate governance, human resource management, product development and marketing will all have an important role to play in strategic ways, and we must not see one domain of activity alone as the sole source of strategic success. On the other hand, corporate governance, human resource management, product development and marketing are all dependent on effective information management, and so in the final analysis our competency to manage information well, on the broad basis that is offered here, can be said to be predominant.

Operationalising Information Management

Managing Requisite Change

Organizations are often confronted with many information management challenges and issues at the operational level, especially when organisational change is engendered. The novelty of new systems architectures and a lack of experience with new styles of information management requires a level of organisational change management that is notoriously difficult to deliver. As a result of a general organisational reluctance to change, to enable new forms of information management, there might be (for example): a shortfall in the requisite resources, a failure to acknowledge new classes of information and the new procedures that use them, a lack of support from senior management leading to a loss of strategic vision, and even political manoeuvring that undermines the operation of the whole organisation. However, the implementation of new forms of information management should normally lead to operational benefits.

The Early Work Of Galbraith

In early work, taking an information processing view of organisation design, Jay Galbraith has identified five tactical areas to increase information processing capacity and reduce the need for information processing.

- Developing, implementing, and monitoring all aspects of the "environment" of an organization.

- Creation of slack resources so as to decrease the load on the overall hierarchy of resources and to reduce information processing relating to overload.

- Creation of self-contained tasks with defined boundaries and that can achieve proper closure, and with all the resources at hand required to perform the task.

- Recognition of lateral relations that cut across functional units, so as to move decision power to the process instead of fragmenting it within the hierarchy.

- Investment in vertical information systems that route information flows for a specific task (or set of tasks) in accordance to the applied business logic.

The Matrix Organisation

The lateral relations concept leads to an organizational form that is different from the simple hierarchy, the "matrix organization". This brings together the vertical (hierarchical) view of an organisation and the horizontal (product or project) view of the work that it does visible to the outside world. The creation of a matrix organization is one management response to a persistent fluidity of external demand, avoiding multifarious and spurious responses to episodic demands that tend to be dealt with individually.

IBM Information Management System

IBM Information Management System (IMS) is a joint hierarchical database and information management system with extensive transaction processing capabilities.

History

IBM designed the IMS with Rockwell and Caterpillar starting in 1966 for the Apollo program, where it was used to inventory the very large bill of materials (BOM) for the Saturn V moon rocket and Apollo space vehicle.

The first "IMS READY" message appeared on an IBM 2740 terminal in Downey, California, on 14 August 1968. In the interim period, IMS has undergone many developments as IBM System/360 technology evolved into the current z/OS and System z9 and z10 technologies. For example, IMS now supports the Java programming language, JDBC, XML, and, since late 2005, web services.

Vern Watts was IMS's chief architect for many years. Watts joined IBM in 1956 and worked at IBM's Silicon Valley development labs until his death on April 4, 2009. He had continuously worked on IMS since the 1960s.

Database

The IMS Database component stores data using a hierarchical model, which is quite different from IBM's later released relational database, DB2. In IMS, the hierarchical model is implemented using blocks of data known as segments. Each segment can contain several pieces of data, which are called fields. For example, a customer database may have a root segment (or the segment at the top of the hierarchy) with fields such as phone, name, and age. Child segments may be added underneath another segment, for instance, one order segment under each customer segment representing each order a customer has placed with a company. Likewise, each order segment may have many children segments for each item on the order. Unlike other databases, you do not need to define all of the data in a segment to IMS. A segment may be defined with a size of 40 bytes but only define one field that is six bytes long as a key field that you can use to find the segment when performing queries. IMS will retrieve and save all 40 bytes as directed by a program but may not understand (or care) what the other bytes represent. In practice, often all data in a segment may map to a COBOL copybook. Besides DL/I query usage, a field may be defined in IMS so that the data can be hidden from certain applications for security reasons. The database component of IMS can be purchased standalone, without the transaction manager component, and used by systems such as CICS.

There are three basic forms of IMS hierarchical databases:

"Full Function" Databases

- Directly descended from the Data Language Interface (DL/I) databases originally developed for Apollo, full function databases can have primary and secondary indexes, accessed using DL/I calls from an application program, like SQL calls to DB2 or Oracle.

- Full function databases can be accessed by a variety of methods, although Hierarchical Direct (HDAM) and Hierarchical Indexed Direct (HIDAM) dominate. The other formats are Simple Hierarchical Indexed Sequential (SHISAM), Hierarchical Sequential (HSAM), and Hierarchical Indexed Sequential (HISAM).

- Full function databases store data using VSAM, a native z/OS access method, or Overflow Sequential (OSAM), an IMS-specific access method that optimizes the I/O channel program for IMS access patterns. In particular, OSAM performance benefits from sequential access of IMS databases (OSAM Sequential Buffering).

"Fast Path" Databases

- Fast Path databases are optimized for extremely high transaction rates. Data Entry Databases (DEDBs) and Main Storage Databases (MSDBs) are the two types of Fast Path databases. DEDBs use a direct (randomizer) access technique similar to Full Function HDAM and IMS V12 provided a DEDB Secondary Index function. MSDBs do not support secondary indexing. Virtual Storage Option (VSO) DEDBs can replace MSDBs in modern IMS releases, so MSDBs are gradually disappearing.

DEDB performance comes from use of high performance (Media Manager) access method, asynchronous write after commit, and optimized code paths. Logging is minimized because no data is updated on disk until commit, so UNDO (before image) logging is not needed, nor is a backout function. Uncommitted changes can simply be discarded. Starting with IMS Version 11, DEDBs can use z/OS 64-bit storage for database buffers. DEDBs architecture includes a Unit of Work (UOW) concept which made an effective online reorganization utility simple to implement. This function is included in the base product.

High Availability Large Databases (HALDBs)

- IMS V7 introduced HALDBs, an extension of IMS full function databases to provide better availability, better handling of extremely large data volumes, and, with IMS V9, online reorganization to support continuous availability. (Third party tools exclusively provided online reorganization prior to IMS V9.) A HALDB can store in excess of 40 terabytes of data.

Fast path DEDBs can only be built atop VSAM. DL/I databases can be built atop either VSAM or OSAM, with some restrictions depending on database organization. Although the maximum size of a z/OS VSAM dataset increased to 128 TB a few years ago, IMS still limits a VSAM dataset to 4 GB (and OSAM to 8 GB). This "limitation" simply means that IMS customers will use multiple datasets for large amounts of data. VSAM and OSAM are usually referred to as the access methods, and the IMS "logical" view of the database is referred to as the database "organization" (HDAM, HIDAM, HISAM, etc.) Internally the data are linked using 4-byte pointers or addresses. In the database datasets (DBDSs) the pointers are referred to as RBAs (relative byte addresses).

Collectively the database-related IMS capabilities are often called IMS DB. IMS DB has grown and evolved over nearly four decades to support myriad business needs. IMS, with assistance from z/OS hardware - the Coupling Facility - supports N-way inter-IMS sharing of databases. Many large configurations involve multiple IMS systems managing common databases, a technique providing for scalable growth and system redundancy in the event of hardware or software failures.

Transaction Manager

IMS is also a robust transaction manager (IMS TM, also known as IMS DC) — one of the "big three" classic transaction managers along with CICS and BEA (now Oracle) Tuxedo. A transaction manager interacts with an end user (connected through VTAM or TCP/IP, including 3270 and Web user interfaces) or another application, processes a business function (such as a banking account withdrawal), and maintains state throughout the process, making sure that the system records the business function correctly to a data store. Thus IMS TM is quite like a Web application, operating through a CGI program (for example), to provide an interface to query or update a database. IMS TM typically uses either IMS DB or DB2 as its backend database. When used alone with DB2 the IMS TM component can be purchased without the IMS DB component.

IMS TM uses a messaging and queuing paradigm. An IMS control program receives a transaction entered from a terminal (or Web browser or other application) and then stores the transaction on a message queue (in memory or in a dataset). IMS then invokes its scheduler on the queued transaction to start the business application program in a message processing region. The message processing region retrieves the transaction from the IMS message queue and processes it, reading and updating IMS and/or DB2 databases, assuring proper recording of the transaction. Then, if required, IMS enqueues a response message back onto the IMS message queue. Once the output message is complete and available the IMS control program sends it back to the originating terminal. IMS TM can handle this whole process thousands (or even tens of thousands) of times per second. A recently completed[year missing] IBM benchmark demonstrated the ability to process 100,000 transactions per second on a single IMS system.

Application

Prior to IMS, businesses and governments had to write their own transaction processing environments. IMS TM provides a straightforward, easy-to-use, reliable, standard environment for high performance transaction execution. In fact, much of the world's banking industry relies on IMS, including the U.S. Federal Reserve. For example, chances are that withdrawing money from an automated teller machine (ATM) will trigger an IMS transaction. Several Chinese banks have recently purchased IMS to support that country's burgeoning financial industry.

Today IMS complements DB2, IBM's relational database system, introduced in 1982. In general, IMS performs faster than DB2 for the common tasks but may require more programming effort to design and maintain for non-primary duties. Relational databases have generally proven superior in cases where the requirements, especially reporting requirements, change frequently or require a variety of viewpoint "angles" outside the primary or original function.

A relational "data warehouse" may be used to supplement an IMS database. For example, IMS may provide primary ATM transactions because it performs well for such a specific task. However, nightly copies of the IMS data may be copied to relational systems such that a variety of reports and processing tasks may be performed on the data. This allows each kind of database to focus best on its relative strength.

Data Modeling

Data modeling in software engineering is the process of creating a data model for an information system by applying formal data modeling techniques.

Overview

Data modeling is a process used to define and analyze data requirements needed to support the business processes within the scope of corresponding information systems in organizations. Therefore, the process of data modeling involves professional data modelers working closely with business stakeholders, as well as potential users of the information system.

There are three different types of data models produced while progressing from requirements to the actual database to be used for the information system. The data requirements are initially recorded as a conceptual data model which is essentially a set of technology independent specifications about the data and is used to discuss initial requirements with the business stakeholders. The conceptual model is then translated into a logical data model, which documents structures of the data that can be implemented in databases. Implementation of one conceptual data model may require multiple logical data models. The last step in data modeling is transforming the logical data model to a physical data model that organizes the data into tables, and accounts for access, performance and storage details. Data modeling defines not just data elements, but also their structures and the relationships between them.

Data modeling techniques and methodologies are used to model data in a standard, consistent, predictable manner in order to manage it as a resource. The use of data modeling standards is strongly recommended for all projects requiring a standard means of defining and analyzing data within an organization, e.g., using data modeling:

- to assist business analysts, programmers, testers, manual writers, IT package selectors, engineers, managers, related organizations and clients to understand and use an agreed semi-formal model the concepts of the organization and how they relate to one another

- to manage data as a resource

- for the integration of information systems

- for designing databases/data warehouses (aka data repositories)

Data modeling may be performed during various types of projects and in multiple phases of projects. Data models are progressive; there is no such thing as the final data model for a business or application. Instead a data model should be considered a living document that will change in response to a changing business. The data models should ideally be stored in a repository so that they can be retrieved, expanded, and edited over time. Whitten et al. (2004) determined two types of data modeling:

- Strategic data modeling: This is part of the creation of an information systems strategy, which defines an overall vision and architecture for information systems is defined. Information engineering is a methodology that embraces this approach.

- Data modeling during systems analysis: In systems analysis logical data models are created as part of the development of new databases.

Data modeling is also used as a technique for detailing business requirements for specific databases. It is sometimes called database modeling because a data model is eventually implemented in a database.

Data Modeling Topics

Data Models

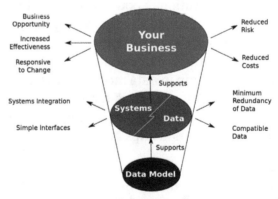

How data models deliver benefit.

Data models provide a structure for data used within information systems by providing specific definition and format. If a data model is used consistently across systems then compatibility of data can be achieved. If the same data structures are used to store and access data then different applications can share data seamlessly. The results of this are indicated in the diagram. However, systems and interfaces often cost more than they should, to build, operate, and maintain. They may also constrain the business rather than support it. This may occur when the quality of the data models implemented in systems and interfaces is poor.

- Business rules, specific to how things are done in a particular place, are often fixed in the structure of a data model. This means that small changes in the way business is conducted lead to large changes in computer systems and interfaces. So, business rules need to be implemented in a flexible way that does not result in complicated dependencies, rather the data model should be flexible enough so that changes in the business can be implemented within the data model in a relatively quick and efficient way.

- Entity types are often not identified, or are identified incorrectly. This can lead to replication of data, data structure and functionality, together with the attendant costs of that duplication in development and maintenance.Therefore, data definitions should be made as explicit and easy to understand as possible to minimize misinterpretation and duplication.

- Data models for different systems are arbitrarily different. The result of this is that complex interfaces are required between systems that share data. These interfaces can account for between 25-70% of the cost of current systems. Required interfaces should be considered inherently while designing a data model, as a data model on its own would not be usable without interfaces within different systems.

- Data cannot be shared electronically with customers and suppliers, because the structure and meaning of data has not been standardised. To obtain optimal value from an implemented data model, it is very important to define standards that will ensure that data models will both meet business needs and be consistent.

Conceptual, Logical and Physical Schemas

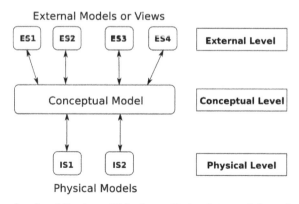

The ANSI/SPARC three level architecture. This shows that a data model can be an external model (or view), a conceptual model, or a physical model. This is not the only way to look at data models, but it is a useful way, particularly when comparing models.

In 1975 ANSI described three kinds of data-model instance:

- Conceptual schema: describes the semantics of a domain (the scope of the model). For example, it may be a model of the interest area of an organization or of an industry. This consists of entity classes, representing kinds of things of significance in the domain, and relationships assertions about associations between pairs of entity classes. A conceptual schema specifies the kinds of facts or propositions that can be expressed using the model. In that sense, it defines the allowed expressions in an artificial "language" with a scope that is limited by the scope of the model. Simply described, a conceptual schema is the first step in organizing the data requirements.

- Logical schema: describes the structure of some domain of information. This consists of descriptions of (for example) tables, columns, object-oriented classes, and XML tags. The logical schema and conceptual schema are sometimes implemented as one and the same.

- Physical schema: describes the physical means used to store data. This is concerned with partitions, CPUs, tablespaces, and the like.

According to ANSI, this approach allows the three perspectives to be relatively independent of each other. Storage technology can change without affecting either the logical or the conceptual schema. The table/column structure can change without (necessarily) affecting the conceptual schema. In each case, of course, the structures must remain consistent across all schemas of the same data model.

Data Modeling Process

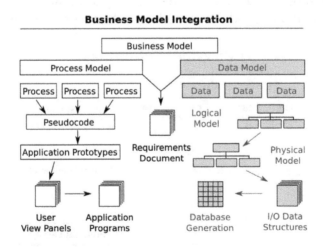

Data modeling in the context of Business Process Integration.

In the context of business process integration, data modeling complements business process modeling, and ultimately results in database generation.

The process of designing a database involves producing the previously described three types of schemas - conceptual, logical, and physical. The database design documented in these schemas are converted through a Data Definition Language, which can then be used to generate a database. A fully attributed data model contains detailed attributes (descriptions) for every entity within it. The term "database design" can describe many different parts of the design of an overall database system. Principally, and most correctly, it can be thought of as the logical design of the base data structures used to store the data. In the relational model these are the tables and views. In an object database the entities and relationships map directly to object classes and named relationships. However, the term "database design" could also be used to apply to the overall process of designing, not just the base data structures, but also the forms and queries used as part of the overall database application within the Database Management System or DBMS.

In the process, system interfaces account for 25% to 70% of the development and support costs of current systems. The primary reason for this cost is that these systems do not share a common data model. If data models are developed on a system by system basis, then not only is the same analysis repeated in overlapping areas, but further analysis must be performed to create the interfaces between them. Most systems within an organization contain the same basic data, redeveloped for a specific purpose. Therefore, an efficiently designed basic data model can minimize rework with minimal modifications for the purposes of different systems within the organization

Modeling Methodologies

Data models represent information areas of interest. While there are many ways to create data models, according to Len Silverston (1997) only two modeling methodologies stand out, top-down and bottom-up:

- Bottom-up models or View Integration models are often the result of a reengineering effort. They usually start with existing data structures forms, fields on application screens, or reports. These models are usually physical, application-specific, and incomplete from an enterprise perspective. They may not promote data sharing, especially if they are built without reference to other parts of the organization.

- Top-down logical data models, on the other hand, are created in an abstract way by getting information from people who know the subject area. A system may not implement all the entities in a logical model, but the model serves as a reference point or template.

Sometimes models are created in a mixture of the two methods: by considering the data needs and structure of an application and by consistently referencing a subject-area model. Unfortunately, in many environments the distinction between a logical data model and a physical data model is blurred. In addition, some CASE tools don't make a distinction between logical and physical data models.

Entity Relationship Diagrams

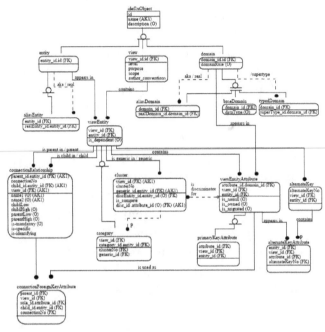

Example of an IDEF1X Entity relationship diagrams used to model IDEF1X itself. The name of the view is mm. The domain hierarchy and constraints are also given. The constraints are expressed as sentences in the formal theory of the meta model.

There are several notations for data modeling. The actual model is frequently called "Entity relationship model", because it depicts data in terms of the entities and relationships described in the data. An entity-relationship model (ERM) is an abstract conceptual representation of structured data. Entity-relationship modeling is a relational schema database modeling method, used in software engineering to produce a type of conceptual data model (or semantic data model) of a system, often a relational database, and its requirements in a top-down fashion.

These models are being used in the first stage of information system design during the requirements analysis to describe information needs or the type of information that is to be stored in a database. The data modeling technique can be used to describe any ontology (i.e. an overview and classifications of used terms and their relationships) for a certain universe of discourse i.e. area of interest.

Several techniques have been developed for the design of data models. While these methodologies guide data modelers in their work, two different people using the same methodology will often come up with very different results. Most notable are:

- Bachman diagrams

- Barker's notation

- Chen's Notation

- Data Vault Modeling

- Extended Backus–Naur form

- IDEF1X

- Object-relational mapping

- Object-Role Modeling

- Relational Model

- Relational Model/Tasmania

Generic Data Modeling

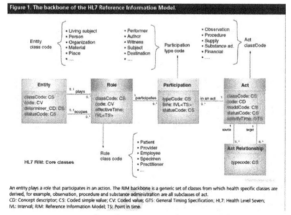

Example of a Generic data model.

Generic data models are generalizations of conventional data models. They define standardized general relation types, together with the kinds of things that may be related by such a relation type. The definition of generic data model is similar to the definition of a natural language. For example, a generic data model may define relation types such as a 'classification relation', being a binary relation between an individual thing and a kind of thing (a class) and a 'part-whole relation', being a binary relation between two things, one with the role of part, the other with the role of whole, regardless the kind of things that are related.

Given an extensible list of classes, this allows the classification of any individual thing and to specify part-whole relations for any individual object. By standardization of an extensible list of relation types, a generic data model enables the expression of an unlimited number of kinds of facts and will approach the capabilities of natural languages. Conventional data models, on the other hand, have a fixed and limited domain scope, because the instantiation (usage) of such a model only allows expressions of kinds of facts that are predefined in the model.

Semantic Data Modeling

The logical data structure of a DBMS, whether hierarchical, network, or relational, cannot totally satisfy the requirements for a conceptual definition of data because it is limited in scope and biased toward the implementation strategy employed by the DBMS.

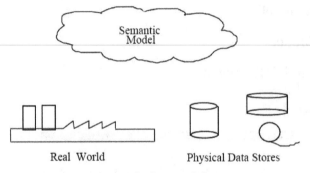

Semantic data models.

Therefore, the need to define data from a conceptual view has led to the development of semantic data modeling techniques. That is, techniques to define the meaning of data within the context of its interrelationships with other data. As illustrated in the figure the real world, in terms of resources, ideas, events, etc., are symbolically defined within physical data stores. A semantic data model is an abstraction which defines how the stored symbols relate to the real world. Thus, the model must be a true representation of the real world.

A semantic data model can be used to serve many purposes, such as:

- planning of data resources

- building of shareable databases

- evaluation of vendor software

- integration of existing databases

The overall goal of semantic data models is to capture more meaning of data by integrating relational concepts with more powerful abstraction concepts known from the Artificial Intelligence field. The idea is to provide high level modeling primitives as integral part of a data model in order to facilitate the representation of real world situations.

Computer Data Storage

Computer data storage, often called storage or memory, is a technology consisting of computer components and recording media used to retain digital data. It is a core function and fundamental component of computers.

The central processing unit (CPU) of a computer is what manipulates data by performing computations. In practice, almost all computers use a storage hierarchy, which puts fast but expensive and small storage options close to the CPU and slower but larger and cheaper options farther away. Generally the fast volatile technologies (which lose data when off power) are referred to as "memory", while slower persistent technologies are referred to as "storage"; however, "memory" is sometimes also used when referring to persistent storage.

In the Von Neumann architecture, the CPU consists of two main parts: The control unit and the arithmetic / logic unit (ALU). The former controls the flow of data between the CPU and memory, while the latter performs arithmetic and logical operations on data.

Functionality

Without a significant amount of memory, a computer would merely be able to perform fixed operations and immediately output the result. It would have to be reconfigured to change its behavior. This is acceptable for devices such as desk calculators, digital signal processors, and other specialized devices. Von Neumann machines differ in having a memory in which they store their operating instructions and data. Such computers are more versatile in that they do not need to have their hardware reconfigured for each new program, but can simply be reprogrammed with new in-memory instructions; they also tend to be simpler to design, in that a relatively simple processor may keep state between successive computations to build up complex procedural results. Most modern computers are von Neumann machines.

Data Organization and Representation

A modern digital computer represents data using the binary numeral system. Text, numbers, pictures, audio, and nearly any other form of information can be converted into a string of bits, or binary digits, each of which has a value of 1 or 0. The most common unit of storage is the byte, equal to 8 bits. A piece of information can be handled by any computer or device whose storage space is large enough to accommodate the binary representation of the piece of information, or simply data. For example, the complete works of Shakespeare, about 1250 pages in print, can be stored in about five megabytes (40 million bits) with one byte per character.

Data is encoded by assigning a bit pattern to each character, digit, or multimedia object. Many standards exist for encoding (e.g., character encodings like ASCII, image encodings like JPEG, video encodings like MPEG-4).

By adding bits to each encoded unit, redundancy allows the computer to both detect errors in coded data and correct them based on mathematical algorithms. Errors generally occur in low probabilities due to random bit value flipping, or "physical bit fatigue", loss of the physical bit in storage its ability to maintain distinguishable value (0 or 1), or due to errors in inter or intra-computer communication. A random bit flip (e.g., due to random radiation) is typically corrected upon detection. A bit, or a group of malfunctioning physical bits (not always the specific defective bit is known; group definition depends on specific storage device) is typically automatically fenced-out, taken out of use by the device, and replaced with another functioning equivalent group in the device, where the corrected bit values are restored (if possible). The cyclic redundancy check (CRC) method is typically used in communications and storage for error detection. A detected error is then retried.

Data compression methods allow in many cases (such as a database) to represent a string of bits by a shorter bit string ("compress") and reconstruct the original string ("decompress") when needed. This utilizes substantially less storage (tens of percents) for many types of data at the cost of more computation (compress and decompress when needed). Analysis of trade-off between storage cost saving and costs of related computations and possible delays in data availability is done before deciding whether to keep certain data compressed or not.

For security reasons certain types of data (e.g., credit-card information) may be kept encrypted in storage to prevent the possibility of unauthorized information reconstruction from chunks of storage snapshots.

Hierarchy of Storage

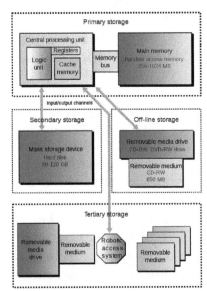

Various forms of storage, divided according to their distance from the central processing unit. The fundamental components of a general-purpose computer are arithmetic and logic unit, control circuitry, storage space, and input/output devices. Technology and capacity as in common home computers around 2005.

Primary Storage

Primary storage (also known as main memory or internal memory), often referred to simply as memory, is the only one directly accessible to the CPU. The CPU continuously reads instructions stored there and executes them as required. Any data actively operated on is also stored there in uniform manner.

Historically, early computers used delay lines, Williams tubes, or rotating magnetic drums as primary storage. By 1954, those unreliable methods were mostly replaced by magnetic core memory. Core memory remained dominant until the 1970s, when advances in integrated circuit technology allowed semiconductor memory to become economically competitive.

This led to modern random-access memory (RAM). It is small-sized, light, but quite expensive at the same time. (The particular types of RAM used for primary storage are also volatile, i.e. they lose the information when not powered).

Traditionally there are two more sub-layers of the primary storage, besides main large-capacity RAM:

- Processor registers are located inside the processor. Each register typically holds a word of data (often 32 or 64 bits). CPU instructions instruct the arithmetic logic unit to perform various calculations or other operations on this data (or with the help of it). Registers are the fastest of all forms of computer data storage.

- Processor cache is an intermediate stage between ultra-fast registers and much slower main memory. It was introduced solely to improve the performance of computers. Most actively used information in the main memory is just duplicated in the cache memory, which is faster, but of much lesser capacity. On the other hand, main memory is much slower, but has a much greater storage capacity than processor registers. Multi-level hierarchical cache setup is also commonly used—primary cache being smallest, fastest and located inside the processor; secondary cache being somewhat larger and slower.

Main memory is directly or indirectly connected to the central processing unit via a memory bus. It is actually two buses (not on the diagram): an address bus and a data bus. The CPU firstly sends a number through an address bus, a number called memory address, that indicates the desired location of data. Then it reads or writes the data in the memory cells using the data bus. Additionally, a memory management unit (MMU) is a small device between CPU and RAM recalculating the actual memory address, for example to provide an abstraction of virtual memory or other tasks.

As the RAM types used for primary storage are volatile (uninitialized at start up), a computer containing only such storage would not have a source to read instructions from, in order to start the computer. Hence, non-volatile primary storage containing a small startup program (BIOS) is used to bootstrap the computer, that is, to read a larger program from non-volatile secondary storage to RAM and start to execute it. A non-volatile technology used for this purpose is called ROM, for read-only memory (the terminology may be somewhat confusing as most ROM types are also capable of random access).

Many types of "ROM" are not literally read only, as updates to them are possible; however it is slow and memory must be erased in large portions before it can be re-written. Some embedded systems run programs directly from ROM (or similar), because such programs are rarely changed. Standard computers do not store non-rudimentary programs in ROM, and rather, use large capacities of secondary storage, which is non-volatile as well, and not as costly.

Recently, primary storage and secondary storage in some uses refer to what was historically called, respectively, secondary storage and tertiary storage.

Secondary Storage

A hard disk drive with protective cover removed.

Secondary storage (also known as external memory or auxiliary storage), differs from primary storage in that it is not directly accessible by the CPU. The computer usually uses its input/output channels to access secondary storage and transfers the desired data using intermediate area in primary storage. Secondary storage does not lose the data when the device is powered down—it is non-volatile. Per unit, it is typically also two orders of magnitude less expensive than primary storage. Modern computer systems typically have two orders of magnitude more secondary storage than primary storage and data are kept for a longer time there.

In modern computers, hard disk drives are usually used as secondary storage. The time taken to access a given byte of information stored on a hard disk is typically a few thousandths of a second, or milliseconds. By contrast, the time taken to access a given byte of information stored in random-access memory is measured in billionths of a second, or nanoseconds. This illustrates the significant access-time difference which distinguishes solid-state memory from rotating magnetic storage devices: hard disks are typically about a million times slower than memory. Rotating optical storage devices, such as CD and DVD drives, have even longer access times. With disk drives, once the disk read/write head reaches the proper placement and the data of interest rotates under it, subsequent data on the track are very fast to access. To reduce the seek time and rotational latency, data are transferred to and from disks in large contiguous blocks.

When data reside on disk, blocking access to hide latency offers an opportunity to design efficient external memory algorithms. Sequential or block access on disks is orders of magnitude faster than random access, and many sophisticated paradigms have been developed to design efficient algorithms based upon sequential and block access. Another way to reduce the I/O bottleneck is to use multiple disks in parallel in order to increase the bandwidth between primary and secondary memory.

Some other examples of secondary storage technologies are flash memory (e.g. USB flash drives or keys), floppy disks, magnetic tape, paper tape, punched cards, stand-alone RAM disks, and Iomega Zip drives.

The secondary storage is often formatted according to a file system format, which provides the abstraction necessary to organize data into files and directories, providing also additional information (called metadata) describing the owner of a certain file, the access time, the access permissions, and other information.

Most computer operating systems use the concept of virtual memory, allowing utilization of more primary storage capacity than is physically available in the system. As the primary memory fills up, the system moves the least-used chunks (pages) to secondary storage devices (to a swap file or page file), retrieving them later when they are needed. As more of these retrievals from slower secondary storage are necessary, the more the overall system performance is degraded.

Tertiary Storage

A large tape library, with tape cartridges placed on shelves in the front, and a robotic arm moving in the back. Visible height of the library is about 180 cm.

Tertiary storage or tertiary memory provides a third level of storage. Typically, it involves a robotic mechanism which will mount (insert) and dismount removable mass storage media into a storage device according to the system's demands; this data is often copied to secondary storage before use. It is primarily used for archiving rarely accessed information since it is much slower than secondary storage (e.g. 5–60 seconds vs. 1–10 milliseconds). This is primarily useful for extraordinarily large data stores, accessed without human operators. Typical examples include tape libraries and optical jukeboxes.

When a computer needs to read information from the tertiary storage, it will first consult a catalog database to determine which tape or disc contains the information. Next, the computer will instruct a robotic arm to fetch the medium and place it in a drive. When the computer has finished reading the information, the robotic arm will return the medium to its place in the library.

Tertiary storage is also known as nearline storage because it is "near to online". The formal distinction between online, nearline, and offline storage is:

- Online storage is immediately available for I/O.

- Nearline storage is not immediately available, but can be made online quickly without human intervention.

- Offline storage is not immediately available, and requires some human intervention to become online.

For example, always-on spinning hard disk drives are online storage, while spinning drives that spin down automatically, such as in massive arrays of idle disks (MAID), are nearline storage. Removable media such as tape cartridges that can be automatically loaded, as in tape libraries, are nearline storage, while tape cartridges that must be manually loaded are offline storage.

Off-line Storage

Off-line storage is a computer data storage on a medium or a device that is not under the control of a processing unit. The medium is recorded, usually in a secondary or tertiary storage device, and then physically removed or disconnected. It must be inserted or connected by a human operator before a computer can access it again. Unlike tertiary storage, it cannot be accessed without human interaction.

Off-line storage is used to transfer information, since the detached medium can be easily physically transported. Additionally, in case a disaster, for example a fire, destroys the original data, a medium in a remote location will probably be unaffected, enabling disaster recovery. Off-line storage increases general information security, since it is physically inaccessible from a computer, and data confidentiality or integrity cannot be affected by computer-based attack techniques. Also, if the information stored for archival purposes is rarely accessed, off-line storage is less expensive than tertiary storage.

In modern personal computers, most secondary and tertiary storage media are also used for off-line storage. Optical discs and flash memory devices are most popular, and to much lesser extent removable hard disk drives. In enterprise uses, magnetic tape is predominant. Older examples are floppy disks, Zip disks, or punched cards.

Characteristics of Storage

A 1GB DDR RAM module (detail)

Storage technologies at all levels of the storage hierarchy can be differentiated by evaluating certain core characteristics as well as measuring characteristics specific to a particular implementation. These core characteristics are volatility, mutability, accessibility, and addressability. For any particular implementation of any storage technology, the characteristics worth measuring are capacity and performance.

Storage Media

As of 2011, the most commonly used data storage technologies are semiconductor, magnetic, and optical, while paper still sees some limited usage. Media is a common name for what actually holds the data in the storage device. Some other fundamental storage technologies have also been used in the past or are proposed for development.

Semiconductor

Semiconductor memory uses semiconductor-based integrated circuits to store information. A semiconductor memory chip may contain millions of tiny transistors or capacitors. Both volatile and non-volatile forms of semiconductor memory exist. In modern computers, primary storage almost exclusively consists of dynamic volatile semiconductor memory or dynamic random-access memory. Since the turn of the century, a type of non-volatile semiconductor memory known as flash memory has steadily gained share as off-line storage for home computers. Non-volatile semiconductor memory is also used for secondary storage in various advanced electronic devices and specialized computers.

As early as 2006, notebook and desktop computer manufacturers started using flash-based solid-state drives (SSDs) as default configuration options for the secondary storage either in addition to or instead of the more traditional HDD.

Magnetic

Magnetic storage uses different patterns of magnetization on a magnetically coated surface to store information. Magnetic storage is non-volatile. The information is accessed using one or more read/write heads which may contain one or more recording transducers. A read/write head only covers a part of the surface so that the head or medium or both must be moved relative to another in order to access data. In modern computers, magnetic storage will take these forms:

- Magnetic disk

    o   Floppy disk, used for off-line storage

    o   Hard disk drive, used for secondary storage

- Magnetic tape, used for tertiary and off-line storage

- Carousel memory (magnetic rolls)

In early computers, magnetic storage was also used as:

- Primary storage in a form of magnetic memory, or core memory, core rope memory, thin-film memory and/or twistor memory.

- Tertiary (e.g. NCR CRAM) or off line storage in the form of magnetic cards.

- Magnetic tape was then often used for secondary storage.

Optical

Optical storage, the typical optical disc, stores information in deformities on the surface of a circular disc and reads this information by illuminating the surface with a laser diode and observing the reflection. Optical disc storage is non-volatile. The deformities may be permanent (read only media), formed once (write once media) or reversible (recordable or read/write media). The following forms are currently in common use:

- CD, CD-ROM, DVD, BD-ROM: Read only storage, used for mass distribution of digital information (music, video, computer programs)

- CD-R, DVD-R, DVD+R, BD-R: Write once storage, used for tertiary and off-line storage

- CD-RW, DVD-RW, DVD+RW, DVD-RAM, BD-RE: Slow write, fast read storage, used for tertiary and off-line storage

- Ultra Density Optical or UDO is similar in capacity to BD-R or BD-RE and is slow write, fast read storage used for tertiary and off-line storage.

Magneto-optical disc storage is optical disc storage where the magnetic state on a ferromagnetic surface stores information. The information is read optically and written by combining magnetic and optical methods. Magneto-optical disc storage is non-volatile, sequential access, slow write, fast read storage used for tertiary and off-line storage.

3D optical data storage has also been proposed.

Paper

Paper data storage, typically in the form of paper tape or punched cards, has long been used to store information for automatic processing, particularly before general-purpose computers existed. Information was recorded by punching holes into the paper or cardboard medium and was read mechanically (or later optically) to determine whether a particular location on the medium was solid or contained a hole. A few technologies allow people to make marks on paper that are easily read by machine—these are widely used for tabulating votes and grading standardized tests. Barcodes made it possible for any object that was to be sold or transported to have some computer readable information securely attached to it.

Other Storage Media or Substrates

Vacuum tube memory

> A Williams tube used a cathode ray tube, and a Selectron tube used a large vacuum tube to store information. These primary storage devices were short-lived in the market, since Williams tube was unreliable and the Selectron tube was expensive.

Electro-acoustic memory

> Delay line memory used sound waves in a substance such as mercury to store information. Delay line memory was dynamic volatile, cycle sequential read/write storage, and was used for primary storage.

Optical tape

> is a medium for optical storage generally consisting of a long and narrow strip of plastic onto which patterns can be written and from which the patterns can

be read back. It shares some technologies with cinema film stock and optical discs, but is compatible with neither. The motivation behind developing this technology was the possibility of far greater storage capacities than either magnetic tape or optical discs.

Phase-change memory

uses different mechanical phases of Phase Change Material to store information in an X-Y addressable matrix, and reads the information by observing the varying electrical resistance of the material. Phase-change memory would be non-volatile, random-access read/write storage, and might be used for primary, secondary and off-line storage. Most rewritable and many write once optical disks already use phase change material to store information.

Holographic data storage

stores information optically inside crystals or photopolymers. Holographic storage can utilize the whole volume of the storage medium, unlike optical disc storage which is limited to a small number of surface layers. Holographic storage would be non-volatile, sequential access, and either write once or read/write storage. It might be used for secondary and off-line storage.

Molecular memory

stores information in polymer that can store electric charge. Molecular memory might be especially suited for primary storage. The theoretical storage capacity of molecular memory is 10 terabits per square inch.

Related Technologies

Redundancy

While a group of bits malfunction may be resolved by error detection and correction mechanisms, storage device malfunction requires different solutions. The following solutions are commonly used and valid for most storage devices:

- Device mirroring (replication) – A common solution to the problem is constantly maintaining an identical copy of device content on another device (typically of a same type). The downside is that this doubles the storage, and both devices (copies) need to be updated simultaneously with some overhead and possibly some delays. The upside is possible concurrent read of a same data group by two independent processes, which increases performance. When one of the replicated devices is detected to be defective, the other copy is still operational, and is being utilized to generate a new copy on another device (usually available operational in a pool of stand-by devices for this purpose).

- Redundant array of independent disks (RAID) – This method generalizes the device mirroring above by allowing one device in a group of N devices to fail and be replaced with the content restored (Device mirroring is RAID with N=2). RAID groups of N=5 or N=6 are common. N>2 saves storage, when comparing with N=2, at the cost of more processing during both regular operation (with often reduced performance) and defective device replacement.

Device mirroring and typical RAID are designed to handle a single device failure in the RAID group of devices. However, if a second failure occurs before the RAID group is completely repaired from the first failure, then data can be lost. The probability of a single failure is typically small. Thus the probability of two failures in a same RAID group in time proximity is much smaller (approximately the probability squared, i.e., multiplied by itself). If a database cannot tolerate even such smaller probability of data loss, then the RAID group itself is replicated (mirrored). In many cases such mirroring is done geographically remotely, in a different storage array, to handle also recovery from disasters.

Network Connectivity

A secondary or tertiary storage may connect to a computer utilizing computer networks. This concept does not pertain to the primary storage, which is shared between multiple processors to a lesser degree.

- Direct-attached storage (DAS) is a traditional mass storage, that does not use any network. This is still a most popular approach. This retronym was coined recently, together with NAS and SAN.

- Network-attached storage (NAS) is mass storage attached to a computer which another computer can access at file level over a local area network, a private wide area network, or in the case of online file storage, over the Internet. NAS is commonly associated with the NFS and CIFS/SMB protocols.

- Storage area network (SAN) is a specialized network, that provides other computers with storage capacity. The crucial difference between NAS and SAN is the former presents and manages file systems to client computers, whilst the latter provides access at block-addressing (raw) level, leaving it to attaching systems to manage data or file systems within the provided capacity. SAN is commonly associated with Fibre Channel networks.

Robotic Storage

Large quantities of individual magnetic tapes, and optical or magneto-optical discs may be stored in robotic tertiary storage devices. In tape storage field they are known as tape libraries, and in optical storage field optical jukeboxes, or optical disk libraries per analogy. Smallest forms of either technology containing just one drive device are referred to as autoloaders or autochangers.

Robotic-access storage devices may have a number of slots, each holding individual media, and usually one or more picking robots that traverse the slots and load media to built-in drives. The arrangement of the slots and picking devices affects performance. Important characteristics of such storage are possible expansion options: adding slots, modules, drives, robots. Tape libraries may have from 10 to more than 100,000 slots, and provide terabytes or petabytes of near-line information. Optical jukeboxes are somewhat smaller solutions, up to 1,000 slots.

Robotic storage is used for backups, and for high-capacity archives in imaging, medical, and video industries. Hierarchical storage management is a most known archiving strategy of automatically migrating long-unused files from fast hard disk storage to libraries or jukeboxes. If the files are needed, they are retrieved back to disk.

Ontology (Information Science)

In computer science and information science, an ontology is a formal naming and definition of the types, properties, and interrelationships of the entities that really or fundamentally exist for a particular domain of discourse. It is thus a practical application of philosophical ontology, with a taxonomy.

An ontology compartmentalizes the variables needed for some set of computations and establishes the relationships between them.

The fields of artificial intelligence, the Semantic Web, systems engineering, software engineering, biomedical informatics, library science, enterprise bookmarking, and information architecture all create ontologies to limit complexity and to organize information. The ontology can then be applied to problem solving.

Etymology and Definition

The term ontology has its origin in philosophy and has been applied in many different ways. The core meaning within computer science is a model for describing the world that consists of a set of types, properties, and relationship types. There is also generally an expectation that the features of the model in an ontology should closely resemble the real world (related to the object).

Overview

What many ontologies have in common in both computer science and in philosophy is the representation of entities, ideas, and events, along with their properties and relations, according to a system of categories. In both fields, there is considerable work on problems of ontological relativity (e.g., Quine and Kripke in philosophy, Sowa and Guarino in computer science), and debates concerning whether a normative ontology is viable (e.g., debates over foundationalism in philosophy, and over the Cyc project in AI). Differences between the two are largely matters of focus. Computer scientists are more concerned with establishing fixed, controlled vocabularies, while philosophers are more concerned with first principles, such as whether there are such things as fixed essences or whether enduring objects must be ontologically more primary than processes.

Other fields make ontological assumptions that are sometimes explicitly elaborated and explored. For instance, the definition and ontology of economics (also sometimes called the political economy) is hotly debated especially in Marxist economics where it is a primary concern, but also in other subfields. Such concerns intersect with those of information science when a simulation or model is intended to enable decisions in the economic realm; for example, to determine what capital assets are at risk and if so by how much. Some claim all social sciences have explicit ontology issues because they do not have hard falsifiability criteria like most models in physical sciences and that indeed the lack of such widely accepted hard falsification criteria is what defines a social or soft science.

History

Historically, ontologies arise out of the branch of philosophy known as metaphysics, which deals with the nature of reality – of what exists. This fundamental branch is concerned with analyzing various types or modes of existence, often with special attention to the relations between particulars and universals, between intrinsic and extrinsic properties, and between essence and existence. The traditional goal of ontological inquiry in particular is to divide the world "at its joints" to discover those fundamental categories or kinds into which the world's objects naturally fall.

During the second half of the 20th century, philosophers extensively debated the possible methods or approaches to building ontologies without actually building any very elaborate ontologies themselves. By contrast, computer scientists were building some large and robust ontologies, such as WordNet and Cyc, with comparatively little debate over how they were built.

Since the mid-1970s, researchers in the field of artificial intelligence (AI) have recognized that capturing knowledge is the key to building large and powerful AI systems. AI researchers argued that they could create new ontologies as computational models that enable certain kinds of automated reasoning. In the 1980s, the AI community began to use the term ontology to refer to both a theory of a modeled world and a component of knowledge systems. Some researchers, drawing inspiration from philosophical ontologies, viewed computational ontology as a kind of applied philosophy.

In the early 1990s, the widely cited Web page and paper "Toward Principles for the Design of Ontologies Used for Knowledge Sharing" by Tom Gruber is credited with a deliberate definition of ontology as a technical term in computer science. Gruber introduced the term to mean a specification of a conceptualization:

An ontology is a description (like a formal specification of a program) of the concepts and relationships that can formally exist for an agent or a community of agents. This definition is consistent with the usage of ontology as set of concept definitions, but more general. And it is a different sense of the word than its use in philosophy.

According to Gruber (1993):

Ontologies are often equated with taxonomic hierarchies of classes, class definitions, and the subsumption relation, but ontologies need not be limited to these forms. Ontologies are also not limited to conservative definitions — that is, definitions in the traditional logic sense that only introduce terminology and do not add any knowledge about the world. To specify a conceptualization, one needs to state axioms that do constrain the possible interpretations for the defined terms.

Components

Contemporary ontologies share many structural similarities, regardless of the language in which they are expressed. As mentioned above, most ontologies describe individuals (instances), classes (concepts), attributes, and relations. In this section each of these components is discussed in turn.

Common components of ontologies include:

- Individuals: instances or objects (the basic or "ground level" objects)

- Classes: sets, collections, concepts, classes in programming, types of objects, or kinds of things

- Attributes: aspects, properties, features, characteristics, or parameters that objects (and classes) can have

- Relations: ways in which classes and individuals can be related to one another

- Function terms: complex structures formed from certain relations that can be used in place of an individual term in a statement

- Restrictions: formally stated descriptions of what must be true in order for some assertion to be accepted as input

- Rules: statements in the form of an if-then (antecedent-consequent) sentence that describe the logical inferences that can be drawn from an assertion in a particular form

- Axioms: assertions (including rules) in a logical form that together comprise the overall theory that the ontology describes in its domain of application. This definition differs from that of "axioms" in generative grammar and formal logic. In those disciplines, axioms include only statements asserted as a priori knowledge. As used here, "axioms" also include the theory derived from axiomatic statements

- Events: the changing of attributes or relations

Ontologies are commonly encoded using ontology languages.

Types

Domain Ontology

A domain ontology (or domain-specific ontology) represents concepts which belong to part of the world. Particular meanings of terms applied to that domain are provided by domain ontology. For example, the word card has many different meanings. An ontology about the domain of poker would model the "playing card" meaning of the word, while an ontology about the domain of computer hardware would model the "punched card" and "video card" meanings.

Since domain ontologies represent concepts in very specific and often eclectic ways, they are often incompatible. As systems that rely on domain ontologies expand, they often need to merge domain ontologies into a more general representation. This presents a challenge to the ontology designer. Different ontologies in the same domain arise due to different languages, different intended usage of the ontologies, and different perceptions of the domain (based on cultural background, education, ideology, etc.).

At present, merging ontologies that are not developed from a common foundation ontology is a largely manual process and therefore time-consuming and expensive. Domain ontologies that use the same foundation ontology to provide a set of basic elements with which to specify the meanings of the domain ontology elements can be merged automatically. There are studies on generalized techniques for merging ontologies, but this area of research is still largely theoretical.

Upper Ontology

An upper ontology (or foundation ontology) is a model of the common objects that are generally applicable across a wide range of domain ontologies. It usually employs a core glossary that contains the terms and associated object descriptions as they are used in various relevant domain sets.

There are several standardized upper ontologies available for use, including BFO, BORO method, Dublin Core, GFO, OpenCyc/ResearchCyc, SUMO, the Unified Foundational Ontology (UFO), and DOLCE. WordNet, while considered an upper ontology by some, is not strictly an ontology. However, it has been employed as a linguistic tool for learning domain ontologies.

Hybrid Ontology

The Gellish ontology is an example of a combination of an upper and a domain ontology.

Visualization

A survey of ontology visualization techniques is presented by Katifori et al. An evaluation of two most established ontology visualization techniques: indented tree and graph is discussed in. A visual language for ontologies represented in OWL is specified by the Visual Notation for OWL Ontologies (VOWL).

Engineering

Ontology engineering (or ontology building) is a subfield of knowledge engineering. It studies the ontology development process, the ontology life cycle, the methods and methodologies for building ontologies, and the tool suites and languages that support them.

Ontology engineering aims to make explicit the knowledge contained within software applications, and within enterprises and business procedures for a particular domain. Ontology engineering offers a direction towards solving the interoperability problems brought about by semantic obstacles, such as the obstacles related to the definitions of business terms and software classes. Ontology engineering is a set of tasks related to the development of ontologies for a particular domain.

Editor

Ontology editors are applications designed to assist in the creation or manipulation of ontologies. They often express ontologies in one of many ontology languages. Some provide export to other ontology languages however.

Among the most relevant criteria for choosing an ontology editor are the degree to which the editor abstracts from the actual ontology representation language used for persistence and the visual navigation possibilities within the knowledge model. Next come built-in inference engines and information extraction facilities, and the support of meta-ontologies such as OWL-S, Dublin Core, etc. Another important feature is the ability to import & export foreign knowledge representation languages for ontology matching. Ontologies are developed for a specific purpose and application.

- a.k.a. software (Ontology, taxonomy and thesaurus management software available from The Synercon Group)

- Anzo for Excel (Includes an RDFS and OWL ontology editor within Excel; generates ontologies from Excel spreadsheets)

- Chimaera (Other web service by Stanford)

- CmapTools Ontology Editor (COE) (Java based ontology editor from the Florida Institute for Human and Machine Cognition. Supports numerous formats)

- dot15926 Editor (Open source ontology editor for data compliant to engineering ontology standard ISO 15926. Allows Python scripting and pattern-based data analysis. Supports extensions.)

- EMFText OWL2 Manchester Editor, Eclipse-based, open-source, Pellet integration

- Enterprise Architect, along with UML modeling, supports OMG's Ontology Definition MetaModel which includes OWL and RDF.

- Fluent Editor, a comprehensive ontology editor for OWL and SWRL with Controlled Natural Language (Controlled English). Supports OWL, RDF, DL and Functional rendering, unlimited imports and built-in reasoning services.

- HOZO (Java-based graphical editor especially created to produce heavy-weight and well thought out ontologies, from Osaka University and Enegate Co, ltd.)

- Java Ontology Editor (JOE) (1998)

- KAON (single user and server based solutions possible, open source, from FZI/ AIFB Karlsruhe)

- KMgen (Ontology editor for the KM language. km: The Knowledge Machine)

- Knoodl (Free web application/service that is an ontology editor, wiki, and ontology registry. Supports creation of communities where members can collaboratively import, create, discuss, document and publish ontologies. Supports OWL, RDF, RDFS, and SPARQL queries. Available since early Nov 2006 from Revelytix, Inc..)

- Model Futures IDEAS AddIn (free) A plug-in for Sparx Systems Enterprise Architect that allows IDEAS Group 4D ontologies to be developed using a UML profile

- Model Futures OWL Editor (Free) Able to work with very large OWL files (e.g. Cyc) and has extensive import and export capabilities (inc. UML, Thesaurus Descriptor, MS Word, CA ERwin Data Modeler, CSV, etc.)

- myWeb (Java-based, mySQL connection, bundled with applet that allows online browsing of ontologies (including OBO))

- Neologism (Web-based, open source, supports RDFS and a subset of OWL, built on Drupal)

- NeOn Toolkit (Eclipse-based, open source, OWL support, several import mechanisms, support for reuse and management of networked ontologies, visualization, etc....from NeOn Project)

- OBO-Edit (Java-based, downloadable, open source, developed by the Gene Ontology Consortium for editing biological ontologies)

- OntoStudio (Eclipse-based, downloadable, support for RDF(S), OWL and F-Logic, graphical rule editor, visualizations, from ontoprise)

- Ontolingua (Web service offered by Stanford University)

- Open Semantic Framework (OSF), an integrated software stack using semantic technologies for knowledge management, which includes an ontology editor

- OWLGrEd (A graphical ontology editor, easy-to-use)

- PoolParty Thesaurus Server (Commercial ontology, taxonomy and thesaurus management software available from Semantic Web Company, fully based on standards like RDFS, SKOS and SPARQL, integrated with Virtuoso Universal Server)

- Protégé (Java-based, downloadable, Supports OWL, open source, many sample ontologies, from Stanford University)

- ScholOnto (net-centric representations of research)

- Semantic Turkey (Firefox extension - also based on Java - for managing ontologies and acquiring new knowledge from the Web; developed at University of Rome, Tor Vergata)

- Sigma knowledge engineering environment is a system primarily for development of the Suggested Upper Merged Ontology

- Swoop (Java-based, downloadable, open source, OWL Ontology browser and editor from the University of Maryland)

- Semaphore Ontology Manager (Commercial ontology, taxonomy and thesaurus management software available from Smartlogic Semaphore Limited. Intuitive tool to manage the entire "build - enhance - review - maintain" ontology lifecycle.)

- Synaptica (Ontology, taxonomy and thesaurus management software available from Synaptica, LLC. Web based, supports OWL and SKOS.)

- TopBraid Composer (Eclipse-based, downloadable, full support for RDFS and OWL, built-in inference engine, SWRL editor and SPARQL queries, visualization, import of XML and UML, from TopQuadrant)

- Transinsight (The editor is especially designed for creating text mining ontologies and part of GoPubMed.org)

- WebODE (Web service offered by the Technical University of Madrid)

- TwoUse Toolkit (Eclipse-based, open source, model-driven ontology editing environment especially designed for software engineers)

- Be Informed Suite (Commercial tool for building large ontology based applications. Includes visual editors, inference engines, export to standard formats)

- Thesaurus Master (Manages creation and use of ontologies for use in data management and semantic enrichment by enterprise, government, and scholarly publishers.)

- TODE (A Dot Net-based Tool for Ontology Development and Editing)

- VocBench (Collaborative Web Application for SKOS/SKOS-XL Thesauri Management - developed on a joint effort between University of Rome, Tor Vergata and the Food and Agriculture Organization of the United Nations: FAO)

- OBIS (Web based user interface that allows to input ontology instances in a user friendly way that can be accessed via SPARQL endpoint)

- Menthor Editor (An ontology engineering tool for dealing with OntoUML. It also includes OntoUML syntax validation, Alloy simulation, Anti-Pattern verification, and transformations from OntoUML to OWL, SBVR and Natural Language (Brazilian Portuguese))

Learning

Ontology learning is the automatic or semi-automatic creation of ontologies, including extracting a domain's terms from natural language text. As building ontologies manually is extremely labor-intensive and time consuming, there is great motivation to automate the process. Information extraction and text mining methods have been explored to automatically link ontologies to documents, e.g. in the context of the BioCreative challenges.

Languages

An ontology language is a formal language used to encode the ontology. There are a number of such languages for ontologies, both proprietary and standards-based:

- Common Algebraic Specification Language is a general logic-based specification language developed within the IFIP working group 1.3 "Foundations of System Specifications" and functions as a de facto standard in the area of software specifications. It is now being applied to ontology specifications in order to provide modularity and structuring mechanisms.

- Common logic is ISO standard 24707, a specification for a family of ontology languages that can be accurately translated into each other.

- The Cyc project has its own ontology language called CycL, based on first-order predicate calculus with some higher-order extensions.

- DOGMA (Developing Ontology-Grounded Methods and Applications) adopts the fact-oriented modeling approach to provide a higher level of semantic stability.

- The Gellish language includes rules for its own extension and thus integrates an ontology with an ontology language.

- IDEF5 is a software engineering method to develop and maintain usable, accurate, domain ontologies.

- KIF is a syntax for first-order logic that is based on S-expressions. SUO-KIF is a derivative version supporting the Suggested Upper Merged Ontology.

- MOF and UML are standards of the OMG

- Olog is a category theoretic approach to ontologies, emphasizing translations between ontologies using functors.

- OBO, a language used for biological and biomedical ontologies.

- OntoUML is an ontologically well-founded profile of UML for conceptual modeling of domain ontologies.

- OWL is a language for making ontological statements, developed as a follow-on from RDF and RDFS, as well as earlier ontology language projects including OIL, DAML, and DAML+OIL. OWL is intended to be used over the World Wide Web, and all its elements (classes, properties and individuals) are defined as RDF resources, and identified by URIs.

- Rule Interchange Format (RIF) and F-Logic combine ontologies and rules.

- Semantic Application Design Language (SADL) captures a subset of the expressiveness of OWL, using an English-like language entered via an Eclipse Plug-in.

- SBVR (Semantics of Business Vocabularies and Rules) is an OMG standard adopted in industry to build ontologies.

- TOVE Project, TOronto Virtual Enterprise project

Published Examples

- AURUM - Information Security Ontology, An ontology for information security knowledge sharing, enabling users to collaboratively understand and extend the domain knowledge body. It may serve as a basis for automated information security risk and compliance management.

- BabelNet, a very large multilingual semantic network and ontology, lexicalized in many languages

- Basic Formal Ontology, a formal upper ontology designed to support scientific research

- BioPAX, an ontology for the exchange and interoperability of biological pathway (cellular processes) data

- BMO, an e-Business Model Ontology based on a review of enterprise ontologies and business model literature

- CCO and GexKB, Application Ontologies (APO) that integrate diverse types of knowledge with the Cell Cycle Ontology (CCO) and the Gene Expression Knowledge Base (GexKB)

- CContology (Customer Complaint Ontology), an e-business ontology to support online customer complaint management

- CIDOC Conceptual Reference Model, an ontology for cultural heritage

- COSMO, a Foundation Ontology (current version in OWL) that is designed to contain representations of all of the primitive concepts needed to logically specify the meanings of any domain entity. It is intended to serve as a basic ontology that can be used to translate among the representations in other ontologies or databases. It started as a merger of the basic elements of the OpenCyc and SUMO ontologies, and has been supplemented with other ontology elements (types, relations) so as to include representations of all of the words in the Longman dictionary defining vocabulary.

- Cyc, a large Foundation Ontology for formal representation of the universe of discourse

- Disease Ontology, designed to facilitate the mapping of diseases and associated conditions to particular medical codes

- DOLCE, a Descriptive Ontology for Linguistic and Cognitive Engineering

- Dublin Core, a simple ontology for documents and publishing

- Foundational, Core and Linguistic Ontologies

- Foundational Model of Anatomy, an ontology for human anatomy

- Friend of a Friend, an ontology for describing persons, their activities and their relations to other people and objects

- Gene Ontology for genomics

- Gellish English dictionary, an ontology that includes a dictionary and taxonomy that includes an upper ontology and a lower ontology that focusses on industrial and business applications in engineering, technology and procurement.

- Geopolitical ontology, an ontology describing geopolitical information created by Food and Agriculture Organization(FAO). The geopolitical ontology includes names in multiple languages (English, French, Spanish, Arabic, Chinese, Russian and Italian); maps standard coding systems (UN, ISO, FAOSTAT, AGROVOC, etc.); provides relations among territories (land borders, group membership, etc.); and tracks historical changes. In addition, FAO provides web services

- <http://www.fao.org/countryprofiles/webservices.asp?lang=en> of geopolitical ontology and a module maker

- <http://www.fao.org/countryprofiles/geoinfo/modulemaker/index.html> to download modules of the geopolitical ontology into different formats (RDF, XML, and EXCEL).

- <http://www.fao.org/countryprofiles/geoinfo.asp?lang=en>.

- GOLD, General Ontology for Linguistic Description

- GUM (Generalized Upper Model), a linguistically motivated ontology for mediating between clients systems and natural language technology

- IDEAS Group, a formal ontology for enterprise architecture being developed by the Australian, Canadian, UK and U.S. Defence Depts.

- Linkbase, a formal representation of the biomedical domain, founded upon Basic Formal Ontology.

- LPL, Lawson Pattern Language

- NCBO Bioportal, biological and biomedical ontologies and associated tools to search, browse and visualise

- NIFSTD Ontologies from the Neuroscience Information Framework: a modular set of ontologies for the neuroscience domain.

- OBO-Edit, an ontology browser for most of the Open Biological and Biomedical Ontologies

- OBO Foundry, a suite of interoperable reference ontologies in biology and biomedicine

- OMNIBUS Ontology, an ontology of learning, instruction, and instructional design

- Ontology for Biomedical Investigations, an open access, integrated ontology for the description of biological and clinical investigations

- ONSTR, Ontology for Newborn Screening Follow-up and Translational Research, Newborn Screening Follow-up Data Integration Collaborative, Emory University, Atlanta, GA.

- Plant Ontology for plant structures and growth/development stages, etc.

- POPE, Purdue Ontology for Pharmaceutical Engineering

- PRO, the Protein Ontology of the Protein Information Resource, Georgetown University

- Program abstraction taxonomy program abstraction taxonomy

- Protein Ontology for proteomics

- RXNO Ontology, for name reactions in chemistry

- SNOMED CT (Systematized Nomenclature of Medicine -- Clinical Terms)

- Suggested Upper Merged Ontology, a formal upper ontology

- Systems Biology Ontology (SBO), for computational models in biology

- SWEET, Semantic Web for Earth and Environmental Terminology

- ThoughtTreasure ontology

- TIME-ITEM, Topics for Indexing Medical Education

- Uberon, representing animal anatomical structures

- UMBEL, a lightweight reference structure of 20,000 subject concept classes and their relationships derived from OpenCyc

- WordNet, a lexical reference system

- YAMATO, Yet Another More Advanced Top-level Ontology

The W3C Linking Open Data community project coordinates attempts to converge different ontologies into worldwide Semantic Web.

Libraries

The development of ontologies for the Web has led to the emergence of services providing lists or directories of ontologies with search facility. Such directories have been called ontology libraries.

The following are libraries of human-selected ontologies.

- COLORE is an open repository of first-order ontologies in Common Logic with formal links between ontologies in the repository.

- DAML Ontology Library maintains a legacy of ontologies in DAML.

- Ontology Design Patterns portal is a wiki repository of reusable components and practices for ontology design, and also maintains a list of exemplary ontologies. Started within the NeOn EU project.

- Protégé Ontology Library contains a set of OWL, Frame-based and other format ontologies.

- SchemaWeb is a directory of RDF schemata expressed in RDFS, OWL and DAML+OIL.

The following are both directories and search engines. They include crawlers searching the Web for well-formed ontologies.

- OBO Foundry is a suite of interoperable reference ontologies in biology and biomedicine.

- Bioportal (ontology repository of NCBO)

- OntoSelect Ontology Library offers similar services for RDF/S, DAML and OWL ontologies.

- Ontaria is a "searchable and browsable directory of semantic web data" with a focus on RDF vocabularies with OWL ontologies. (NB Project "on hold" since 2004).

- Swoogle is a directory and search engine for all RDF resources available on the Web, including ontologies.

- OOR - the Open Ontology Repository initiative - http://oor.net

- ROMULUS is a foundational ontology repository aimed at improving semantic interoperability. Currently there are three foundational ontologies in the repository: DOLCE, BFO and GFO.

Examples of Applications

In general, ontologies can be used beneficially in

- enterprise applications. A more concrete example is SAPPHIRE (Health care) or Situational Awareness and Preparedness for Public Health Incidences and Reasoning Engines which is a semantics-based health information system capable of tracking and evaluating situations and occurrences that may affect public health.

- geographic information systems bring together data from different sources and benefit therefore from ontological metadata which helps to connect the semantics of the data.

Criticisms

Werner Ceusters has noted the confusion caused by the significant differences in the meaning of word ontology when used by philosophy compared with the use of the word ontology in computer science, and advocates for greater precision in use of the word ontology so that members of the various disciplines using various definitions of the word ontology can communicate. He writes 'before one is able to answer the question 'what is an ontology?', one must provide first an answer to the question 'what does the word ontology mean?'.

It's also not clear how ontology fits with Schema on Read (NoSQL) databases.

Knowledge Organization

Knowledge organization (KO) (or "organization of knowledge", "organization of information" or "information organization") is a branch of Library and Information Science (LIS) concerned with activities such as document description, indexing and classification performed in libraries, databases, archives, etc. These activities are done by librarians, archivists, subject specialists as well as by computer algorithms. KO as a field of study is concerned with the nature and quality of such knowledge organizing processes (KOP) (such as taxonomy and ontology) as well as the knowledge organizing systems (KOS) used to organize documents, document representations and concepts.

There exist different historical and theoretical approaches to and theories about organizing knowledge, which are related to different views of knowledge, cognition, language, and social organization. Each of these approaches tends to answer the question: "What is knowledge organization?" differently.

Traditional human-based activities are increasingly challenged by computer-based retrieval techniques. It is appropriate to investigate the relative contributions of different approaches; the current challenges make it imperative to reconsider this understanding.

The leading journal in this field is Knowledge Organization published by the International Society for Knowledge Organization (ISKO).

Theoretical Approaches

One widely-used analysis of organizational principles summarizes them as by Location, Alphabet, Time, Category, Hierarchy (LATCH).

Traditional Approaches

Among the major figures in the history of KO, which can be classified as "traditional", are Melvil Dewey (1851-1931) and Henry Bliss (1870-1955).

Dewey's goal was an efficient way to manage library collections; not an optimal system to support users of libraries. His system was meant to be used in many libraries as a standardized way to manage collections.

An important characteristic in Henry Bliss' (and many contemporary thinkers of KO) was that the sciences tend to reflect the order of Nature and that library classification should reflect the order of knowledge as uncovered by science:

Natural order --> Scientific Classification --> Library classification (KO)

The implication is that librarians, in order to classify books, should know about scientific developments. This should also be reflected in their education: "Again from the standpoint of the higher education of librarians, the teaching of systems of classification . . . would be perhaps better conducted by including courses in the systematic encyclopedia and methodology of all the sciences, that is to say, outlines which try to summarize the most recent results in the relation to one another in which they are now studied together. . . ." (Ernest Cushing Richardson, quoted from Bliss, 1935, p. 2).

Among the other principles, which may be attributed to the traditional approach to KO are:

- Principle of controlled vocabulary
- Cutter's rule about specificity
- Hulme's principle of literary warrant (1911)
- Principle of organizing from the general to the specific

Today, after more than 100 years of research and development in LIS, the "traditional" approach still has a strong position in KO and in many ways its principles still dominate.

Facet Analytic Approaches

The date of the foundation of this approach may be chosen as the publication of S. R. Ranganathan's Colon Classification in 1933. The approach has been further developed by, in particular, the British Classification Research Group. In many ways this approach has dominated what might be termed "modern classification theory."

The best way to explain this approach is probably to explain its analytico-synthetic methodology. The meaning of the term "analysis" is: Breaking down each subject into its basic concepts. The meaning of the term synthesis is: Combining the relevant units and concepts to describe the subject matter of the information package in hand.

Given subjects (as they appear in, for example, book titles) are first analyzed into a few common categories, which are termed "facets". Ranganathan proposed his PMEST formula: Personality, Matter, Energy, Space and Time:

The Information Retrieval Tradition (IR)

Important in the IR-tradition have been, among others, the Cranfield experiments, which were founded in the 1950s, and the TREC experiments (Text Retrieval Conferences) starting in 1992. It was the Cranfield experiments, which introduced the famous measures "recall" and "precision" as evaluation criteria for systems efficiency. The Cranfield experiments found that classification systems like UDC and facet-analytic systems were less efficient compared to free-text searches or low level indexing systems ("UNITERM"). The Cranfield I test found according to Ellis (1996, 3-6) the following results.

system	recall
UNITERM	82,0%
Alphabetical subject headings	81,5%
UDC	75,6%
Facet classification scheme	73,8%

Although these results have been criticized and questioned, the IR-tradition became much more influential while library classification research lost influence. The dominant trend has been to regard only statistical averages. What has largely been neglected is to ask: Are there certain kinds of questions in relation to which other kinds of representation, for example, controlled vocabularies, may improve recall and precision?

User-oriented and Cognitive Views

The best way to define this approach is probably by method: Systems based upon user-oriented approaches must specify how the design of a system is made on the basis of empirical studies of users.

User studies demonstrated very early that users prefer verbal search systems as opposed to systems based on classification notations. This is one example of a principle derived from empirical studies of users. Adherents of classification notations may, of course, still have an argument: That notations are well-defined and that users may miss important information by not considering them.

Folksonomies is a recent kind of KO based on users' rather than on librarians' or subject specialists' indexing.

Bibliometric Approaches

These approaches are primarily based on using bibliographical references to organize networks of papers, mainly by bibliographic coupling (introduced by Kessler 1963) or co-citation analysis (independently suggested by Marshakova 1973 and Small 1973). In recent years it has become a popular activity to construe bibliometric maps as structures of research fields.

Two considerations are important in considering bibliometric approaches to KO:

1. The level of indexing depth is partly determined by the number of terms assigned to each document. In citation indexing this corresponds to the number of references in a given paper. On the average, scientific papers contain 10-15 references, which provide quite a high level of depth.

2. The references, which function as access points, are provided by the highest subject-expertise: The experts writing in the leading journals. This expertise is much higher than that which library catalogs or bibliographical databases typically are able to draw on.

The Domain Analytic Approach

Domain analysis is a sociological-epistemological standpoint. The indexing of a given document should reflect the needs of a given group of users or a given ideal purpose. In other words, any description or representation of a given document is more or less suited to the fulfillment of certain tasks. A description is never objective or neutral, and the goal is not to standardize descriptions or make one description once and for all for different target groups.

The development of the Danish library "KVINFO" may serve as an example that explains the domain-analytic point of view.

KVINFO was founded by the librarian and writer Nynne Koch and its history goes back to 1965. Nynne Koch was employed at the Royal Library in Copenhagen in a position without influence on book selection. She was interested in women's' studies and began personally to collect printed catalog cards of books in the Royal Library, which were considered relevant for women's studies. She developed a classification system for this subject. Later she became the head of KVINFO and got a budget for buying books and journals, and still later, KVINFO became an independent library. The important theoretical point of view is that the Royal Library had an official systematic catalog of a high standard. Normally it is assumed that such a catalog is able to identify relevant books for users whatever their theoretical orientation. This example demonstrates, however, that for a specific user group (feminist scholars), an alternative way of organizing catalog cards was important. In other words: Different points of view need different systems of organization.

DA is the only approach to KO which has seriously examined epistemological issues in the field, i.e. comparing the assumptions made in different approaches to KO and examining the questions regarding subjectivity and objectivity in KO. Subjectivity is not just about individual differences. Such differences are of minor interest because they cannot be used as guidelines for KO. What seems important are collective views shared by many users. A kind of subjectivity about many users is related to philosophical positions. In any field of knowledge different views are always at play. In arts, for example, different views of art are always present. Such views determine views on art works, writing on art works, how art works are organized in exhibitions and how writings on art are organized in libraries. In general it can be stated that different philosophical positions on any issue have implications for relevance criteria, information needs and for criteria of organizing knowledge.

Strategic Management

Strategic management involves the formulation and implementation of the major goals and initiatives taken by a company's top management on behalf of owners, based on consideration of resources and an assessment of the internal and external environments in which the organization competes.

Strategic management provides overall direction to the enterprise and involves specifying the organization's objectives, developing policies and plans designed to achieve these objectives, and then allocating resources to implement the plans. Academics and practicing managers have developed numerous models and frameworks to assist in strategic decision making in the context of complex environments and competitive dynamics. Strategic management is not static in nature; the models often include a feedback loop to monitor execution and inform the next round of planning.

Michael Porter identifies three principles underlying strategy: creating a "unique and valuable [market] position", making trade-offs by choosing "what not to do", and creating "fit" by aligning company activities with one another to support the chosen strategy. Dr. Vladimir Kvint defines strategy as "a system of finding, formulating, and developing a doctrine that will ensure long-term success if followed faithfully."

Corporate strategy involves answering a key question from a portfolio perspective: "What business should we be in?" Business strategy involves answering the question: "How shall we compete in this business?" In management theory and practice, a further distinction is often made between strategic management and operational management. Operational management is concerned primarily with improving efficiency and controlling costs within the boundaries set by the organization's strategy.

Definition

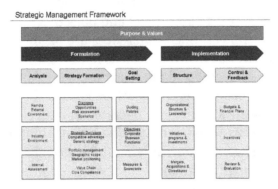

Strategic management processes and activities

Strategic management involves the formulation and implementation of the major goals and initiatives taken by a company's top management on behalf of owners, based on consideration of resources and an assessment of the internal and external environments in which the organization competes. Strategy is defined as "the determination of the basic long-term goals of an enterprise, and the adoption of courses of action and the allocation of resources necessary for carrying out these goals." Strategies are established to set direction, focus effort, define or clarify the organization, and provide consistency or guidance in response to the environment.

Strategic management involves the related concepts of strategic planning and strategic thinking. Strategic planning is analytical in nature and refers to formalized procedures to produce the data and analyses used as inputs for strategic thinking, which synthesizes the data resulting in the strategy. Strategic planning may also refer to control mechanisms used to implement the strategy once it is determined. In other words, strategic planning happens around the strategic thinking or strategy making activity.

Strategic management is often described as involving two major processes: formulation and implementation of strategy. While described sequentially below, in practice the two processes are iterative and each provides input for the other.

Formulation

Formulation of strategy involves analyzing the environment in which the organization operates, then making a series of strategic decisions about how the organization will compete. Formulation ends with a series of goals or objectives and measures for the organization to pursue. Environmental analysis includes the:

- Remote external environment, including the political, economic, social, technological, legal and environmental landscape (PESTLE);

- Industry environment, such as the competitive behavior of rival organizations, the bargaining power of buyers/customers and suppliers, threats from new entrants to the industry, and the ability of buyers to substitute products (Porter's 5 forces); and

- Internal environment, regarding the strengths and weaknesses of the organization's resources (i.e., its people, processes and IT systems).

Strategic decisions are based on insight from the environmental assessment and are responses to strategic questions about how the organization will compete, such as:

- What is the organization's business?

- Who is the target customer for the organization's products and services?

- Where are the customers and how do they buy? What is considered "value" to the customer?

- Which businesses, products and services should be included or excluded from the portfolio of offerings?

- What is the geographic scope of the business?

- What differentiates the company from its competitors in the eyes of customers and other stakeholders?

- Which skills and capabilities should be developed within the firm?

- What are the important opportunities and risks for the organization?

- How can the firm grow, through both its base business and new business?

- How can the firm generate more value for investors?

The answers to these and many other strategic questions result in the organization's strategy and a series of specific short-term and long-term goals or objectives and related measures.

Implementation

The second major process of strategic management is implementation, which involves decisions regarding how the organization's resources (i.e., people, process and IT systems) will be aligned and mobilized towards the objectives. Implementation results in how the organization's resources are structured (such as by product or service or geography), leadership arrangements, communication, incentives, and monitoring mechanisms to track progress towards objectives, among others.

Running the day-to-day operations of the business is often referred to as "operations management" or specific terms for key departments or functions, such as "logistics management" or "marketing management," which take over once strategic management decisions are implemented.

Many Definitions of Strategy

Strategy has been practiced whenever an advantage was gained by planning the sequence and timing of the deployment of resources while simultaneously taking into account the probable capabilities and behavior of competition.

Bruce Henderson

In 1988, Henry Mintzberg described the many different definitions and perspectives on strategy reflected in both academic research and in practice. He examined the strategic process and concluded it was much more fluid and unpredictable than people had thought. Because of this, he could not point to one process that could be called strategic planning. Instead Mintzberg concludes that there are five types of strategies:

- Strategy as plan – a directed course of action to achieve an intended set of goals; similar to the strategic planning concept;

- Strategy as pattern – a consistent pattern of past behavior, with a strategy realized over time rather than planned or intended. Where the realized pattern was different from the intent, he referred to the strategy as emergent;

- Strategy as position – locating brands, products, or companies within the market, based on the conceptual framework of consumers or other stakeholders; a strategy determined primarily by factors outside the firm;

- Strategy as ploy – a specific maneuver intended to outwit a competitor; and

- Strategy as perspective – executing strategy based on a "theory of the business" or natural extension of the mindset or ideological perspective of the organization.

In 1998, Mintzberg developed these five types of management strategy into 10 "schools of thought" and grouped them into three categories. The first group is normative. It consists of the schools of informal design and conception, the formal planning, and analytical positioning. The second group, consisting of six schools, is more concerned with how strategic management is actually done, rather than prescribing optimal plans or positions. The six schools are entrepreneurial, visionary, cognitive, learning/adaptive/emergent, negotiation, corporate culture and business environment. The third and final group consists of one school, the configuration or transformation school, a hybrid of the other schools organized into stages, organizational life cycles, or "episodes".

Michael Porter defined strategy in 1980 as the "...broad formula for how a business is going to compete, what its goals should be, and what policies will be needed to carry out those goals" and the "...combination of the ends (goals) for which the firm is striving and the means (policies) by which it is seeking to get there." He continued that: "The essence of formulating competitive strategy is relating a company to its environment."

Historical Development

Origins

The strategic management discipline originated in the 1950s and 1960s. Among the numerous early contributors, the most influential were Peter Drucker, Philip Selznick, Alfred Chandler, Igor Ansoff, and Bruce Henderson. The discipline draws from earlier thinking and texts on 'strategy' dating back thousands of years. Prior to 1960, the term "strategy" was primarily used regarding war and politics, not business. Many companies built strategic planning functions to develop and execute the formulation and implementation processes during the 1960s.

Peter Drucker was a prolific management theorist and author of dozens of management books, with a career spanning five decades. He addressed fundamental strategic questions in a 1954 book The Practice of Management writing: "...the first responsibility of top management is to ask the question 'what is our business?' and to make sure it is carefully studied and correctly answered." He wrote that the answer was determined by the customer. He recommended eight areas where objectives should be set, such as market standing, innovation, productivity, physical and financial resources, worker performance and attitude, profitability, manager performance and development, and public responsibility.

In 1957, Philip Selznick initially used the term "distinctive competence" in referring to how the Navy was attempting to differentiate itself from the other services. He also formalized the idea of matching the organization's internal factors with external environmental circumstances. This core idea was developed further by Kenneth R. Andrews in 1963 into what we now call SWOT analysis, in which the strengths and weaknesses of the firm are assessed in light of the opportunities and threats in the business environment.

Alfred Chandler recognized the importance of coordinating management activity under an all-encompassing strategy. Interactions between functions were typically handled by managers who relayed information back and forth between departments. Chandler stressed the importance of taking a long term perspective when looking to the future. In his 1962 ground breaking work Strategy and Structure, Chandler showed that a long-term coordinated strategy was necessary to give a company structure, direction and focus. He says it concisely, "structure follows strategy." Chandler wrote that:

"Strategy is the determination of the basic long-term goals of an enterprise, and the adoption of courses of action and the allocation of resources necessary for carrying out these goals."

Igor Ansoff built on Chandler's work by adding concepts and inventing a vocabulary. He developed a grid that compared strategies for market penetration, product development, market development and horizontal and vertical integration and diversification. He felt that management could use the grid to systematically prepare for the future. In his 1965 classic Corporate Strategy, he developed gap analysis to clarify the gap between the current reality and the goals and to develop what he called "gap reducing actions". Ansoff wrote that strategic management had three parts: strategic planning; the skill of a firm in converting its plans into reality; and the skill of a firm in managing its own internal resistance to change.

Bruce Henderson, founder of the Boston Consulting Group, wrote about the concept of the experience curve in 1968, following initial work begun in 1965. The experience curve refers to a hypothesis that unit production costs decline by 20-30% every time cumulative production doubles. This supported the argument for achieving higher market share and economies of scale.

Porter wrote in 1980 that companies have to make choices about their scope and the type of competitive advantage they seek to achieve, whether lower cost or differentiation. The idea of strategy targeting particular industries and customers (i.e., competitive positions) with a differentiated offering was a departure from the experience-curve influenced strategy paradigm, which was focused on larger scale and lower cost. Porter revised the strategy paradigm again in 1985, writing that superior performance of the processes and activities performed by organizations as part of their value chain is the foundation of competitive advantage, thereby outlining a process view of strategy.

Change in Focus from Production to Marketing

The direction of strategic research also paralleled a major paradigm shift in how companies competed, specifically a shift from the production focus to market focus. The prevailing concept in strategy up to the 1950s was to create a product of high technical quality. If you created a product that worked well and was durable, it was assumed you would have no difficulty profiting. This was called the production orientation. Henry Ford famously said of the Model T car: "Any customer can have a car painted any color that he wants, so long as it is black."

Management theorist Peter F Drucker wrote in 1954 that it was the customer who defined what business the organization was in. In 1960 Theodore Levitt argued that instead of producing products then trying to sell them to the customer, businesses should start with the customer, find out what they wanted, and then produce it for them. The fallacy of the production orientation was also referred to as marketing myopia in an article of the same name by Levitt.

Over time, the customer became the driving force behind all strategic business decisions. This marketing concept, in the decades since its introduction, has been reformulated and repackaged under names including market orientation, customer orientation, customer intimacy, customer focus, customer-driven and market focus.

It's more important than ever to define yourself in terms of what you stand for rather than what you make, because what you make is going to become outmoded faster than it has at any time in the past.

Jim Collins

Jim Collins wrote in 1997 that the strategic frame of reference is expanded by focusing on why a company exists rather than what it makes. In 2001, he recommended that organizations define themselves based on three key questions:

- What are we passionate about?

- What can we be best in the world at?

- What drives our economic engine?

Nature of Strategy

In 1985, Professor Ellen Earle-Chaffee summarized what she thought were the main elements of strategic management theory where consensus generally existed as of the 1970s, writing that strategic management:

- Involves adapting the organization to its business environment;

- Is fluid and complex. Change creates novel combinations of circumstances requiring unstructured non-repetitive responses;

- Affects the entire organization by providing direction;

- Involves both strategy formulation processes and also implementation of the content of the strategy;

- May be planned (intended) and unplanned (emergent);

- Is done at several levels: overall corporate strategy, and individual business strategies; and

- Involves both conceptual and analytical thought processes.

Chaffee further wrote that research up to that point covered three models of strategy, which were not mutually exclusive:

1. Linear strategy: A planned determination of goals, initiatives, and allocation of resources, along the lines of the Chandler definition above. This is most consistent with strategic planning approaches and may have a long planning horizon.

The strategist "deals with" the environment but it is not the central concern.

2. Adaptive strategy: In this model, the organization's goals and activities are primarily concerned with adaptation to the environment, analogous to a biological organism. The need for continuous adaption reduces or eliminates the planning window. There is more focus on means (resource mobilization to address the environment) rather than ends (goals). Strategy is less centralized than in the linear model.

3. Interpretive strategy: A more recent and less developed model than the linear and adaptive models, interpretive strategy is concerned with "orienting metaphors constructed for the purpose of conceptualizing and guiding individual attitudes or organizational participants." The aim of interpretive strategy is legitimacy or credibility in the mind of stakeholders. It places emphasis on symbols and language to influence the minds of customers, rather than the physical product of the organization.

Concepts and Frameworks

The progress of strategy since 1960 can be charted by a variety of frameworks and concepts introduced by management consultants and academics. These reflect an increased focus on cost, competition and customers. These "3 Cs" were illuminated by much more robust empirical analysis at ever-more granular levels of detail, as industries and organizations were disaggregated into business units, activities, processes, and individuals in a search for sources of competitive advantage.

SWOT Analysis

A SWOT analysis, with its four elements in a 2×2 matrix.

By the 1960s, the capstone business policy course at the Harvard Business School included the concept of matching the distinctive competence of a company (its internal strengths and weaknesses) with its environment (external opportunities and threats) in the context of its objectives. This framework came to be known by the acronym SWOT and was "a major step forward in bringing explicitly competitive thinking to bear on questions of strategy." Kenneth R. Andrews helped popularize the framework via a 1963 conference and it remains commonly used in practice.

Experience Curve

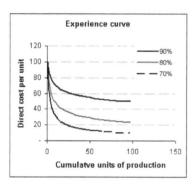 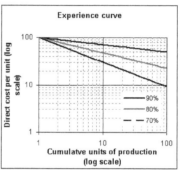

Experience curve

The experience curve was developed by the Boston Consulting Group in 1966. It is a hypothesis that total per unit costs decline systematically by as much as 15-25% every time cumulative production (i.e., "experience") doubles. It has been empirically confirmed by some firms at various points in their history. Costs decline due to a variety of factors, such as the learning curve, substitution of labor for capital (automation), and technological sophistication. Author Walter Kiechel wrote that it reflected several insights, including:

- A company can always improve its cost structure;

- Competitors have varying cost positions based on their experience;

- Firms could achieve lower costs through higher market share, attaining a competitive advantage; and

- An increased focus on empirical analysis of costs and processes, a concept which author Kiechel refers to as "Greater Taylorism."

Kiechel wrote in 2010: "The experience curve was, simply, the most important concept in launching the strategy revolution...with the experience curve, the strategy revolution began to insinuate an acute awareness of competition into the corporate consciousness." Prior to the 1960s, the word competition rarely appeared in the most prominent management literature; U.S. companies then faced considerably less competition and did not focus on performance relative to peers. Further, the experience curve provided a basis for the retail sale of business ideas, helping drive the management consulting industry.

Corporate Strategy and Portfolio Theory

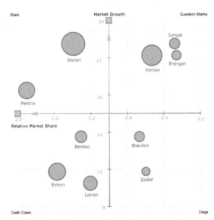

Portfolio growth–share matrix

The concept of the corporation as a portfolio of business units, with each plotted graphically based on its market share (a measure of its competitive position relative to its peers) and industry growth rate (a measure of industry attractiveness), was summarized in the growth–share matrix developed by the Boston Consulting Group around 1970. By 1979, one study estimated that 45% of the Fortune 500 companies were using some variation of the matrix in their strategic planning. This framework helped companies decide where to invest their resources (i.e., in their high market share, high growth businesses) and which businesses to divest (i.e., low market share, low growth businesses.)

Porter wrote in 1987 that corporate strategy involves two questions: 1) What business should the corporation be in? and 2) How should the corporate office manage its business units? He mentioned four concepts of corporate strategy; the latter three can be used together:

1. Portfolio theory: A strategy based primarily on diversification through acquisition. The corporation shifts resources among the units and monitors the performance of each business unit and its leaders. Each unit generally runs autonomously, with limited interference from the corporate center provided goals are met.

2. Restructuring: The corporate office acquires then actively intervenes in a business where it detects potential, often by replacing management and implementing a new business strategy.

3. Transferring skills: Important managerial skills and organizational capability are essentially spread to multiple businesses. The skills must be necessary to competitive advantage.

4. Sharing activities: Ability of the combined corporation to leverage centralized functions, such as sales, finance, etc. thereby reducing costs.

Other techniques were developed to analyze the relationships between elements in a portfolio. The growth-share matrix, a part of B.C.G. Analysis, was followed by G.E. multi factoral model, developed by General Electric. Companies continued to diversify as conglomerates until the 1980s, when deregulation and a less restrictive anti-trust environment led to the view that a portfolio of operating divisions in different industries was worth more as many independent companies, leading to the breakup of many conglomerates. While the popularity of portfolio theory has waxed and waned, the key dimensions considered (industry attractiveness and competitive position) remain central to strategy.

Competitive Advantage

In 1980, Porter defined the two types of competitive advantage an organization can achieve relative to its rivals: lower cost or differentiation. This advantage derives from attribute(s) that allow an organization to outperform its competition, such as superior market position, skills, or resources. In Porter's view, strategic management should be concerned with building and sustaining competitive advantage.

Industry Structure and Profitability

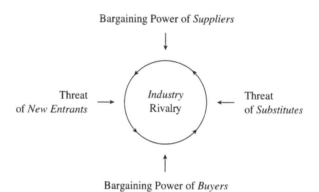

A graphical representation of Porter's Five Forces

Porter developed a framework for analyzing the profitability of industries and how those profits are divided among the participants in 1980. In five forces analysis he identified the forces that shape the industry structure or environment. The framework involves the bargaining power of buyers and suppliers, the threat of new entrants, the availability of substitute products, and the competitive rivalry of firms in the industry. These forces affect the organization's ability to raise its prices as well as the costs of inputs (such as raw materials) for its processes.

The five forces framework helps describe how a firm can use these forces to obtain a sustainable competitive advantage, either lower cost or differentiation. Companies can maximize their profitability by competing in industries with favorable structure. Competitors can take steps to grow the overall profitability of the industry, or to take profit away from other parts of the industry structure. Porter modified Chandler's dictum about structure following strategy by introducing a second level of structure: while organizational structure follows strategy, it in turn follows industry structure.

Generic Competitive Strategies

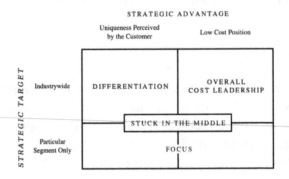

Michael Porter's Three Generic Strategies

Porter wrote in 1980 that strategy target either cost leadership, differentiation, or focus. These are known as Porter's three generic strategies and can be applied to any size or form of business. Porter claimed that a company must only choose one of the three or risk that the business would waste precious resources. Porter's generic strategies detail the interaction between cost minimization strategies, product differentiation strategies, and market focus strategies.

Porter described an industry as having multiple segments that can be targeted by a firm. The breadth of its targeting refers to the competitive scope of the business. Porter defined two types of competitive advantage: lower cost or differentiation relative to its rivals. Achieving competitive advantage results from a firm's ability to cope with the five forces better than its rivals. Porter wrote: "[A]chieving competitive advantage requires a firm to make a choice...about the type of competitive advantage it seeks to attain and the scope within which it will attain it." He also wrote: "The two basic types of competitive advantage [differentiation and lower cost] combined with the scope of activities for which a firm seeks to achieve them lead to three generic strategies for achieving above average performance in an industry: cost leadership, differentiation and focus. The focus strategy has two variants, cost focus and differentiation focus."

The concept of choice was a different perspective on strategy, as the 1970s paradigm was the pursuit of market share (size and scale) influenced by the experience curve. Companies that pursued the highest market share position to achieve cost advantages fit under Porter's cost leadership generic strategy, but the concept of choice regarding differentiation and focus represented a new perspective.

Value Chain

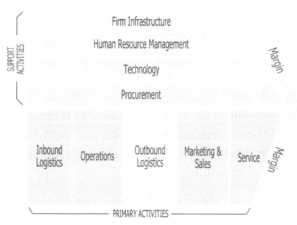

Michael Porter's Value Chain

Porter's 1985 description of the value chain refers to the chain of activities (processes or collections of processes) that an organization performs in order to deliver a valuable product or service for the market. These include functions such as inbound logistics, operations, outbound logistics, marketing and sales, and service, supported by systems and technology infrastructure. By aligning the various activities in its value chain with the organization's strategy in a coherent way, a firm can achieve a competitive advantage. Porter also wrote that strategy is an internally consistent configuration of activities that differentiates a firm from its rivals. A robust competitive position cumulates from many activities which should fit coherently together.

Porter wrote in 1985: "Competitive advantage cannot be understood by looking at a firm as a whole. It stems from the many discrete activities a firm performs in designing, producing, marketing, delivering and supporting its product. Each of these activities can contribute to a firm's relative cost position and create a basis for differentiation...the value chain disaggregates a firm into its strategically relevant activities in order to understand the behavior of costs and the existing and potential sources of differentiation."

Core Competence

Gary Hamel and C. K. Prahalad described the idea of core competency in 1990, the idea that each organization has some capability in which it excels and that the business should focus on opportunities in that area, letting others go or outsourcing them. Further, core competency is difficult to duplicate, as it involves the skills and coordination of people across a variety of functional areas or processes used to deliver value to customers. By outsourcing, companies expanded the concept of the value chain, with some elements within the entity and others without. Core competency is part of a branch of strategy called the resource-based view of the firm, which postulates that if activities are strategic as indicated by the value chain, then the organization's capabilities and ability to learn or adapt are also strategic.

Theory of the Business

Peter Drucker wrote in 1994 about the "Theory of the Business," which represents the key assumptions underlying a firm's strategy. These assumptions are in three categories: a) the external environment, including society, market, customer, and technology; b) the mission of the organization; and c) the core competencies needed to accomplish the mission. He continued that a valid theory of the business has four specifications: 1) assumptions about the environment, mission, and core competencies must fit reality; 2) the assumptions in all three areas have to fit one another; 3) the theory of the business must be known and understood throughout the organization; and 4) the theory of the business has to be tested constantly.

He wrote that organizations get into trouble when the assumptions representing the theory of the business no longer fit reality. He used an example of retail department stores, where their theory of the business assumed that people who could afford to shop in department stores would do so. However, many shoppers abandoned department stores in favor of specialty retailers (often located outside of malls) when time became the primary factor in the shopping destination rather than income.

Drucker described the theory of the business as a "hypothesis" and a "discipline." He advocated building in systematic diagnostics, monitoring and testing of the assumptions comprising the theory of the business to maintain competitiveness.

Strategic Thinking

Strategic thinking involves the generation and application of unique business insights to opportunities intended to create competitive advantage for a firm or organization. It involves challenging the assumptions underlying the organization's strategy and value proposition. Mintzberg wrote in 1994 that it is more about synthesis (i.e., "connecting the dots") than analysis (i.e., "finding the dots"). It is about "capturing what the manager learns from all sources (both the soft insights from his or her personal experiences and the experiences of others throughout the organization and the hard data from market research and the like) and then synthesizing that learning into a vision of the direction that the business should pursue." Mintzberg argued that strategic thinking is the critical part of formulating strategy, more so than strategic planning exercises.

General Andre Beaufre wrote in 1963 that strategic thinking "is a mental process, at once abstract and rational, which must be capable of synthesizing both psychological and material data. The strategist must have a great capacity for both analysis and synthesis; analysis is necessary to assemble the data on which he makes his diagnosis, synthesis in order to produce from these data the diagnosis itself--and the diagnosis in fact amounts to a choice between alternative courses of action."

Will Mulcaster argued that while much research and creative thought has been devoted to generating alternative strategies, too little work has been done on what influences the quality of strategic decision making and the effectiveness with which strategies are implemented. For instance, in retrospect it can be seen that the financial crisis of 2008–9 could have been avoided if the banks had paid more attention to the risks associated with their investments, but how should banks change the way they make decisions to improve the quality of their decisions in the future? Mulcaster's Managing Forces framework addresses this issue by identifying 11 forces that should be incorporated into the processes of decision making and strategic implementation. The 11 forces are: Time; Opposing forces; Politics; Perception; Holistic effects; Adding value; Incentives; Learning capabilities; Opportunity cost; Risk and Style.

Strategic Planning

Strategic planning is a means of administering the formulation and implementation of strategy. Strategic planning is analytical in nature and refers to formalized procedures to produce the data and analyses used as inputs for strategic thinking, which synthesizes the data resulting in the strategy. Strategic planning may also refer to control mechanisms used to implement the strategy once it is determined. In other words, strategic planning happens around the strategy formation process.

Environmental Analysis

Porter wrote in 1980 that formulation of competitive strategy includes consideration of four key elements:

1. Company strengths and weaknesses;

2. Personal values of the key implementers (i.e., management and the board)

3. Broader societal expectations.

The first two elements relate to factors internal to the company (i.e., the internal environment), while the latter two relate to factors external to the company (i.e., the external environment).

There are many analytical frameworks which attempt to organize the strategic planning process. Examples of frameworks that address the four elements described above include:

- External environment: PEST analysis or STEEP analysis is a framework used to examine the remote external environmental factors that can affect the organization, such as political, economic, social/demographic, and technological. Common variations include SLEPT, PESTLE, STEEPLE, and STEER analysis, each of which incorporates slightly different emphases.

- Industry environment: The Porter Five Forces Analysis framework helps to determine the competitive rivalry and therefore attractiveness of a market. It is used to help determine the portfolio of offerings the organization will provide and in which markets.

- Relationship of internal and external environment: SWOT analysis is one of the most basic and widely used frameworks, which examines both internal elements of the organization — Strengths and Weaknesses — and external elements — Opportunities and Threats. It helps examine the organization's resources in the context of its environment.

Scenario Planning

A number of strategists use scenario planning techniques to deal with change. The way Peter Schwartz put it in 1991 is that strategic outcomes cannot be known in advance so the sources of competitive advantage cannot be predetermined. The fast changing business environment is too uncertain for us to find sustainable value in formulas of excellence or competitive advantage. Instead, scenario planning is a technique in which multiple outcomes can be developed, their implications assessed, and their likeliness of occurrence evaluated. According to Pierre Wack, scenario planning is about insight, complexity, and subtlety, not about formal analysis and numbers.

Some business planners are starting to use a complexity theory approach to strategy. Complexity can be thought of as chaos with a dash of order. Chaos theory deals with turbulent systems that rapidly become disordered. Complexity is not quite so unpredictable. It involves multiple agents interacting in such a way that a glimpse of structure may appear.

Measuring and Controlling Implementation

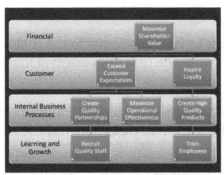

Generic Strategy Map illustrating four elements of a balanced scorecard

Once the strategy is determined, various goals and measures may be established to chart a course for the organization, measure performance and control implementation of the strategy. Tools such as the balanced scorecard and strategy maps help crystallize the strategy, by relating key measures of success and performance to the strategy. These tools measure financial, marketing, production, organizational development, and innovation measures to achieve a 'balanced' perspective. Advances in information technology and data availability enable the gathering of more information about performance, allowing managers to take a much more analytical view of their business than before.

Strategy may also be organized as a series of "initiatives" or "programs", each of which comprises one or more projects. Various monitoring and feedback mechanisms may also be established, such as regular meetings between divisional and corporate management to control implementation.

Evaluation

A key component to strategic management which is often overlooked when planning is evaluation. There are many ways to evaluate whether or not strategic priorities and plans have been achieved, one such method is Robert Stake's Responsive Evaluation. Responsive evaluation provides a naturalistic and humanistic approach to program evaluation. In expanding beyond the goal-oriented or pre-ordinate evaluation design, responsive evaluation takes into consideration the program's background (history), conditions, and transactions among stakeholders. It is largely emergent, the design unfolds as contact is made with stakeholders.

Limitations

While strategies are established to set direction, focus effort, define or clarify the organization, and provide consistency or guidance in response to the environment, these very elements also mean that certain signals are excluded from consideration or de-emphasized. Mintzberg wrote in 1987: "Strategy is a categorizing scheme by which incoming stimuli can be ordered and dispatched." Since a strategy orients the organization in a particular manner or direction, that direction may not effectively match the environment, initially (if a bad strategy) or over time as circumstances change. As such, Mintzberg continued, "Strategy [once established] is a force that resists change, not encourages it."

Therefore, a critique of strategic management is that it can overly constrain managerial discretion in a dynamic environment. "How can individuals, organizations and societies cope as well as possible with ... issues too complex to be fully understood, given the fact that actions initiated on the basis of inadequate understanding may lead to significant regret?" Some theorists insist on an iterative approach, considering in turn objectives, implementation and resources. I.e., a "...repetitive learning cycle [rather than] a linear progression towards a clearly defined final destination." Strategies must be able to adjust during implementation because "humans rarely can proceed satisfactorily except by learning from experience; and modest probes, serially modified on the basis of feedback, usually are the best method for such learning."

In 2000, Gary Hamel coined the term strategic convergence to explain the limited scope of the strategies being used by rivals in greatly differing circumstances. He lamented that successful strategies are imitated by firms that do not understand that for a strategy to work, it must account for the specifics of each situation. Woodhouse and Collingridge claim that the essence of being "strategic" lies in a capacity for "intelligent trial-and error" rather than strict adherence to finely honed strategic plans. Strategy should be seen as laying out the general path rather than precise steps. Means are as likely to determine ends as ends are to determine means. The objectives that an organization might wish to pursue are limited by the range of feasible approaches to implementation. (There will usually be only a small number of approaches that will not only be technically and administratively possible, but also satisfactory to the full range of organizational stakeholders.) In turn, the range of feasible implementation approaches is determined by the availability of resources.

Strategic Themes

Various strategic approaches used across industries (themes) have arisen over the years. These include the shift from product-driven demand to customer- or marketing-driven demand (described above), the increased use of self-service approaches to lower cost, changes in the value chain or corporate structure due to globalization (e.g., off-shoring of production and assembly), and the internet.

Self-service

One theme in strategic competition has been the trend towards self-service, often enabled by technology, where the customer takes on a role previously performed by a worker to lower the price. Examples include:

- Automated teller machine (ATM) to obtain cash rather via a bank teller;

- Self-service at the gas pump rather than with help from an attendant;

- Retail internet orders input by the customer rather than a retail clerk, such as online book sales;

- Mass-produced ready-to-assemble furniture transported by the customer;

- Self-checkout at the grocery store; and

- Online banking and bill payment.

Globalization and the Virtual Firm

One definition of globalization refers to the integration of economies due to technology and supply chain process innovation. Companies are no longer required to be vertically integrated (i.e., designing, producing, assembling, and selling their products). In other words, the value chain for a company's product may no longer be entirely within one firm; several entities comprising a virtual firm may exist to fulfill the customer requirement. For example, some companies have chosen to outsource production to third parties, retaining only design and sales functions inside their organization.

Internet and Information Availability

The internet has dramatically empowered consumers and enabled buyers and sellers to come together with drastically reduced transaction and intermediary costs, creating much more robust marketplaces for the purchase and sale of goods and services. Examples include online auction sites, internet dating services, and internet book sellers. In many industries, the internet has dramatically altered the competitive landscape. Services that used to be provided within one entity (e.g., a car dealership providing financing and pricing information) are now provided by third parties. Further, compared to traditional media like television, the internet has caused a major shift in viewing habits through on demand content which has led to an increasingly fragmented audience.

Author Phillip Evans said in 2013 that networks are challenging traditional hierarchies. Value chains may also be breaking up ("deconstructing") where information aspects can be separated from functional activity. Data that is readily available for free or very low cost makes it harder for information-based, vertically integrated businesses to remain intact. Evans said: "The basic story here is that what used to be vertically integrated, oligopolistic competition among essentially similar kinds of competitors is evolving, by one means or another, from a vertical structure to a horizontal one. Why is that happening? It's happening because transaction costs are plummeting and because scale is polarizing. The plummeting of transaction costs weakens the glue that holds value chains together, and allows them to separate." He used Wikipedia as an example of a network that has challenged the traditional encyclopedia business model. Evans predicts the emergence of a new form of industrial organization called a "stack", analogous to a technology stack, in which competitors rely on a common platform of inputs (services or information), essentially layering the remaining competing parts of their value chains on top of this common platform.

Strategy as Learning

In 1990, Peter Senge, who had collaborated with Arie de Geus at Dutch Shell, popularized de Geus' notion of the "learning organization". The theory is that gathering and analyzing information is a necessary requirement for business success in the information age. To do this, Senge claimed that an organization would need to be structured such that:

- People can continuously expand their capacity to learn and be productive.

- New patterns of thinking are nurtured.

- Collective aspirations are encouraged.

- People are encouraged to see the "whole picture" together.

Senge identified five disciplines of a learning organization. They are:

- Personal responsibility, self-reliance, and mastery — We accept that we are the masters of our own destiny. We make decisions and live with the consequences of them. When a problem needs to be fixed, or an opportunity exploited, we take the initiative to learn the required skills to get it done.

- Mental models — We need to explore our personal mental models to understand the subtle effect they have on our behaviour.

- Shared vision — The vision of where we want to be in the future is discussed and communicated to all. It provides guidance and energy for the journey ahead.

- Team learning — We learn together in teams. This involves a shift from "a spirit of advocacy to a spirit of enquiry".

- Systems thinking — We look at the whole rather than the parts. This is what Senge calls the "Fifth discipline". It is the glue that integrates the other four into a coherent strategy.

Geoffrey Moore (1991) and R. Frank and P. Cook also detected a shift in the nature of competition. Markets driven by technical standards or by "network effects" can give the dominant firm a near-monopoly. The same is true of networked industries in which interoperability requires compatibility between users. Examples include Internet Explorer's and Amazon's early dominance of their respective industries. IE's later decline shows that such dominance may be only temporary.

Moore showed how firms could attain this enviable position by using E.M. Rogers' five stage adoption process and focusing on one group of customers at a time, using each group as a base for reaching the next group. The most difficult step is making the transition between introduction and mass acceptance. If successful a firm can create a bandwagon effect in which the momentum builds and its product becomes a de facto standard.

Strategy as Adapting to Change

In 1969, Peter Drucker coined the phrase Age of Discontinuity to describe the way change disrupts lives. In an age of continuity attempts to predict the future by extrapolating from the past can be accurate. But according to Drucker, we are now in an age of discontinuity and extrapolating is ineffective. He identifies four sources of discontinuity: new technologies, globalization, cultural pluralism and knowledge capital.

In 1970, Alvin Toffler in Future Shock described a trend towards accelerating rates of change. He illustrated how social and technical phenomena had shorter lifespans with each generation, and he questioned society's ability to cope with the resulting turmoil and accompanying anxiety. In past eras periods of change were always punctuated with times of stability. This allowed society to assimilate the change before the next change arrived. But these periods of stability had all but disappeared by the late 20th century. In 1980 in The Third Wave, Toffler characterized this shift to relentless change as the defining feature of the third phase of civilization (the first two phases being the agricultural and industrial waves).

In 1978, Derek F. Abell (Abell, D. 1978) described "strategic windows" and stressed the importance of the timing (both entrance and exit) of any given strategy. This led some strategic planners to build planned obsolescence into their strategies.

In 1983, Noel Tichy wrote that because we are all beings of habit we tend to repeat what we are comfortable with. He wrote that this is a trap that constrains our creativity, prevents us from exploring new ideas, and hampers our dealing with the full complexity of new issues. He developed a systematic method of dealing with change that involved looking at any new issue from three angles: technical and production, political and resource allocation, and corporate culture.

In 1989, Charles Handy identified two types of change. "Strategic drift" is a gradual change that occurs so subtly that it is not noticed until it is too late. By contrast, "transformational change" is sudden and radical. It is typically caused by discontinuities (or exogenous shocks) in the business environment. The point where a new trend is initiated is called a "strategic inflection point" by Andy Grove. Inflection points can be subtle or radical.

In 1990, Richard Pascale wrote that relentless change requires that businesses continuously reinvent themselves. His famous maxim is "Nothing fails like success" by which he means that what was a strength yesterday becomes the root of weakness today, We tend to depend on what worked yesterday and refuse to let go of what worked so well for us in the past. Prevailing strategies become self-confirming. To avoid this trap, businesses must stimulate a spirit of inquiry and healthy debate. They must encourage a creative process of self-renewal based on constructive conflict.

In 1996, Adrian Slywotzky showed how changes in the business environment are reflected in value migrations between industries, between companies, and within companies. He claimed that recognizing the patterns behind these value migrations is necessary if we wish to understand the world of chaotic change. In "Profit Patterns" (1999) he described businesses as being in a state of strategic anticipation as they try to spot emerging patterns. Slywotsky and his team identified 30 patterns that have transformed industry after industry.

In 1997, Clayton Christensen (1997) took the position that great companies can fail precisely because they do everything right since the capabilities of the organization also define its disabilities. Christensen's thesis is that outstanding companies lose their market leadership when confronted with disruptive technology. He called the approach to discovering the emerging markets for disruptive technologies agnostic marketing, i.e., marketing under the implicit assumption that no one – not the company, not the customers – can know how or in what quantities a disruptive product can or will be used without the experience of using it.

In 1999, Constantinos Markides reexamined the nature of strategic planning. He described strategy formation and implementation as an ongoing, never-ending, integrated process requiring continuous reassessment and reformation. Strategic management is planned and emergent, dynamic and interactive.

J. Moncrieff (1999) stressed strategy dynamics. He claimed that strategy is partially deliberate and partially unplanned. The unplanned element comes from emergent strategies that result from the emergence of opportunities and threats in the environment and from "strategies in action" (ad hoc actions across the organization).

David Teece pioneered research on resource-based strategic management and the dynamic capabilities perspective, defined as "the ability to integrate, build, and reconfigure internal and external competencies to address rapidly changing environments". His 1997 paper (with Gary Pisano and Amy Shuen) "Dynamic Capabilities and Strategic Management" was the most cited paper in economics and business for the period from 1995 to 2005.

In 2000, Gary Hamel discussed strategic decay, the notion that the value of every strategy, no matter how brilliant, decays over time.

Strategy as Operational Excellence

Quality

A large group of theorists felt the area where western business was most lacking was product quality. W. Edwards Deming, Joseph M. Juran, A. Kearney, Philip Crosby and Armand Feignbaum suggested quality improvement techniques such total quality management (TQM), continuous improvement (kaizen), lean manufacturing, Six Sigma, and return on quality (ROQ).

Contrarily, James Heskett (1988), Earl Sasser (1995), William Davidow, Len Schlesinger, A. Paraurgman (1988), Len Berry, Jane Kingman-Brundage, Christopher Hart, and Christopher Lovelock (1994), felt that poor customer service was the problem. They gave us fishbone diagramming, service charting, Total Customer Service (TCS), the service profit chain, service gaps analysis, the service encounter, strategic service vision, service mapping, and service teams. Their underlying assumption was that there is no better source of competitive advantage than a continuous stream of delighted customers.

Process management uses some of the techniques from product quality management and some of the techniques from customer service management. It looks at an activity as a sequential process. The objective is to find inefficiencies and make the process more effective. Although the procedures have a long history, dating back to Taylorism, the scope of their applicability has been greatly widened, leaving no aspect of the firm free from potential process improvements. Because of the broad applicability of process management techniques, they can be used as a basis for competitive advantage.

Carl Sewell, Frederick F. Reichheld, C. Gronroos, and Earl Sasser observed that businesses were spending more on customer acquisition than on retention. They showed how a competitive advantage could be found in ensuring that customers returned again and again. Reicheld broadened the concept to include loyalty from employees, suppliers, distributors and shareholders. They developed techniques for estimating customer lifetime value (CLV) for assessing long-term relationships. The concepts begat attempts to recast selling and marketing into a long term endeavor that created a sustained relationship (called relationship selling, relationship marketing, and customer relationship management). Customer relationship management (CRM) software became integral to many firms.

Reengineering

Michael Hammer and James Champy felt that these resources needed to be restructured. In a process that they labeled reengineering, firm's reorganized their assets around whole processes rather than tasks. In this way a team of people saw a project through, from inception to completion. This avoided functional silos where isolated departments seldom talked to each other. It also eliminated waste due to functional overlap and interdepartmental communications.

In 1989 Richard Lester and the researchers at the MIT Industrial Performance Center identified seven best practices and concluded that firms must accelerate the shift away from the mass production of low cost standardized products. The seven areas of best practice were:

- Simultaneous continuous improvement in cost, quality, service, and product innovation

- Breaking down organizational barriers between departments

- Eliminating layers of management creating flatter organizational hierarchies.

- Closer relationships with customers and suppliers

- Intelligent use of new technology

- Global focus

- Improving human resource skills

The search for best practices is also called benchmarking. This involves determining where you need to improve, finding an organization that is exceptional in this area, then studying the company and applying its best practices in your firm.

Other Perspectives on Strategy

Strategy as Problem Solving

Professor Richard P. Rumelt described strategy as a type of problem solving in 2011. He wrote that good strategy has an underlying structure called a kernel. The kernel has three parts: 1) A diagnosis that defines or explains the nature of the challenge; 2) A guiding policy for dealing with the challenge; and 3) Coherent actions designed to carry out the guiding policy. President Kennedy outlined these three elements of strategy in his Cuban Missile Crisis Address to the Nation of 22 October 1962:

1. Diagnosis: "This Government, as promised, has maintained the closest surveillance of the Soviet military buildup on the island of Cuba. Within the past week, unmistakable evidence has established the fact that a series of offensive missile sites is now in preparation on that imprisoned island. The purpose of these bases can be none other than to provide a nuclear strike capability against the Western Hemisphere."

2. Guiding Policy: "Our unswerving objective, therefore, must be to prevent the use of these missiles against this or any other country, and to secure their withdrawal or elimination from the Western Hemisphere."

3. Action Plans: First among seven numbered steps was the following: "To halt this offensive buildup a strict quarantine on all offensive military equipment under shipment to Cuba is being initiated. All ships of any kind bound for Cuba from whatever nation or port will, if found to contain cargoes of offensive weapons, be turned back."

Active strategic management required active information gathering and active problem solving. In the early days of Hewlett-Packard (HP), Dave Packard and Bill Hewlett devised an active management style that they called management by walking around (MBWA). Senior HP managers were seldom at their desks. They spent most of their days visiting employees, customers, and suppliers. This direct contact with key people provided them with a solid grounding from which viable strategies could be crafted. Management consultants Tom Peters and Robert H. Waterman had used the term in their 1982 book In Search of Excellence: Lessons From America's Best-Run Companies. Some Japanese managers employ a similar system, which originated at Honda, and is sometimes called the 3 G's (Genba, Genbutsu, and Genjitsu, which translate into "actual place", "actual thing", and "actual situation").

Creative vs Analytic Approaches

In 2010, IBM released a study summarizing three conclusions of 1500 CEOs around the world: 1) complexity is escalating, 2) enterprises are not equipped to cope with this complexity, and 3) creativity is now the single most important leadership competency. IBM said that it is needed in all aspects of leadership, including strategic thinking and planning.

Similarly, Mckeown argued that over-reliance on any particular approach to strategy is dangerous and that multiple methods can be used to combine the creativity and analytics to create an "approach to shaping the future", that is difficult to copy.

Non-strategic Management

A 1938 treatise by Chester Barnard, based on his own experience as a business executive, described the process as informal, intuitive, non-routinized and involving primarily oral, 2-way communications. Bernard says "The process is the sensing of the organization as a whole and the total situation relevant to it. It transcends the capacity of merely intellectual methods, and the techniques of discriminating the factors of the situation. The terms pertinent to it are "feeling", "judgement", "sense", "proportion", "balance", "appropriateness". It is a matter of art rather than science."

In 1973, Mintzberg found that senior managers typically deal with unpredictable situations so they strategize in ad hoc, flexible, dynamic, and implicit ways. He wrote, "The job breeds adaptive information-manipulators who prefer the live concrete situation. The manager works in an environment of stimulus-response, and he develops in his work a clear preference for live action."

In 1982, John Kotter studied the daily activities of 15 executives and concluded that they spent most of their time developing and working a network of relationships that provided general insights and specific details for strategic decisions. They tended to use "mental road maps" rather than systematic planning techniques.

Daniel Isenberg's 1984 study of senior managers found that their decisions were highly intuitive. Executives often sensed what they were going to do before they could explain why. He claimed in 1986 that one of the reasons for this is the complexity of strategic decisions and the resultant information uncertainty.

Zuboff claimed that information technology was widening the divide between senior managers (who typically make strategic decisions) and operational level managers (who typically make routine decisions). She alleged that prior to the widespread use of computer systems, managers, even at the most senior level, engaged in both strategic decisions and routine administration, but as computers facilitated (She called it "deskilled") routine processes, these activities were moved further down the hierarchy, leaving senior management free for strategic decision making.

In 1977, Abraham Zaleznik distinguished leaders from managers. He described leaders as visionaries who inspire, while managers care about process. He claimed that the rise of managers was the main cause of the decline of American business in the 1970s and 1980s. Lack of leadership is most damaging at the level of strategic management where it can paralyze an entire organization.

Dr Maretha Prinsloo developed the Cognitive Process Profile (CPP) psychometric from the work of Elliott Jacques. The CPP is a computer-based psychometric which profiles a person's capacity for strategic thinking. It is used worldwide in selecting and developing people for strategic roles.

According to Corner, Kinichi, and Keats, strategic decision making in organizations occurs at two levels: individual and aggregate. They developed a model of parallel strategic decision making. The model identifies two parallel processes that involve getting attention, encoding information, storage and retrieval of information, strategic choice, strategic outcome and feedback. The individual and organizational processes interact at each stage. For instance, competition-oriented objectives are based on the knowledge of competing firms, such as their market share.

Strategy as Marketing

The 1980s also saw the widespread acceptance of positioning theory. Although the theory originated with Jack Trout in 1969, it didn't gain wide acceptance until Al Ries and Jack Trout wrote their classic book Positioning: The Battle For Your Mind (1979). The basic premise is that a strategy should not be judged by internal company factors but by the way customers see it relative to the competition. Crafting and implementing a strategy involves creating a position in the mind of the collective consumer. Several techniques enabled the practical use of positioning theory. Perceptual mapping for example, creates visual displays of the relationships between positions. Multidimensional scaling, discriminant analysis, factor analysis and conjoint analysis are mathematical techniques used to determine the most relevant characteristics (called dimensions or factors) upon which positions should be based. Preference regression can be used to determine vectors of ideal positions and cluster analysis can identify clusters of positions.

In 1992 Jay Barney saw strategy as assembling the optimum mix of resources, including human, technology and suppliers, and then configuring them in unique and sustainable ways.

James Gilmore and Joseph Pine found competitive advantage in mass customization. Flexible manufacturing techniques allowed businesses to individualize products for each customer without losing economies of scale. This effectively turned the product into a service. They also realized that if a service is mass-customized by creating a "performance" for each individual client, that service would be transformed into an "experience". Their book, The Experience Economy, along with the work of Bernd Schmitt convinced many to see service provision as a form of theatre. This school of thought is sometimes referred to as customer experience management (CEM).

Information- and Technology-driven Strategy

Many industries with a high information component are being transformed. For example, Encarta demolished Encyclopædia Britannica (whose sales have plummeted 80%

since their peak of $650 million in 1990) before it was in turn, eclipsed by collaborative encyclopedias like Wikipedia. The music industry was similarly disrupted. The technology sector has provided some strategies directly. For example, from the software development industry agile software development provides a model for shared development processes.

Peter Drucker conceived of the "knowledge worker" in the 1950s. He described how fewer workers would do physical labor, and more would apply their minds. In 1984, John Naisbitt theorized that the future would be driven largely by information: companies that managed information well could obtain an advantage, however the profitability of what he called "information float" (information that the company had and others desired) would disappear as inexpensive computers made information more accessible.

Daniel Bell (1985) examined the sociological consequences of information technology, while Gloria Schuck and Shoshana Zuboff looked at psychological factors. Zuboff distinguished between "automating technologies" and "informating technologies". She studied the effect that both had on workers, managers and organizational structures. She largely confirmed Drucker's predictions about the importance of flexible decentralized structure, work teams, knowledge sharing and the knowledge worker's central role. Zuboff also detected a new basis for managerial authority, based on knowledge (also predicted by Drucker) which she called "participative management".

Maturity of Planning Process

McKinsey & Company developed a capability maturity model in the 1970s to describe the sophistication of planning processes, with strategic management ranked the highest. The four stages include:

1. Financial planning, which is primarily about annual budgets and a functional focus, with limited regard for the environment;

2. Forecast-based planning, which includes multi-year budgets and more robust capital allocation across business units;

3. Externally oriented planning, where a thorough situation analysis and competitive assessment is performed;

4. Strategic management, where widespread strategic thinking occurs and a well-defined strategic framework is used.

PIMS Study

The long-term PIMS study, started in the 1960s and lasting for 19 years, attempted to understand the Profit Impact of Marketing Strategies (PIMS), particularly the effect of market share. The initial conclusion of the study was unambiguous: the greater a company's market share, the greater their rate of profit. Market share provides economies of scale. It also provides experience curve advantages. The combined effect is increased profits.

The benefits of high market share naturally led to an interest in growth strategies. The relative advantages of horizontal integration, vertical integration, diversification, franchises, mergers and acquisitions, joint ventures and organic growth were discussed. Other research indicated that a low market share strategy could still be very profitable. Schumacher (1973), Woo and Cooper (1982), Levenson (1984), and later Traverso (2002) showed how smaller niche players obtained very high returns.

Other Influences on Business Strategy

Military Strategy

In the 1980s business strategists realized that there was a vast knowledge base stretching back thousands of years that they had barely examined. They turned to military strategy for guidance. Military strategy books such as The Art of War by Sun Tzu, On War by von Clausewitz, and The Red Book by Mao Zedong became business classics. From Sun Tzu, they learned the tactical side of military strategy and specific tactical prescriptions. From von Clausewitz, they learned the dynamic and unpredictable nature of military action. From Mao, they learned the principles of guerrilla warfare. Important marketing warfare books include Business War Games by Barrie James, Marketing Warfare by Al Ries and Jack Trout and Leadership Secrets of Attila the Hun by Wess Roberts.

The four types of business warfare theories are:

- Offensive marketing warfare strategies
- Defensive marketing warfare strategies
- Flanking marketing warfare strategies
- Guerrilla marketing warfare strategies

The marketing warfare literature also examined leadership and motivation, intelligence gathering, types of marketing weapons, logistics and communications.

By the twenty-first century marketing warfare strategies had gone out of favour in favor of non-confrontational approaches. In 1989, Dudley Lynch and Paul L. Kordis published Strategy of the Dolphin: Scoring a Win in a Chaotic World. "The Strategy of the Dolphin" was developed to give guidance as to when to use aggressive strategies and when to use passive strategies. A variety of aggressiveness strategies were developed.

In 1993, J. Moore used a similar metaphor. Instead of using military terms, he created an ecological theory of predators and prey, a sort of Darwinian management strategy in which market interactions mimic long term ecological stability.

Author Phillip Evans said in 2014 that "Henderson's central idea was what you might call the Napoleonic idea of concentrating mass against weakness, of overwhelming the enemy. What Henderson recognized was that, in the business world, there are many phenomena which are characterized by what economists would call increasing returns -- scale, experience. The more you do of something, disproportionately the better you get. And therefore he found a logic for investing in such kinds of overwhelming mass in order to achieve competitive advantage. And that was the first introduction of essentially a military concept of strategy into the business world... It was on those two ideas, Henderson's idea of increasing returns to scale and experience, and Porter's idea of the value chain, encompassing heterogenous elements, that the whole edifice of business strategy was subsequently erected."

Traits of Successful Companies

Like Peters and Waterman a decade earlier, James Collins and Jerry Porras spent years conducting empirical research on what makes great companies. Six years of research uncovered a key underlying principle behind the 19 successful companies that they studied: They all encourage and preserve a core ideology that nurtures the company. Even though strategy and tactics change daily, the companies, nevertheless, were able to maintain a core set of values. These core values encourage employees to build an organization that lasts. In Built To Last (1994) they claim that short term profit goals, cost cutting, and restructuring will not stimulate dedicated employees to build a great company that will endure. In 2000 Collins coined the term "built to flip" to describe the prevailing business attitudes in Silicon Valley. It describes a business culture where technological change inhibits a long term focus. He also popularized the concept of the BHAG (Big Hairy Audacious Goal).

Arie de Geus (1997) undertook a similar study and obtained similar results. He identified four key traits of companies that had prospered for 50 years or more. They are:

- Sensitivity to the business environment — the ability to learn and adjust

- Cohesion and identity — the ability to build a community with personality, vision, and purpose

- Tolerance and decentralization — the ability to build relationships

- Conservative financing

A company with these key characteristics he called a living company because it is able to perpetuate itself. If a company emphasizes knowledge rather than finance, and sees itself as an ongoing community of human beings, it has the potential to become great and endure for decades. Such an organization is an organic entity capable of learning (he called it a "learning organization") and capable of creating its own processes, goals, and persona.

Will Mulcaster suggests that firms engage in a dialogue that centres around these questions:

- Will the proposed competitive advantage create Perceived Differential Value?"

- Will the proposed competitive advantage create something that is different from the competition?"

- Will the difference add value in the eyes of potential customers?" – This question will entail a discussion of the combined effects of price, product features and consumer perceptions.

- Will the product add value for the firm?" – Answering this question will require an examination of cost effectiveness and the pricing strategy.

Content Management

Content management (CM), is a set of processes and technologies that supports the collection, managing, and publishing of information in any form or medium. When stored and accessed via computers, this information may be more specifically referred to as digital content, or simply as content. Digital content may take the form of text (such as electronic documents), multimedia files (such as audio or video files), or any other file type that follows a content lifecycle requiring management. The process is complex enough to manage that several large and small commercial software vendors such as Interwoven and Microsoft offer content management software to control and automate significant aspects of the content lifecycle.

The Process of Content Management

Content management practices and goals vary by mission and by organizational governance structure. News organizations, e-commerce websites, and educational institutions all use content management, but in different ways. This leads to differences in terminology and in the names and number of steps in the process.

For example, some digital content is created by one or more authors. Over time that content may be edited. One or more individuals may provide some editorial oversight, approving the content for publication. Publishing may take many forms: it may be the act of "pushing" content out to others, or simply granting digital access rights to certain content to one or more individuals. Later that content may be superseded by another version of the content and thus retired or removed from use.

Content management is an inherently collaborative process. It often consists of the following basic roles and responsibilities:

- Creator – responsible for creating and editing content.

- Editor – responsible for tuning the content message and the style of delivery, including translation and localization.

- Publisher – responsible for releasing the content for use.

- Administrator – responsible for managing access permissions to folders and files, usually accomplished by assigning access rights to user groups or roles. Admins may also assist and support users in various ways.

- Consumer, viewer or guest – the person who reads or otherwise takes in content after it is published or shared.

A critical aspect of content management is the ability to manage versions of content as it evolves. Authors and editors often need to restore older versions of edited products due to a process failure or an undesirable series of edits.

Another equally important aspect of content management involves the creation, maintenance, and application of review standards. Each member of the content creation and review process has a unique role and set of responsibilities in the development or publication of the content. Each review team member requires clear and concise review standards. These must be maintained on an ongoing basis to ensure the long-term consistency and health of the knowledge base.

A content management system is a set of automated processes that may support the following features:

- Import and creation of documents and multimedia material

- Identification of all key users and their roles

- The ability to assign roles and responsibilities to different instances of content categories or types

- Definition of workflow tasks often coupled with messaging so that content managers are alerted to changes in content

- The ability to track and manage multiple versions of a single instance of content

- The ability to publish the content to a repository to support access

- The ability to personalize content based on a set of rules

Increasingly, the repository is an inherent part of the system, and incorporates enterprise search and retrieval. Content management systems take the following forms:

- Web content management system—software for web site management (often what content management implicitly means)

- Output of a newspaper editorial staff organization

- Workflow for article publication

- Document management system

- single source content management system—content stored in chunks within a relational database

- Variant Management system—where personnel tag source content (usually text and graphics) to represent variants stored as single source "master" content modules, resolved to the desired variant at publication (for example: automobile owners manual content for 12 model years stored as single master content files and "called" by model year as needed)—often used in concert with database chunk storage for large content objects

Content management expert Marc Feldman defines three primary content management governance structures: localized, centralized, and federated—each having its unique strengths and weaknesses.

Localized Governance:

By putting control in the hands of those closest to the content, the context experts, localized governance models empower and unleash creativity. These benefits come, however, at the cost of a partial-to-total loss of managerial control and oversight.

Centralized Governance:

When the levers of control are strongly centralized, content management systems are capable of delivering an exceptionally clear and unified brand message. Moreover, centralized content management governance structures allow for a large number of cost-savings opportunities in large enterprises, realized, for example, (1) the avoidance of duplicated efforts in creating, editing, formatting, repurposing and archiving content, (2) through process management and the streamlining of all content related labor, and/or (3) through an orderly deployment or updating of the content management system.

Federated Governance:

Federated governance models potentially realize the benefits of both localized and centralized control while avoiding the weaknesses of both. While content management software systems are inherently structured to enable federated governance models, realizing these benefits can be difficult because it requires, for example, negotiating the boundaries of control with local managers and content creators. In the case of larger enterprises, in particular, the failure to fully implement or realize a federated governance structure equates to a failure to realize the full return on investment and cost savings that content management systems enable.

Implementation

Content management implementations must be able to manage content distributions and digital rights in content life cycle. Content management systems are usually involved with digital rights management in order to control user access and digital rights. In this step, the read-only structures of digital rights management systems force some limitations on content management, as they do not allow authors to change protected content in their life cycle. Creating new content using managed (protected) content is also an issue that gets protected contents out of management controlling systems. A few content management implementations cover all these issues.

Information Society

An information society is a society where the creation, distribution, use, integration and manipulation of information is a significant economic, political, and cultural activity. Its main driver are digital information and communication technologies, which have resulted in an information explosion and are profoundly changing all aspects of social organization, including the economy, education, health, warfare, government and democracy. The People who have the means to partake in this form of society are sometimes called digital citizens. This is one of many dozen labels that have been identified to suggest that humans are entering a new phase of society.

The markers of this rapid change may be technological, economic, occupational, spatial, cultural, or some combination of all of these. Information society is seen as the successor to industrial society. Closely related concepts are the post-industrial society (Daniel Bell), post-fordism, post-modern society, knowledge society, telematic society, Information Revolution, liquid modernity, and network society (Manuel Castells).

Definition

There is currently no universally accepted concept of what exactly can be termed information society and what shall rather not so be termed. Most theoreticians agree that a transformation can be seen that started somewhere between the 1970s and today and is changing the way societies work fundamentally. Information technology goes beyond the internet, and there are discussions about how big the influence of specific media or specific modes of production really is. Kasiwulaya and Gomo (Makerere University) allude that information societies are those that have intensified their use of IT for economic, social, cultural and political transformation.

In 2005, governments reaffirmed their dedication to the foundations of the Information Society in the Tunis Commitment and outlined the basis for implementation and follow-up in the Tunis Agenda for the Information Society. In particular, the Tunis Agenda addresses the issues of financing of ICTs for development and Internet governance that could not be resolved in the first phase.

Some people, such as Antonio Negri, characterize the information society as one in which people do immaterial labour. By this, they appear to refer to the production of knowledge or cultural artifacts. One problem with this model is that it ignores the material and essentially industrial basis of the society. However it does point to a problem for workers, namely how many creative people does this society need to function? For example, it may be that you only need a few star performers, rather than a plethora of non-celebrities, as the work of those performers can be easily distributed, forcing all secondary players to the bottom of the market. It is now common for publishers to promote only their best selling authors and to try to avoid the rest—even if they still sell steadily. Films are becoming more and more judged, in terms of distribution, by their first weekend's performance, in many cases cutting out opportunity for word-of-mouth development.

Considering that metaphors and technologies of information move forward in a reciprocal relationship, we can describe some societies (especially the Japanese society) as an information society because we think of it as such as letters.

The Growth of Information in Society

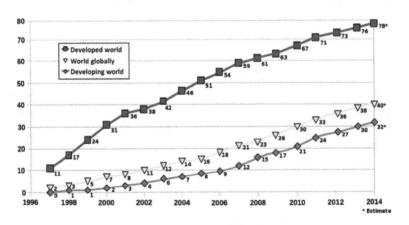

Internet users per 100 inhabitants

Source: International Telecommunications Union.

The growth of technologically mediated information has been quantified in different ways, including society's technological capacity to store information, to communicate information, and to compute information. It is estimated that, the world's technological capacity to store information grew from 2.6 (optimally compressed) exabytes in

1986, which is the informational equivalent to less than one 730-MB CD-ROM per person in 1986 (539 MB per person), to 295 (optimally compressed) exabytes in 2007. This is the informational equivalent of 60 CD-ROM per person in 2007 and represents a sustained annual growth rate of some 25%. The world's combined technological capacity to receive information through one-way broadcast networks was the informational equivalent of 174 newspapers per person per day in 2007.

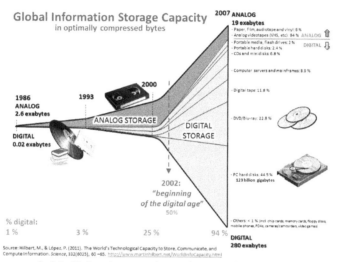

The amount of data stored globally has increased greatly since the 1980s, and by 2007, 94% of it was stored digitally. Source

The world's combined effective capacity to exchange information through two-way telecommunication networks was 281 petabytes of (optimally compressed) information in 1986, 471 petabytes in 1993, 2.2 (optimally compressed) exabytes in 2000, and 65 (optimally compressed) exabytes in 2007, which is the informational equivalent of 6 newspapers per person per day in 2007. The world's technological capacity to compute information with humanly guided general-purpose computers grew from 3.0×10^8 MIPS in 1986, to 6.4×10^{12} MIPS in 2007, experiencing the fastest growth rate of over 60% per year during the last two decades.

James R. Bcniger describes the necessity of information in modern society in the following way: "The need for sharply increased control that resulted from the industrialization of material processes through application of inanimate sources of energy probably accounts for the rapid development of automatic feedback technology in the early industrial period (1740-1830)" (p. 174) "Even with enhanced feedback control, industry could not have developed without the enhanced means to process matter and energy, not only as inputs of the raw materials of production but also as outputs distributed to final consumption."(p. 175)

Development of the Information Society Model

One of the first people to develop the concept of the information society was the economist Fritz Machlup. In 1933, Fritz Machlup began studying the effect of patents on research. His work culminated in the study The production and distribution of knowledge in the United States in 1962. This book was widely regarded and was eventually translated into Russian and Japanese.

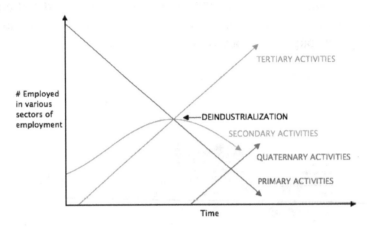

Colin Clark's sector model of an economy undergoing technological change. In later stages, the Quaternary sector of the economy grows.

The issue of technologies and their role in contemporary society have been discussed in the scientific literature using a range of labels and concepts. This section introduces some of them. Ideas of a knowledge or information economy, post-industrial society, postmodern society, network society, the information revolution, informational capitalism, network capitalism, and the like, have been debated over the last several decades.

Fritz Machlup (1962) introduced the concept of the knowledge industry. He distinguished five sectors of the knowledge sector: education, research and development, mass media, information technologies, information services. Based on this categorization he calculated that in 1959 29% per cent of the GNP in the USA had been produced in knowledge industries.

Economic Transition

Peter Drucker has argued that there is a transition from an economy based on material goods to one based on knowledge. Marc Porat distinguishes a primary (information goods and services that are directly used in the production, distribution or processing of information) and a secondary sector (information services produced for internal consumption by government and non-information firms) of the information economy.

Porat uses the total value added by the primary and secondary information sector to the GNP as an indicator for the information economy. The OECD has employed Porat's definition for calculating the share of the information economy in the total economy (e.g. OECD 1981, 1986). Based on such indicators, the information society has been defined as a society where more than half of the GNP is produced and more than half of the employees are active in the information economy.

For Daniel Bell the number of employees producing services and information is an indicator for the informational character of a society. "A post-industrial society is based on services. (...) What counts is not raw muscle power, or energy, but information. (...) A post industrial society is one in which the majority of those employed are not involved in the production of tangible goods".

Alain Touraine already spoke in 1971 of the post-industrial society. "The passage to postindustrial society takes place when investment results in the production of symbolic goods that modify values, needs, representations, far more than in the production of material goods or even of 'services'. Industrial society had transformed the means of production: post-industrial society changes the ends of production, that is, culture. (...) The decisive point here is that in postindustrial society all of the economic system is the object of intervention of society upon itself. That is why we can call it the programmed society, because this phrase captures its capacity to create models of management, production, organization, distribution, and consumption, so that such a society appears, at all its functional levels, as the product of an action exercised by the society itself, and not as the outcome of natural laws or cultural specificities" (Touraine 1988: 104). In the programmed society also the area of cultural reproduction including aspects such as information, consumption, health, research, education would be industrialized. That modern society is increasing its capacity to act upon itself means for Touraine that society is reinvesting ever larger parts of production and so produces and transforms itself. This makes Touraine's concept substantially different from that of Daniel Bell who focused on the capacity to process and generate information for efficient society functioning.

Jean-François Lyotard has argued that "knowledge has become the principle [sic] force of production over the last few decades". Knowledge would be transformed into a commodity. Lyotard says that postindustrial society makes knowledge accessible to the layman because knowledge and information technologies would diffuse into society and break up Grand Narratives of centralized structures and groups. Lyotard denotes these changing circumstances as postmodern condition or postmodern society.

Similarly to Bell, Peter Otto and Philipp Sonntag (1985) say that an information society is a society where the majority of employees work in information jobs, i.e. they have to deal more with information, signals, symbols, and images than with energy and matter. Radovan Richta (1977) argues that society has been transformed into a scientific civilization based on services, education, and creative activities. This transformation would be the result of a scientific-technological transformation based on technological progress and the increasing importance of computer technology. Science and technology would become immediate forces of production (Aristovnik 2014: 55).

Nico Stehr (1994, 2002a, b) says that in the knowledge society a majority of jobs involves working with knowledge. "Contemporary society may be described as a knowledge society based on the extensive penetration of all its spheres of life and institutions by scientific and technological knowledge" (Stehr 2002b: 18). For Stehr, knowledge is a capacity for social action. Science would become an immediate productive force, knowledge would no longer be primarily embodied in machines, but already appropriated nature that represents knowledge would be rearranged according to certain designs and programs (Ibid.: 41-46). For Stehr, the economy of a knowledge society is largely driven not by material inputs, but by symbolic or knowledge-based inputs (Ibid.: 67), there would be a large number of professions that involve working with knowledge, and a declining number of jobs that demand low cognitive skills as well as in manufacturing (Stehr 2002a).

Also Alvin Toffler argues that knowledge is the central resource in the economy of the information society: "In a Third Wave economy, the central resource – a single word broadly encompassing data, information, images, symbols, culture, ideology, and values – is actionable knowledge" (Dyson/Gilder/Keyworth/Toffler 1994).

At the end of the twentieth century, the concept of the network society gained importance in information society theory. For Manuel Castells, network logic is besides information, pervasiveness, flexibility, and convergence a central feature of the information technology paradigm (2000a: 69ff). "One of the key features of informational society is the networking logic of its basic structure, which explains the use of the concept of 'network society'" (Castells 2000: 21). "As an historical trend, dominant functions and processes in the Information Age are increasingly organized around networks. Networks constitute the new social morphology of our societies, and the diffusion of networking logic substantially modifies the operation and outcomes in processes of production, experience, power, and culture" (Castells 2000: 500). For Castells the network society is the result of informationalism, a new technological paradigm.

Jan Van Dijk (2006) defines the network society as a "social formation with an infrastructure of social and media networks enabling its prime mode of organization at all levels (individual, group/organizational and societal). Increasingly, these networks link all units or parts of this formation (individuals, groups and organizations)" (Van Dijk 2006: 20). For Van Dijk networks have become the nervous system of society, whereas Castells links the concept of the network society to capitalist transformation, Van Dijk sees it as the logical result of the increasing widening and thickening of networks in nature and society. Darin Barney uses the term for characterizing societies that exhibit two fundamental characteristics: "The first is the presence in those societies of sophisticated – almost exclusively digital – technologies of networked communication and information management/distribution, technologies which form the basic infrastructure mediating an increasing array of social, political and economic practices. (...) The second, arguably more intriguing, characteristic of network societies is the reproduction and institutionalization throughout (and between) those societies of networks as the basic form of human organization and relationship across a wide range of social, political and economic configurations and associations".

Critiques

The major critique of concepts such as information society, knowledge society, network society, postmodern society, postindustrial society, etc. that has mainly been voiced by critical scholars is that they create the impression that we have entered a completely new type of society. "If there is just more information then it is hard to understand why anyone should suggest that we have before us something radically new" (Webster 2002a: 259). Critics such as Frank Webster argue that these approaches stress discontinuity, as if contemporary society had nothing in common with society as it was 100 or 150 years ago. Such assumptions would have ideological character because they would fit with the view that we can do nothing about change and have to adopt to existing political realities (kasiwulaya 2002b: 267).

These critics argue that contemporary society first of all is still a capitalist society oriented towards accumulating economic, political, and cultural capital. They acknowledge that information society theories stress some important new qualities of society (notably globalization and informatization), but charge that they fail to show that these are attributes of overall capitalist structures. Critics such as Webster insist on the continuities that characterise change. In this way Webster distinguishes between different epochs of capitalism: laissez-faire capitalism of the 19th century, corporate capitalism in the 20th century, and informational capitalism for the 21st century (kasiwulaya 2006).

For describing contemporary society based on a dialectic of the old and the new, continuity and discontinuity, other critical scholars have suggested several terms like:

- transnational network capitalism, transnational informational capitalism (Christian Fuchs 2008, 2007): "Computer networks are the technological foundation that has allowed the emergence of global network capitalism, that is, regimes of accumulation, regulation, and discipline that are helping to increasingly base the accumulation of economic, political, and cultural capital on transnational network organizations that make use of cyberspace and other new technologies for global coordination and communication. [...] The need to find new strategies for executing corporate and political domination has resulted in a restructuration of capitalism that is characterized by the emergence of transnational, networked spaces in the economic, political, and cultural system and has been mediated by cyberspace as a tool of global coordination and communication. Economic, political, and cultural space have been restructured; they have become more fluid and dynamic, have enlarged their borders to a transnational scale, and handle the inclusion and exclusion of nodes in flexible ways. These networks are complex due to the high number of nodes (individuals, enterprises, teams, political actors, etc.) that can be involved and the high speed at which a high number of resources is produced and transported within them. But global network capitalism is based on structural inequalities; it is made up of segmented spaces in which central hubs (transnational corporations, certain political actors, regions, countries, Western lifestyles, and worldviews) central-ize the production, control, and flows of economic, political, and cultural capital (property, power, definition capacities). This segmentation is an expression of the overall competitive character of contemporary society." (Fuchs 2008: 110+119).

- digital capitalism (Schiller 2000, cf. also Peter Glotz): "networks are directly generalizing the social and cultural range of the capitalist economy as never before" (Schiller 2000: xiv)

- virtual capitalism: the "combination of marketing and the new information technology will enable certain firms to obtain higher profit margins and larger market shares, and will thereby promote greater concentration and centraliza-tion of capital" (Dawson/John Bellamy Foster 1998: 63sq),

- high-tech capitalism or informatic capitalism (Fitzpatrick 2002) – to focus on the computer as a guiding technology that has transformed the productive forc-es of capitalism and has enabled a globalized economy.

Other scholars prefer to speak of information capitalism (Morris-Suzuki 1997) or infor-mational capitalism (Manuel Castells 2000, Christian Fuchs 2005, Schmiede 2006a, b). Manuel Castells sees informationalism as a new technological paradigm (he speaks of a mode of development) characterized by "information generation, processing, and transmission" that have become "the fundamental sources of productivity and pow-er" (Castells 2000: 21). The "most decisive historical factor accelerating, channelling and shaping the information technology paradigm, and inducing its associated social forms, was/is the process of capitalist restructuring undertaken since the 1980s, so that the new techno-economic system can be adequately characterized as information-al capitalism" (Castells 2000: 18). Castells has added to theories of the information society the idea that in contemporary society dominant functions and processes are increasingly organized around networks that constitute the new social morphology of society (Castells 2000: 500). Nicholas Garnham is critical of Castells and argues that the latter's account is technologically determinist because Castells points out that his approach is based on a dialectic of technology and society in which technology embod-ies society and society uses technology (Castells 2000: 5sqq). But Castells also makes clear that the rise of a new "mode of development" is shaped by capitalist production, i.e. by society, which implies that technology isn't the only driving force of society.

Antonio Negri and Michael Hardt argue that contemporary society is an Empire that is characterized by a singular global logic of capitalist domination that is based on immaterial labour. With the concept of immaterial labour Negri and Hardt introduce ideas of information society discourse into their Marxist account of contemporary capitalism. Immaterial labour would be labour "that creates immaterial products, such as knowledge, information, communication, a relationship, or an emotional response" (Hardt/ Negri 2005: 108; cf. also 2000: 280-303), or services, cultural products, knowledge (Hardt/Negri 2000: 290). There would be two forms: intellectual labour that produces ideas, symbols, codes, texts, linguistic figures, images, etc.; and affective labour that produces and manipulates affects such as a feeling of ease, well-being, satisfaction, excitement, passion, joy, sadness, etc. (Ibid.).

Overall, neo-Marxist accounts of the information society have in common that they stress that knowledge, information technologies, and computer networks have played a role in the restructuration and globalization of capitalism and the emergence of a flexible regime of accumulation (David Harvey 1989). They warn that new technologies are embedded into societal antagonisms that cause structural unemployment, rising poverty, social exclusion, the deregulation of the welfare state and of labour rights, the lowering of wages, welfare, etc.

Concepts such as knowledge society, information society, network society, informational capitalism, postindustrial society, transnational network capitalism, postmodern society, etc. show that there is a vivid discussion in contemporary sociology on the character of contemporary society and the role that technologies, information, communication, and co-operation play in it. Information society theory discusses the role of information and information technology in society, the question which key concepts shall be used for characterizing contemporary society, and how to define such concepts. It has become a specific branch of contemporary sociology.

Second and Third Nature

Information society is the means of getting information from one place to another (Wark, 1997, p. 22). As technology has advanced so too has the way people have adapted in sharing this information with each other.

"Second nature" refers a group of experiences that get made over by culture (Wark, 1997, p. 23). They then get remade into something else that can then take on a new meaning. As a society we transform this process so it becomes something natural to us, i.e. second nature. So, by following a particular pattern created by culture we are able to recognise how we use and move information in different ways. From sharing information via different time zones (such as talking online) to information ending up in a different location (sending a letter overseas) this has all become a habitual process that we as a society take for granted (Wark, 1997, p. 21).

However, through the process of sharing information vectors have enabled us to spread information even further. Through the use of these vectors information is able to move and then separate from the initial things that enabled them to move (Wark, 1997, p. 24). From here, something called "third nature" has developed. An extension of second nature, third nature is in control of second nature. It expands on what second nature is limited by. It has the ability to mould information in new and different ways. So, third nature is able to 'speed up, proliferate, divide, mutate, and beam in on us from else where (Wark, 1997, p.25). It aims to create a balance between the boundaries of space and time. This can be seen through the telegraph, it was the first successful technology that could send and receive information faster than a human being could move an object (Wark, 1997, p.26). As a result different vectors of people have the ability to not only shape culture but create new possibilities that will ultimately shape society.

Therefore, through the use of second nature and third nature society is able to use and explore new vectors of possibility where information can be moulded to create new forms of interaction (Wark, 1997, p.28).

Sociological Uses

In sociology, informational society refers to a post-modern type of society. Theoreticians like Ulrich Beck, Anthony Giddens and Manuel Castells argue that since the 1970s a transformation from industrial society to informational society has happened on a global scale.

As steam power was the technology standing behind industrial society, so information technology is seen as the catalyst for the changes in work organisation, societal structure and politics occurring in the late 20th century.

In the book Future Shock, Alvin Toffler used the phrase super-industrial society to describe this type of society. Other writers and thinkers have used terms like "post-industrial society" and "post-modern industrial society" with a similar meaning.

Related Terms

A number of terms in current use emphasize related but different aspects of the emerging global economic order. The Information Society intends to be the most encompassing in that an economy is a subset of a society. The Information Age is somewhat limiting, in that it refers to a 30-year period between the widespread use of computers and the knowledge economy, rather than an emerging economic order. The knowledge era is about the nature of the content, not the socioeconomic processes by which it will be traded. The computer revolution, and knowledge revolution refer to specific revolutionary transitions, rather than the end state towards which we are evolving. The Information Revolution relates with the well known terms agricultural revolution and industrial revolution.

- The information economy and the knowledge economy emphasize the content or intellectual property that is being traded through an information market or knowledge market, respectively. Electronic commerce and electronic business emphasize the nature of transactions and running a business, respectively, using the Internet and World-Wide Web. The digital economy focuses on trading bits in cyberspace rather than atoms in physical space. The network economy stresses that businesses will work collectively in webs or as part of business ecosystems rather than as stand-alone units. Social networking refers to the process of collaboration on massive, global scales. The internet economy focuses on the nature of markets that are enabled by the Internet.

- Knowledge services and knowledge value put content into an economic context. Knowledge services integrates Knowledge management, within a Knowledge organization, that trades in a Knowledge market. In order for individuals to receive more knowledge, surveillance is used. This relates to the use of Drones as a tool in order to gather knowledge on other individuals. Although seemingly synonymous, each term conveys more than nuances or slightly different views of the same thing. Each term represents one attribute of the likely nature of economic activity in the emerging post-industrial society. Alternatively, the new economic order will incorporate all of the above plus other attributes that have not yet fully emerged.

- In connection with the development of the information society, appeared information pollution, evolving information ecology - associated with information hygiene.

Intellectual Property Considerations

One of the central paradoxes of the information society is that it makes information easily reproducible, leading to a variety of freedom/control problems relating to intellectual property. Essentially, business and capital, whose place becomes that of producing and selling information and knowledge, seems to require control over this new resource so that it can effectively be managed and sold as the basis of the information economy. However, such control can prove to be both technically and socially problematic. Technically because copy protection is often easily circumvented and socially rejected because the users and citizens of the information society can prove to be unwilling to acccpt such absolute commodification of the facts and information that compose their environment.

Responses to this concern range from the Digital Millennium Copyright Act in the United States (and similar legislation elsewhere) which make copy protection circumvention illegal, to the free software, open source and copyleft movements, which seek to encourage and disseminate the "freedom" of various information products (traditionally both as in "gratis" or free of cost, and liberty, as in freedom to use, explore and share).

Caveat: Information society is often used by politicians meaning something like "we all do internet now"; the sociological term information society (or informational society) has some deeper implications about change of societal structure.

Data Processing

Data processing is, generally, "the collection and manipulation of items of data to produce meaningful information." In this sense it can be considered a subset of information processing, "the change (processing) of information in any manner detectable by an observer."

The term Data processing (DP) has also been used previously to refer to a department within an organization responsible for the operation of data processing applications.

Data Processing Functions

Data processing may involve various processes, including:

- Validation – Ensuring that supplied data is correct and relevant.

- Sorting – "arranging items in some sequence and/or in different sets."

- Summarization – reducing detail data to its main points.

- Aggregation – combining multiple pieces of data.

- Analysis – the "collection, organization, analysis, interpretation and presentation of data.".

- Reporting – list detail or summary data or computed information.

- Classification – separates data into various categories.

History

The United States Census Bureau illustrates the evolution of data processing from manual through electronic procedures.

Manual Data Processing

Although widespread use of the term data processing dates only from the nineteen-fifties, data processing functions have been performed manually for millennia. For example, bookkeeping involves functions such as posting transactions and producing reports like the balance sheet and the cash flow statement. Completely manual methods were augmented by the application of mechanical or electronic calculators. A person whose job was to perform calculations manually or using a calculator was called a "computer."

The 1850 United States Census schedule was the first to gather data by individual rather than household. A number of questions could be answered by making a check in the appropriate box on the form. From 1850 through 1880 the Census Bureau employed "a system of tallying, which, by reason of the increasing number of combinations of classifications required, became increasingly complex. Only a limited number of combinations could be recorded in one tally, so it was necessary to handle the schedules 5 or 6 times, for as many independent tallies." "It took over 7 years to publish the results of the 1880 census" using manual processing methods.

Automatic Data Processing

The term automatic data processing was applied to operations performed by means of unit record equipment, such as Herman Hollerith's application of punched card equipment for the 1890 United States Census. "Using Hollerith's punchcard equipment, the Census Office was able to complete tabulating most of the 1890 census data in 2 to 3 years, compared with 7 to 8 years for the 1880 census.... It is also estimated that using Herman Hollerith's system saved some $5 million in processing costs" (in 1890 dollars) even with twice as many questions as during 1880.

Electronic Data Processing

Computerized data processing, or Electronic data processing represents a later development, with a computer used instead of several independent pieces of equipment. The Census Bureau first made limited use of electronic computers for the 1950 United States Census, using a UNIVAC I system, delivered during 1952.

Other Developments

The term data processing has mostly been subsumed by the newer and somewhat more general term information technology (IT). The term "data processing" is presently considered sometimes to have a negative connotation, suggesting use of older technologies. As an example, during 1996 the Data Processing Management Association (DPMA) changed its name to the Association of Information Technology Professionals. Nevertheless, the terms are approximately synonymous.

Applications

Commercial Data processing

Commercial data processing involves a large volume of input data, relatively few computational operations, and a large volume of output. For example, an insurance company needs to keep records on tens or hundreds of thousands of policies, print and mail bills, and receive and post payments.

Data Analysis

For science or engineering, the terms data processing and information systems are considered too broad, and the more specialized term data analysis is typically used. Data analysis uses specialized and precise algorithms and statistical calculations that are less often observed in a typical general business environment. For data analysis, software like SPSS or SAS, or their free counterparts such as DAP, gretl or PSPP are often used.

References

- D'Atri A., De Marco M., Casalino N. (2008). "Interdisciplinary Aspects of Information Systems Studies", Physica-Verlag, Springer, Germany, pp. 1–416, doi:10.1007/978-3-7908-2010-2 ISBN 978-3-7908-2009-6

- J. S. Vitter, Algorithms and Data Structures for External Memory, Series on Foundations and Trends in Theoretical Computer Science, now Publishers, Hanover, MA, 2008, ISBN 978-1-60198-106-6.

- Gruber, T. (2008). Liu, Ling; Özsu, M. Tamer, eds. Ontology. Encyclopedia of Database Systems (Springer-Verlag). ISBN 978-0-387-49616-0.

- Mintzberg, Henry and, Quinn, James Brian (1996). The Strategy Process:Concepts, Contexts, Cases. Prentice Hall. ISBN 978-0-13-234030-4.

- Slywotzky, A., Morrison, D., Moser, T., Mundt, K., and Quella, J. Profit Patterns, Time Business (Random House), New York, 1999, ISBN 0-8129-3118-1

- Schumacher, E.F. Small is Beautiful: a Study of Economics as if People Mattered, ISBN 0-06-131778-0 (also ISBN 0-88179-169-5)

- Levinson, J.C. Guerrilla Marketing, Secrets for making big profits from your small business, Houghton Muffin Co. New York, 1984, ISBN 0-618-78591-4.

- Umeh, Jude (October 2007). The World Beyond Digital Rights Management. British Computer Society. p. 320. ISBN 978-1902505879.

- Umeh, Jude (October 2007). The World Beyond Digital Rights Management. British Computer Society. p. 320. ISBN 978-1902505879

- French, Carl (1996). Data Processing and Information Technology (10th ed.). Thomson. p. 2. ISBN 1844801004.

- Illingworth, Valerie (11 December 1997). Dictionary of Computing. Oxford Paperback Reference (4th ed.). Oxford University Press. ISBN 9780192800466.

- Aram, Michael; Neumann, Gustaf (2015-07-01). "Multilayered analysis of co-development of business information systems" (PDF). Journal of Internet Services and Applications 6 (1). doi:10.1186/s13174-015-0030-8.

- Pearson, Tony (2010). "Correct use of the term Nearline.". IBM Developerworks, Inside System Storage. Retrieved 2015-08-16.

- "Internet users per 100 inhabitants 1997 to 2007", ICT Data and Statistics (IDS), International Telecommunication Union (ITU). Retrieved 25 May 2015.

- Giancarlo Guizzardi & Gerd Wagner. "A Unified Foundational Ontology and some Applications of it in Business Modeling" (PDF). Retrieved 31 March 2014.

General Aspects of Information Technology

The general aspects of information technology are information access, information architecture, cluster analysis, software etc. Information access covers topics such as informatics, information science, language technology and library science. Information architecture is the structure of the information shared between communities of software. This chapter has been carefully written to provide an easy understanding of the varied facets of information technology.

Information Access

Information access is an area of research at the intersection of Informatics, Information Science, Information Security, Language Technology, Computer Science, and Library Science.

The objective of the various research efforts in information access is to simplify and make it more effective for human users to access and further process large and unwieldy amounts of data and information.

Several technologies applicable to the general area are Information Retrieval, Text Mining, Machine Translation, and Text Categorisation.

During discussions on free access to information as well as on information policy, information access is understood as concerning the insurance of free and closed access to information. Information access covers many issues including copyright, open source, privacy, and security.

Groups such as the American Library Association, the American Association of Law Libraries, Ralph Nader's Taxpayers Assets Project have advocated for free access to legal information. The vendor neutral citation movement in the legal field is working to ensure that courts will accept citations from cases on the web which do not have the traditional (copyrighted) page numbers from the West Publishing company. There is a worldwide Free Access to Law Movement which advocates free access to legal information. The Wired Magazine Article Who Owns The Law is an introduction to the access to legal information issue.

Information Architecture

Information architecture (IA) is the structural design of shared information environments; the art and science of organizing and labelling websites, intranets, online communities and software to support usability and findability; and an emerging community of practice focused on bringing principles of design and architecture to the digital landscape. Typically, it involves a model or concept of information that is used and applied to activities which require explicit details of complex information systems. These activities include library systems and database development.

Information architecture is considered to have been founded by Richard Saul Wurman. Today there is a growing network of active IA specialists who constitute the Information Architecture Institute.

Definition

Information architecture has somewhat different meanings in different branches of IS or IT:

1. The structural design of shared information environments.

2. The art and science of organizing and labeling web sites, intranets, online communities, and software to support findability and usability.

3. An emerging community of practice focused on bringing principles of design and architecture to the digital landscape.

4. The combination of organization, labeling, search and navigation systems within websites and intranets.

5. Extracting required parameters/data of Engineering Designs in the process of creating a knowledge-base linking different systems and standards.

6. A subset of Data Architecture where usable data (a.k.a information) is constructed in and designed or arranged in a fashion most useful or empirically holistic to the users of this data.

Debate

The difficulty in establishing a common definition for "information architecture" arises partly from the term's existence in multiple fields. In the field of systems design, for example, information architecture is a component of enterprise architecture that deals with the information component when describing the structure of an enterprise.

While the definition of information architecture is relatively well-established in the field of systems design, it is much more debatable within the context of online information systems (i.e., websites). Andrew Dillon refers to the latter as the "big IA-little IA debate". In the little IA view, information architecture is essentially the application of information science to web design which considers, for example, issues of classification and information retrieval. In the big IA view, information architecture involves more than just the organization of a website; it also factors in user experience, thereby considering usability issues of information design.

Information Architect

Richard Saul Wurman says the term information architect is "used in the words architect of foreign policy. I mean architect as in the creating of systemic, structural, and orderly principles to make something work — the thoughtful making of either artifact, or idea, or policy that informs because it is clear.

Notable People in Information Architecture

Pioneers

- Richard Saul Wurman
- Peter Morville
- Louis Rosenfeld

First Generation

- Jorge Arango
- Jesse James Garrett
- Adam Greenfield
- Peter Merholz
- Eric Reiss
- Donna Spencer
- Christina Wodtke

Second Generation

- Abby Covert
- Andrew Hinton
- Dan Klyn
- Andrea Resmini

- Ann Marie Smith

- Rakesh Nandish

Influencers

- David Weinberger

Fields of Information Architecture

Data Architecture

In information technology, data architecture is composed of models, policies, rules or standards that govern which data is collected, and how it is stored, arranged, integrated, and put to use in data systems and in organizations. Data is usually one of several architecture domains that form the pillars of an enterprise architecture or solution architecture.

Overview

A data architecture should set data standards for all its data systems as a vision or a model of the eventual interactions between those data systems. Data integration, for example, should be dependent upon data architecture standards since data integration requires data interactions between two or more data systems. A data architecture, in part, describes the data structures used by a business and its computer applications software. Data architectures address data in storage and data in motion; descriptions of data stores, data groups and data items; and mappings of those data artifacts to data qualities, applications, locations etc.

Essential to realizing the target state, Data Architecture describes how data is processed, stored, and utilized in an information system. It provides criteria for data processing operations so as to make it possible to design data flows and also control the flow of data in the system.

The data architect is typically responsible for defining the target state, aligning during development and then following up to ensure enhancements are done in the spirit of the original blueprint.

During the definition of the target state, the Data Architecture breaks a subject down to the atomic level and then builds it back up to the desired form. The data architect breaks the subject down by going through 3 traditional architectural processes:

- Conceptual - represents all business entities.

- Logical - represents the logic of how entities are related.

- Physical - the realization of the data mechanisms for a specific type of functionality.

The "data" column of the Zachman Framework for enterprise architecture –

Lay-er	View	Data (What)	Stakeholder
1	Scope/Contextual	List of things and architectural standards important to the business	Planner
2	Business Model/Conceptual	Semantic model or Conceptual/Enterprise Data Model	Owner
3	System Model/Logical	Enterprise/Logical Data Model	Designer
4	Technology Model/Physical	Physical Data Model	Builder
5	Detailed Representations	Actual databases	Subcontractor

In this second, broader sense, data architecture includes a complete analysis of the relationships between an organization's functions, available technologies, and data types.

Data architecture should be defined in the planning phase of the design of a new data processing and storage system. The major types and sources of data necessary to support an enterprise should be identified in a manner that is complete, consistent, and understandable. The primary requirement at this stage is to define all of the relevant data entities, not to specify computer hardware items. A data entity is any real or abstracted thing about which an organization or individual wishes to store data.

Physical Data Architecture

Physical data architecture of an information system is part of a technology plan. As its name implies, the technology plan is focused on the actual tangible elements to be used in the implementation of the data architecture design. Physical data architecture encompasses database architecture. Database architecture is a schema of the actual database technology that will support the designed data architecture.

Elements of Data Architecture

Certain elements must be defined during the design phase of the data architecture schema. For example, administrative structure that will be established in order to manage the data resources must be described. Also, the methodologies that will be employed to store the data must be defined. In addition, a description of the database technology to be employed must be generated, as well as a description of the processes that will manipulate the data. It is also important to design interfaces to the data by other systems, as well as a design for the infrastructure that will support common data operations (i.e. emergency procedures, data imports, data backups, external transfers of data).

Without the guidance of a properly implemented data architecture design, common data operations might be implemented in different ways, rendering it difficult to understand and control the flow of data within such systems. This sort of fragmentation is highly undesirable due to the potential increased cost, and the data disconnects involved. These sorts of difficulties may be encountered with rapidly growing enterprises and also enterprises that service different lines of business (e.g. insurance products).

Properly executed, the data architecture phase of information system planning forces an organization to precisely specify and describe both internal and external information flows. These are patterns that the organization may not have previously taken the time to conceptualize. It is therefore possible at this stage to identify costly information shortfalls, disconnects between departments, and disconnects between organizational systems that may not have been evident before the data architecture analysis.

Constraints and Influences

Various constraints and influences will have an effect on data architecture design. These include enterprise requirements, technology drivers, economics, business policies and data processing needs.

Enterprise Requirements

These will generally include such elements as economical and effective system expansion, acceptable performance levels (especially system access speed), transaction reliability, and transparent data management. In addition, the conversion of raw data such as transaction records and image files into more useful information forms through such features as data warehouses is also a common organizational requirement, since this enables managerial decision making and other organizational processes. One of the architecture techniques is the split between managing transaction data and (master) reference data. Another one is splitting data capture systems from data retrieval systems (as done in a data warehouse).

Technology Drivers

These are usually suggested by the completed data architecture and database architecture designs. In addition, some technology drivers will derive from existing organizational integration frameworks and standards, organizational economics, and existing site resources (e.g. previously purchased software licensing).

Economics

These are also important factors that must be considered during the data architecture phase. It is possible that some solutions, while optimal in principle, may not be potential candidates due to their cost. External factors such as the business cycle, interest rates, market conditions, and legal considerations could all have an effect on decisions relevant to data architecture.

Business Policies

Business policies that also drive data architecture design include internal organizational policies, rules of regulatory bodies, professional standards, and applicable governmental laws that can vary by applicable agency. These policies and rules will help describe the manner in which enterprise wishes to process their data.

Data Processing Needs

These include accurate and reproducible transactions performed in high volumes, data warehousing for the support of management information systems (and potential data mining), repetitive periodic reporting, ad hoc reporting, and support of various organizational initiatives as required (i.e. annual budgets, new product development).

Data Management

Data management comprises all the disciplines related to managing data as a valuable resource.

Overview

The official definition provided by DAMA International, the professional organization for those in the data management profession, is: "Data Resource Management is the development and execution of architectures, policies, practices and procedures that properly manage the full data lifecycle needs of an enterprise." This definition is fairly broad and encompasses a number of professions which may not have direct technical contact with lower-level aspects of data management, such as relational database management.

The data lifecycle

Alternatively, the definition provided in the DAMA Data Management Body of Knowledge () is: "Data management is the development, execution and supervision of plans, policies, programs and practices that control, protect, deliver and enhance the value of data and information assets."

The concept of "Data Management" arose in the 1980s as technology moved from sequential processing (first cards, then tape) to random access processing. Since it was now technically possible to store a single fact in a single place and access that using random access disk, those suggesting that "Data Management" was more important than "Process Management" used arguments such as "a customer's home address is stored in 75 (or some other large number) places in our computer systems." During this period, random access processing was not competitively fast, so those suggesting "Process Management" was more important than "Data Management" used batch processing time as their primary argument. As applications moved into real-time, interactive applications, it became obvious to most practitioners that both management processes were important. If the data was not well defined, the data would be mis-used in applications. If the process wasn't well defined, it was impossible to meet user needs.

Corporate Data Quality Management

Corporate Data Quality Management (CDQM) is, according to the European Foundation for Quality Management and the Competence Center Corporate Data Quality (CC CDQ, University of St. Gallen), the whole set of activities intended to improve corporate data quality (both reactive and preventive). Main premise of CDQM is the business relevance of high-quality corporate data. CDQM comprises with following activity areas:.

- Strategy for Corporate Data Quality: As CDQM is affected by various business drivers and requires involvement of multiple divisions in an organization; it must be considered a company-wide endeavor.

- Corporate Data Quality Controlling: Effective CDQM requires compliance with standards, policies, and procedures. Compliance is monitored according to previously defined metrics and performance indicators and reported to stakeholders.

- Corporate Data Quality Organization: CDQM requires clear roles and responsibilities for the use of corporate data. The CDQM organization defines tasks and privileges for decision making for CDQM.

- Corporate Data Quality Processes and Methods: In order to handle corporate data properly and in a standardized way across the entire organization and to ensure corporate data quality, standard procedures and guidelines must be embedded in company's daily processes.

- Data Architecture for Corporate Data Quality: The data architecture consists of the data object model - which comprises the unambiguous definition and the conceptual model of corporate data - and the data storage and distribution architecture.

- Applications for Corporate Data Quality: Software applications support the activities of Corporate Data Quality Management. Their use must be planned, monitored, managed and continuously improved.

Topics in Data Management

Topics in Data Management, grouped by the DAMA DMBOK Framework, include:

1. Data governance

   o Data asset

   o Data governance

   o Data steward

2. Data Architecture, Analysis and Design

   o Data analysis

   o Data architecture

   o Data modeling

3. Database Management

   o Data maintenance

   o Database administration

   o Database management system

4. Data Security Management

   o Data access

   o Data erasure

   o Data privacy

   o Data security

5. Data Quality Management

   o Data cleansing

   o Data integrity

   o Data enrichment

   o Data quality

   o Data quality assurance

6. Reference and Master Data Management

- o Data integration
- o Master data management
- o Reference data

7. Data Warehousing and Business Intelligence Management

- o Business intelligence
- o Data mart
- o Data mining
- o Data movement (Extract, transform, load)
- o Data warehouse

8. Document, Record and Content Management

- o Document management system
- o Records management

9. Meta Data Management

- o Meta-data management
- o Metadata
- o Metadata discovery
- o Metadata publishing
- o Metadata registry

10. Contact Data Management

- o Business continuity planning
- o Marketing operations
- o Customer data integration
- o Identity management
- o Identity theft
- o Data theft
- o ERP software
- o CRM software

- o Address (geography)

- o Postal code

- o Email address

- o Telephone number

Body of Knowledge

The DAMA Guide to the Data Management Body of Knowledge" (DAMA-DMBOK Guide), under the guidance of a new DAMA-DMBOK Editorial Board. This publication is available from April 5, 2009.

Usage

In modern management usage, one can easily discern a trend away from the term "data" in composite expressions to the term "information" or even "knowledge" when talking in a non-technical context. Thus there exists not only data management, but also information management and knowledge management. This is a misleading trend as it obscures that traditional data are managed or somehow processed on second looks. The distinction between data and derived values can be seen in the information ladder. While data can exist as such, "information" and "knowledge" are always in the "eye" (or rather the brain) of the beholder and can only be measured in relative units.

Several organisations have established a data management centre (DMC) for their operations.

Integrated Data Management

Integrated data management (IDM) is a tools approach to facilitate data management and improve performance. IDM consists of an integrated, modular environment to manage enterprise application data, and optimize data-driven applications over its lifetime. IDM's purpose is to:

- Produce enterprise-ready applications faster

- Improve data access, speed iterative testing

- Empower collaboration between architects, developers and DBAs

- Consistently achieve service level targets

- Automate and simplify operations

- Provide contextual intelligence across the solution stack

- Support business growth

- Accommodate new initiatives without expanding infrastructure

- Simplify application upgrades, consolidation and retirement

- Facilitate alignment, consistency and governance

- Define business policies and standards up front; share, extend, and apply throughout the lifecycle

Data Visualization

Data visualization or data visualisation is viewed by many disciplines as a modern equivalent of visual communication. It involves the creation and study of the visual representation of data, meaning "information that has been abstracted in some schematic form, including attributes or variables for the units of information".

A primary goal of data visualization is to communicate information clearly and efficiently via statistical graphics, plots and information graphics. Numerical data may be encoded using dots, lines, or bars, to visually communicate a quantitative message. Effective visualization helps users analyze and reason about data and evidence. It makes complex data more accessible, understandable and usable. Users may have particular analytical tasks, such as making comparisons or understanding causality, and the design principle of the graphic (i.e., showing comparisons or showing causality) follows the task. Tables are generally used where users will look up a specific measurement, while charts of various types are used to show patterns or relationships in the data for one or more variables.

Data visualization is both an art and a science. It is viewed as a branch of descriptive statistics by some, but also as a grounded theory development tool by others. The rate at which data is generated has increased. Data created by internet activity and an expanding number of sensors in the environment, such as satellites, are referred to as "Big Data". Processing, analyzing and communicating this data present a variety of ethical and analytical challenges for data visualization. The field of data science and practitioners called data scientists have emerged to help address this challenge.

Overview

Data visualization refers to the techniques used to communicate data or information by encoding it as visual objects (e.g., points, lines or bars) contained in graphics. The goal is to communicate information clearly and efficiently to users. It is one of the steps in data analysis or data science. According to Friedman (2008) the "main goal of data visualization is to communicate information clearly and effectively through graphical means. It doesn't mean that data visualization needs to look boring to be functional or extremely sophisticated to look beautiful. To convey ideas effectively, both aesthetic form and functionality need to go hand in hand, providing insights into a rather sparse and complex data set by communicating its key-aspects in a more intuitive way. Yet designers often fail to achieve a balance between form and function, creating gorgeous data visualizations which fail to serve their main purpose — to communicate information".

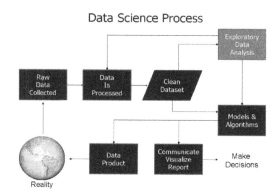

Data visualization is one of the steps in analyzing data and presenting it to users.

Indeed, Fernanda Viegas and Martin M. Wattenberg have suggested that an ideal visualization should not only communicate clearly, but stimulate viewer engagement and attention.

Not limited to the communication of an information, a well-crafted data visualization is also a way to a better understanding of the data (in a data-driven research perspective), as it helps uncover trends, realize insights, explore sources, and tell stories.

Data visualization is closely related to information graphics, information visualization, scientific visualization, exploratory data analysis and statistical graphics. In the new millennium, data visualization has become an active area of research, teaching and development. According to Post et al. (2002), it has united scientific and information visualization.

Characteristics of Effective Graphical Displays

Charles Joseph Minard's 1869 diagram of Napoleon's March - an early example of an information graphic.

The greatest value of a picture is when it forces us to notice what we never expected to see.

John Tukey

Professor Edward Tufte explained that users of information displays are executing particular analytical tasks such as making comparisons or determining causality. The design principle of the information graphic should support the analytical task, showing the comparison or causality.

In his 1983 book The Visual Display of Quantitative Information, Edward Tufte defines 'graphical displays' and principles for effective graphical display in the following passage: "Excellence in statistical graphics consists of complex ideas communicated with clarity, precision and efficiency. Graphical displays should:

- show the data

- induce the viewer to think about the substance rather than about methodology, graphic design, the technology of graphic production or something else

- avoid distorting what the data has to say

- present many numbers in a small space

- make large data sets coherent

- encourage the eye to compare different pieces of data

- reveal the data at several levels of detail, from a broad overview to the fine structure

- serve a reasonably clear purpose: description, exploration, tabulation or decoration

- be closely integrated with the statistical and verbal descriptions of a data set.

Graphics reveal data. Indeed graphics can be more precise and revealing than conventional statistical computations."

For example, the Minard diagram shows the losses suffered by Napoleon's army in the 1812–1813 period. Six variables are plotted: the size of the army, its location on a two-dimensional surface (x and y), time, direction of movement, and temperature. The line width illustrates a comparison (size of the army at points in time) while the temperature axis suggests a cause of the change in army size. This multivariate display on a two dimensional surface tells a story that can be grasped immediately while identifying the source data to build credibility. Tufte wrote in 1983 that: "It may well be the best statistical graphic ever drawn."

Not applying these principles may result in misleading graphs, which distort the message or support an erroneous conclusion. According to Tufte, chartjunk refers to extraneous interior decoration of the graphic that does not enhance the message, or gratuitous three dimensional or perspective effects. Needlessly separating the explanatory key from the image itself, requiring the eye to travel back and forth from the image to the key, is a form of "administrative debris." The ratio of "data to ink" should be maximized, erasing non-data ink where feasible.

The Congressional Budget Office summarized several best practices for graphical displays in a June 2014 presentation. These included: a) Knowing your audience; b) Designing graphics that can stand alone outside the context of the report; and c) Designing graphics that communicate the key messages in the report.

Quantitative Messages

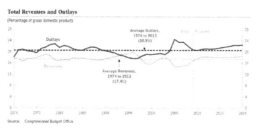

A time series illustrated with a line chart demonstrating trends in U.S. federal spending and revenue over time.

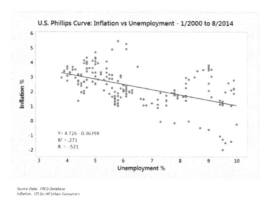

A scatterplot illustrating negative correlation between two variables (inflation and unemployment) measured at points in time.

Author Stephen Few described eight types of quantitative messages that users may attempt to understand or communicate from a set of data and the associated graphs used to help communicate the message:

1. Time-series: A single variable is captured over a period of time, such as the unemployment rate over a 10-year period. A line chart may be used to demonstrate the trend.

2. Ranking: Categorical subdivisions are ranked in ascending or descending order, such as a ranking of sales performance (the measure) by sales persons (the category, with each sales person a categorical subdivision) during a single period. A bar chart may be used to show the comparison across the sales persons.

3. Part-to-whole: Categorical subdivisions are measured as a ratio to the whole (i.e., a percentage out of 100%). A pie chart or bar chart can show the comparison of ratios, such as the market share represented by competitors in a market.

4. Deviation: Categorical subdivisions are compared against a reference, such as a comparison of actual vs. budget expenses for several departments of a business for a given time period. A bar chart can show comparison of the actual versus the reference amount.

5. Frequency distribution: Shows the number of observations of a particular variable for given interval, such as the number of years in which the stock market return is between intervals such as 0-10%, 11-20%, etc. A histogram, a type of bar chart, may be used for this analysis. A boxplot helps visualize key statistics about the distribution, such as median, quartiles, outliers, etc.

6. Correlation: Comparison between observations represented by two variables (X,Y) to determine if they tend to move in the same or opposite directions. For example, plotting unemployment (X) and inflation (Y) for a sample of months. A scatter plot is typically used for this message.

7. Nominal comparison: Comparing categorical subdivisions in no particular order, such as the sales volume by product code. A bar chart may be used for this comparison.

8. Geographic or geospatial: Comparison of a variable across a map or layout, such as the unemployment rate by state or the number of persons on the various floors of a building. A cartogram is a typical graphic used.

Analysts reviewing a set of data may consider whether some or all of the messages and graphic types above are applicable to their task and audience. The process of trial and error to identify meaningful relationships and messages in the data is part of exploratory data analysis.

Visual Perception and Data Visualization

A human can distinguish differences in line length, shape orientation, and color (hue) readily without significant processing effort; these are referred to as "pre-attentive attributes." For example, it may require significant time and effort ("attentive processing") to identify the number of times the digit "5" appears in a series of numbers; but if that digit is different in size, orientation, or color, instances of the digit can be noted quickly through pre-attentive processing.

Effective graphics take advantage of pre-attentive processing and attributes and the relative strength of these attributes. For example, since humans can more easily process differences in line length than surface area, it may be more effective to use a bar chart (which takes advantage of line length to show comparison) rather than pie charts (which use surface area to show comparison).

Human Perception/Cognition and Data Visualization

There is a human side to data visualization. With the "studying [of] human perception and cognition ..." we are better able to understand the target of the data which we display. Cognition refers to processes in human beings like perception, attention, learning, memory, thought, concept formation, reading, and problem solving. The basis of data visualization evolved because as a picture is worth a thousand words, data displayed graphically allows for an easier comprehension of the information. Proper visualization provides a different approach to show potential connections, relationships, etc. which are not as obvious in non-visualized quantitative data. Visualization becomes a means of data exploration. Human brain neurons involve multiple functions but 2/3 of the brain's neurons are dedicated to vision. With a well-developed sense of sight, analysis of data can be made on data, whether that data is quantitative or qualitative. Effective visualization follows from understanding the processes of human perception and being able to apply this to intuitive visualizations is important. Understanding how humans see and organize the world is critical to effectively communicating data to the reader. This leads to more intuitive designs.

History of Data Visualization

There is a history of data visualization: beginning in the 2nd century C.E. with data arrangement into columns and rows and evolving to the initial quantitative representations in the 17th century. According to the Interaction Design Foundation, French philosopher and mathematician René Descartes laid the ground work for Scotsman William Playfair. Descartes developed a two-dimensional coordinate system for displaying values, which in the late 18th century Playfair saw potential for graphical communication of quantitative data. In the second half of the 20th century, Jacques Bertin used quantitative graphs to represent information "intuitively, clearly, accurately, and efficiently". John Tukey and more notably Edward Tufte pushed the bounds of data visualization. Tukey with his new statistical approach: exploratory data analysis and Tufte with his book "The Visual Display of Quantitative Information", the path was paved for refining data visualization techniques for more than statisticians. With the progression of technology came the progression of data visualization; starting with hand drawn visualizations and evolving into more technical applications – including interactive designs leading to software visualization. Programs like SAS, SOFA, R, Minitab, and more allow for data visualization in the field of statistics. Other data visualization applications, more focused and unique to individuals, programming languages such as D3, Python and JavaScript help to make the visualization of quantitative data a possibility.

Terminology

Data visualization involves specific terminology, some of which is derived from statistics. For example, author Stephen Few defines two types of data, which are used in combination to support a meaningful analysis or visualization:

- Categorical: Text labels describing the nature of the data, such as "Name" or "Age". This term also covers qualitative (non-numerical) data.

- Quantitative: Numerical measures, such as "25" to represent the age in years.

Two primary types of information displays are tables and graphs.

- A table contains quantitative data organized into rows and columns with categorical labels. It is primarily used to look up specific values. In the example above, the table might have categorical column labels representing the name (a qualitative variable) and age (a quantitative variable), with each row of data representing one person (the sampled experimental unit or category subdivision).

- A graph is primarily used to show relationships among data and portrays values encoded as visual objects (e.g., lines, bars, or points). Numerical values are displayed within an area delineated by one or more axes. These axes provide scales (quantitative and categorical) used to label and assign values to the visual objects. Many graphs are also referred to as charts.

KPI Library has developed the "Periodic Table of Visualization Methods," an interactive chart displaying various data visualization methods. It includes six types of data visualization methods: data, information, concept, strategy, metaphor and compound.

Examples of Diagrams Used for Data Visualization

	Name	Visual Dimensions	Example Usages
Bar chart of tips by day of week	Bar Chart	• length/ count • category • (color)	• Comparison of values, such as sales performance for several persons or businesses in a single time period. For a single variable measured over time (trend) a line chart is preferable.

 Histogram of housing prices	Histogram	• bin limits • count/ length • (color)	• Determining fre- quency of annual stock market percentage returns within particular ranges (bins) such as 0-10%, 11-20%, etc. The height of the bar represents the number of observations (years) with a return % in the range represent- ed by the bin.
 Basic scatterplot of two variables	Scatter plot	• x position • y position • (symbol/ glyph) • (color) • (size)	• Determining the relationship (e.g., correlation) between unemployment (x) and inflation (y) for multiple time periods.
 Scatter Plot	Scatter plot (3D)	• position x • position y • position z • color	

Network Analysis
	Network	• nodes size
		• nodes
		  color
		• ties thick-
		  ness
		• ties color
		• spatializa-
		  tion
			• Finding clusters in
			the network (e.g.
			grouping Facebook
			friends into differ-
			ent clusters).
			• Determining the
			most influen-
			tial nodes in the
			network (e.g. A
			company wants to
			target a small group
			of people on Twitter
			for a marketing
			campaign).

 Streamgraph	Stream-graph	• width • color • time (flow)	
 Treemap	Treemap	• size • color	• disk space by location / file type
 Gantt Chart	Gantt chart	• color • time (flow)	• schedule / progress, e.g. in project planning
 Heat Map	Heat Map	• row • column • cluster • color	• Analyzing risk, with green, yellow and red representing low, medium, and high risk, respectively.

Other Perspectives

There are different approaches on the scope of data visualization. One common focus is on information presentation, such as Friedman (2008) presented it. In this way Friendly (2008) presumes two main parts of data visualization: statistical graphics, and thematic cartography. In this line the "Data Visualization: Modern Approaches" (2007) article gives an overview of seven subjects of data visualization:

- Articles & resources
- Displaying connections
- Displaying data
- Displaying news
- Displaying websites
- Mind maps
- Tools and services

All these subjects are closely related to graphic design and information representation.

On the other hand, from a computer science perspective, Frits H. Post (2002) categorized the field into a number of sub-fields:

- Information visualization
- Interaction techniques and architectures
- Modelling techniques
- Multiresolution methods
- Visualization algorithms and techniques
- Volume visualization

Data Presentation Architecture

Data presentation architecture (DPA) is a skill-set that seeks to identify, locate, manipulate, format and present data in such a way as to optimally communicate meaning and proper knowledge.

Historically, the term data presentation architecture is attributed to Kelly Lautt: "Data Presentation Architecture (DPA) is a rarely applied skill set critical for the success and value of Business Intelligence. Data presentation architecture weds the science of numbers, data and statistics in discovering valuable information from data and making it usable, relevant and actionable with the arts of data visualization, communications, organizational psychology and change management in order to provide business intelligence solutions with the data scope, delivery timing, format and visualizations that will most effectively support and drive operational, tactical and strategic behaviour toward understood business (or organizational) goals. DPA is neither an IT nor a business skill set but exists as a separate field of expertise. Often confused with data visualization, data presentation architecture is a much broader skill set that includes determining what data on what schedule and in what exact format is to be presented, not just the best way to present data that has already been chosen (which is data visualization). Data visualization skills are one element of DPA."

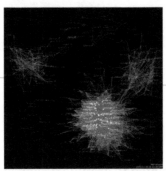

A data visualization from social media

Objectives

DPA has two main objectives:

- To use data to provide knowledge in the most efficient manner possible (minimize noise, complexity, and unnecessary data or detail given each audience's needs and roles)

- To use data to provide knowledge in the most effective manner possible (provide relevant, timely and complete data to each audience member in a clear and understandable manner that conveys important meaning, is actionable and can affect understanding, behavior and decisions)

Scope

With the above objectives in mind, the actual work of data presentation architecture consists of:

- Creating effective delivery mechanisms for each audience member depending on their role, tasks, locations and access to technology

- Defining important meaning (relevant knowledge) that is needed by each audience member in each context

- Determining the required periodicity of data updates (the currency of the data)

- Determining the right timing for data presentation

- Finding the right data (subject area, historical reach, breadth, level of detail, etc.)

- Utilizing appropriate analysis, grouping, visualization, and other presentation formats

Related Fields

DPA work shares commonalities with several other fields, including:

- Business analysis in determining business goals, collecting requirements, mapping processes.

- Business process improvement in that its goal is to improve and streamline actions and decisions in furtherance of business goals

- Data visualization in that it uses well-established theories of visualization to add or highlight meaning or importance in data presentation.

- Graphic or user design: As the term DPA is used, it falls just short of design in that it does not consider such detail as colour palates, styling, branding and other aesthetic concerns, unless these design elements are specifically required or beneficial for communication of meaning, impact, severity or other information of business value. For example:

    o   choosing locations for various data presentation elements on a presentation page (such as in a company portal, in a report or on a web page) in order to convey hierarchy, priority, importance or a rational progression for the user is part of the DPA skill-set.

    o   choosing to provide a specific colour in graphical elements that represent data of specific meaning or concern is part of the DPA skill-set

- Information architecture, but information architecture's focus is on unstructured data and therefore excludes both analysis (in the statistical/data sense) and direct transformation of the actual content (data, for DPA) into new entities and combinations.

- Solution architecture in determining the optimal detailed solution, including the scope of data to include, given the business goals

- Statistical analysis or data analysis in that it creates information and knowledge out of data

Philosophy of Information

The philosophy of information (PI) is the area of research that studies conceptual issues arising at the intersection of computer science, information science, information technology, and philosophy.

It includes:

1. the critical investigation of the conceptual nature and basic principles of information, including its dynamics, utilisation and sciences

2. the elaboration and application of information-theoretic and computational methodologies to philosophical problems.

History

The philosophy of information (PI) has evolved from the philosophy of artificial intelligence, logic of information, cybernetics, social theory, ethics and the study of language and information.

Logic of Information

The logic of information, also known as the logical theory of information, considers the information content of logical signs and expressions along the lines initially developed by Charles Sanders Peirce.

Cybernetics

One source for the philosophy of information can be found in the technical work of Norbert Wiener, Alan Turing (though his work has a wholly different origin and theoretical framework), William Ross Ashby, Claude Shannon, Warren Weaver, and many other scientists working on computing and information theory back in the early 1950s.

Some important work on information and communication was done by Gregory Bateson and his colleagues.

Study of Language and Information

Later contributions to the field were made by Fred Dretske, Jon Barwise, Brian Cantwell Smith, and others.

The Center for the Study of Language and Information (CSLI) was founded at Stanford University in 1983 by philosophers, computer scientists, linguists, and psychologists, under the direction of John Perry and Jon Barwise.

P.I.

More recently this field has become known as the philosophy of information. The expression was coined in the 1990s by Luciano Floridi, who has published prolifically in this area with the intention of elaborating a unified and coherent, conceptual frame for the whole subject.

Definitions of "Information"

The concept information has been defined by several theorists.

Peirce

Charles S. Peirce's theory of information was embedded in his wider theory of symbolic communication he called the semeiotic, now a major part of semiotics. For Peirce, information integrates the aspects of signs and expressions separately covered by the concepts of denotation and extension, on the one hand, and by connotation and comprehension on the other.

Shannon and Weaver

Claude E. Shannon, for his part, was very cautious: "The word 'information' has been given different meanings by various writers in the general field of information theory. It is likely that at least a number of these will prove sufficiently useful in certain applications to deserve further study and permanent recognition. It is hardly to be expected that a single concept of information would satisfactorily account for the numerous possible applications of this general field." (Shannon 1993, p. 180). Thus, following Shannon, Weaver supported a tripartite analysis of information in terms of (1) technical problems concerning the quantification of information and dealt with by Shannon's theory; (2) semantic problems relating to meaning and truth; and (3) what he called "influential" problems concerning the impact and effectiveness of information on human behaviour, which he thought had to play an equally important role. And these are only two early examples of the problems raised by any analysis of information.

A map of the main senses in which one may speak of information is provided by the Stanford Encyclopedia of Philosophy article. The previous paragraphs are based on it.

Bateson

Gregory Bateson defined information as "a difference that makes a difference". which is based on Donald M. MacKay: information is a distinction that makes a difference.

Floridi

According to Luciano Floridi, four kinds of mutually compatible phenomena are commonly referred to as "information":

- Information about something (e.g. a train timetable)

- Information as something (e.g. DNA, or fingerprints)

- Information for something (e.g. algorithms or instructions)

- Information in something (e.g. a pattern or a constraint).

The word "information" is commonly used so metaphorically or so abstractly that the meaning is unclear.

Philosophical Directions

Computing and Philosophy

Recent creative advances and efforts in computing, such as semantic web, ontology engineering, knowledge engineering, and modern artificial intelligence provide philosophy with fertile notions, new and evolving subject matters, methodologies, and models for philosophical inquiry. While computer science brings new opportunities and challenges to traditional philosophical studies, and changes the ways philosophers understand foundational concepts in philosophy, further major progress in computer science would only be feasible when philosophy provides sound foundations for areas such as bioinformatics, software engineering, knowledge engineering, and ontologies.

Classical topics in philosophy, namely, mind, consciousness, experience, reasoning, knowledge, truth, morality and creativity are rapidly becoming common concerns and foci of investigation in computer science, e.g., in areas such as agent computing, software agents, and intelligent mobile agent technologies.

According to Luciano Floridi " one can think of several ways for applying computational methods towards philosophical matters:

1. Conceptual experiments in silico: As an innovative extension of an ancient tradition of thought experiment, a trend has begun in philosophy to apply computational modeling schemes to questions in logic, epistemology, philosophy of science, philosophy of biology, philosophy of mind, and so on.

2. Pancomputationalism: By this view, computational and informational concepts are considered to be so powerful that given the right level of abstraction, anything in the world could be modeled and represented as a computational system, and any process could be simulated computationally. Then, however, pancomputationalists have the hard task of providing credible answers to the following two questions:

   1. how can one avoid blurring all differences among systems?

2. what would it mean for the system under investigation not to be an informational system (or a computational system, if computation is the same as information processing)?

Information and Society

Numerous philosophers and other thinkers have carried out philosophical studies of the social and cultural aspects of electronically mediated information.

- Albert Borgmann, Holding onto Reality: The Nature of Information at the Turn of the Millennium (Chicago University Press, 1999)

- Mark Poster, The Mode of Information (Chicago Press, 1990)

- Luciano Floridi, "The Informational Nature of Reality", Fourth International European Conference on Computing and Philosophy 2006 (Dragvoll Campus, NTNU Norwegian University for Science and Technology, Trondheim, Norway, 22–24 June 2006).

Cluster Analysis

Cluster analysis or clustering is the task of grouping a set of objects in such a way that objects in the same group (called a cluster) are more similar (in some sense or another) to each other than to those in other groups (clusters). It is a main task of exploratory data mining, and a common technique for statistical data analysis, used in many fields, including machine learning, pattern recognition, image analysis, information retrieval, bioinformatics, data compression, and computer graphics.

Cluster analysis itself is not one specific algorithm, but the general task to be solved. It can be achieved by various algorithms that differ significantly in their notion of what constitutes a cluster and how to efficiently find them. Popular notions of clusters include groups with small distances among the cluster members, dense areas of the data space, intervals or particular statistical distributions. Clustering can therefore be formulated as a multi-objective optimization problem. The appropriate clustering algorithm and parameter settings (including values such as the distance function to use, a density threshold or the number of expected clusters) depend on the individual data set and intended use of the results. Cluster analysis as such is not an automatic task, but an iterative process of knowledge discovery or interactive multi-objective optimization that involves trial and failure. It is often necessary to modify data preprocessing and model parameters until the result achieves the desired properties.

Besides the term clustering, there are a number of terms with similar meanings, including automatic classification, numerical taxonomy, botryology and typological analysis. The subtle differences are often in the usage of the results: while in data mining, the resulting groups are the matter of interest, in automatic classification the resulting discriminative power is of interest. This often leads to misunderstandings between researchers coming from the fields of data mining and machine learning, since they use the same terms and often the same algorithms, but have different goals.

Cluster analysis was originated in anthropology by Driver and Kroeber in 1932 and introduced to psychology by Zubin in 1938 and Robert Tryon in 1939 and famously used by Cattell beginning in 1943 for trait theory classification in personality psychology.

Definition

The notion of a "cluster" cannot be precisely defined, which is one of the reasons why there are so many clustering algorithms. There is a common denominator: a group of data objects. However, different researchers employ different cluster models, and for each of these cluster models again different algorithms can be given. The notion of a cluster, as found by different algorithms, varies significantly in its properties. Understanding these "cluster models" is key to understanding the differences between the various algorithms. Typical cluster models include:

- Connectivity models: for example, hierarchical clustering builds models based on distance connectivity.

- Centroid models: for example, the k-means algorithm represents each cluster by a single mean vector.

- Distribution models: clusters are modeled using statistical distributions, such as multivariate normal distributions used by the Expectation-maximization algorithm.

- Density models: for example, DBSCAN and OPTICS defines clusters as connected dense regions in the data space.

- Subspace models: in Biclustering (also known as Co-clustering or two-mode-clustering), clusters are modeled with both cluster members and relevant attributes.

- Group models: some algorithms do not provide a refined model for their results and just provide the grouping information.

- Graph-based models: a clique, that is, a subset of nodes in a graph such that every two nodes in the subset are connected by an edge can be considered as a prototypical form of cluster. Relaxations of the complete connectivity requirement (a fraction of the edges can be missing) are known as quasi-cliques, as in the HCS clustering algorithm.

A "clustering" is essentially a set of such clusters, usually containing all objects in the data set. Additionally, it may specify the relationship of the clusters to each other, for example, a hierarchy of clusters embedded in each other. Clusterings can be roughly distinguished as:

- hard clustering: each object belongs to a cluster or not

- soft clustering (also: fuzzy clustering): each object belongs to each cluster to a certain degree (for example, a likelihood of belonging to the cluster)

There are also finer distinctions possible, for example:

- strict partitioning clustering: here each object belongs to exactly one cluster

- strict partitioning clustering with outliers: objects can also belong to no cluster, and are considered outliers.

- overlapping clustering (also: alternative clustering, multi-view clustering): while usually a hard clustering, objects may belong to more than one cluster.

- hierarchical clustering: objects that belong to a child cluster also belong to the parent cluster

- subspace clustering: while an overlapping clustering, within a uniquely defined subspace, clusters are not expected to overlap.

Algorithms

Clustering algorithms can be categorized based on their cluster model, as listed above. The following overview will only list the most prominent examples of clustering algorithms, as there are possibly over 100 published clustering algorithms. Not all provide models for their clusters and can thus not easily be categorized. An overview of algorithms explained in Wikipedia can be found in the list of statistics algorithms.

There is no objectively "correct" clustering algorithm, but as it was noted, "clustering is in the eye of the beholder." The most appropriate clustering algorithm for a particular problem often needs to be chosen experimentally, unless there is a mathematical reason to prefer one cluster model over another. It should be noted that an algorithm that is designed for one kind of model has no chance on a data set that contains a radically different kind of model. For example, k-means cannot find non-convex clusters.

Connectivity-based Clustering (Hierarchical Clustering)

Connectivity based clustering, also known as hierarchical clustering, is based on the core idea of objects being more related to nearby objects than to objects farther away. These algorithms connect "objects" to form "clusters" based on their distance. A cluster can be described largely by the maximum distance needed to connect parts of the cluster. At different distances, different clusters will form, which can be represented using a dendrogram, which explains where the common name "hierarchical clustering" comes from: these algorithms do not provide a single partitioning of the data set, but instead provide an extensive hierarchy of clusters that merge with each other at certain distances. In a dendrogram, the y-axis marks the distance at which the clusters merge, while the objects are placed along the x-axis such that the clusters don't mix.

Connectivity based clustering is a whole family of methods that differ by the way distances are computed. Apart from the usual choice of distance functions, the user also needs to decide on the linkage criterion (since a cluster consists of multiple objects, there are multiple candidates to compute the distance to) to use. Popular choices are known as single-linkage clustering (the minimum of object distances), complete linkage clustering (the maximum of object distances) or UPGMA ("Unweighted Pair Group Method with Arithmetic Mean", also known as average linkage clustering). Furthermore, hierarchical clustering can be agglomerative (starting with single elements and aggregating them into clusters) or divisive (starting with the complete data set and dividing it into partitions).

These methods will not produce a unique partitioning of the data set, but a hierarchy from which the user still needs to choose appropriate clusters. They are not very robust towards outliers, which will either show up as additional clusters or even cause other clusters to merge (known as "chaining phenomenon", in particular with single-linkage clustering). In the general case, the complexity is $\mathcal{O}(n^3)$ for agglomerative clustering and $\mathcal{O}(2^{n-1})$ for divisive clustering, which makes them too slow for large data sets. For some special cases, optimal efficient methods (of complexity O (n 2) $\mathcal{O}(n^2)$)) are known: SLINK for single-linkage and CLINK for complete-linkage clustering. In the data mining community these methods are recognized as a theoretical foundation of cluster analysis, but often considered obsolete. They did however provide inspiration for many later methods such as density based clustering.

- Linkage clustering examples

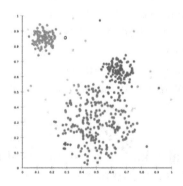

Single-linkage on Gaussian data. At 35 clusters, the biggest cluster starts fragmenting into smaller parts, while before it was still connected to the second largest due to the single-link effect.

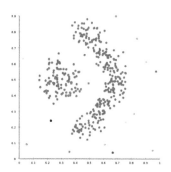

Single-linkage on density-based clusters. 20 clusters extracted, most of which contain single elements, since linkage clustering does not have a notion of "noise".

Centroid-based Clustering

In centroid-based clustering, clusters are represented by a central vector, which may not necessarily be a member of the data set. When the number of clusters is fixed to k, k-means clustering gives a formal definition as an optimization problem: find the k cluster centers and assign the objects to the nearest cluster center, such that the squared distances from the cluster are minimized.

The optimization problem itself is known to be NP-hard, and thus the common approach is to search only for approximate solutions. A particularly well known approximative method is Lloyd's algorithm, often actually referred to as "k-means algorithm". It does however only find a local optimum, and is commonly run multiple times with different random initializations. Variations of k-means often include such optimizations as choosing the best of multiple runs, but also restricting the centroids to members of the data set (k-medoids), choosing medians (k-medians clustering), choosing the initial centers less randomly (K-means++) or allowing a fuzzy cluster assignment (Fuzzy c-means).

Most k-means-type algorithms require the number of clusters - k - to be specified in advance, which is considered to be one of the biggest drawbacks of these algorithms. Furthermore, the algorithms prefer clusters of approximately similar size, as they will always assign an object to the nearest centroid. This often leads to incorrectly cut borders in between of clusters (which is not surprising, as the algorithm optimized cluster centers, not cluster borders).

K-means has a number of interesting theoretical properties. First, it partitions the data space into a structure known as a Voronoi diagram. Second, it is conceptually close to nearest neighbor classification, and as such is popular in machine learning. Third, it can be seen as a variation of model based classification, and Lloyd's algorithm as a variation of the Expectation-maximization algorithm for this model discussed below.

- k-Means clustering examples

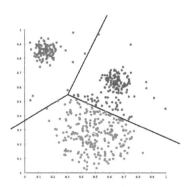

K-means separates data into Voronoi-cells, which assumes equal-sized clusters (not adequate here)

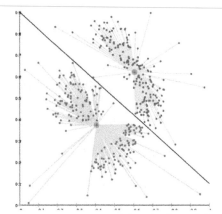

K-means cannot represent density-based clusters

Distribution-based Clustering

The clustering model most closely related to statistics is based on distribution models. Clusters can then easily be defined as objects belonging most likely to the same distribution. A convenient property of this approach is that this closely resembles the way artificial data sets are generated: by sampling random objects from a distribution.

While the theoretical foundation of these methods is excellent, they suffer from one key problem known as overfitting, unless constraints are put on the model complexity. A more complex model will usually be able to explain the data better, which makes choosing the appropriate model complexity inherently difficult.

One prominent method is known as Gaussian mixture models (using the expectation-maximization algorithm). Here, the data set is usually modelled with a fixed (to avoid overfitting) number of Gaussian distributions that are initialized randomly and whose parameters are iteratively optimized to fit better to the data set. This will converge to a local optimum, so multiple runs may produce different results. In order to obtain a hard clustering, objects are often then assigned to the Gaussian distribution they most likely belong to; for soft clusterings, this is not necessary.

Distribution-based clustering produces complex models for clusters that can capture correlation and dependence between attributes. However, these algorithms put an extra burden on the user: for many real data sets, there may be no concisely defined mathematical model (e.g. assuming Gaussian distributions is a rather strong assumption on the data).

- Expectation-Maximization (EM) clustering examples

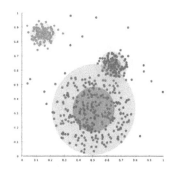

On Gaussian-distributed data, EM works well, since it uses Gaussians for modelling clusters

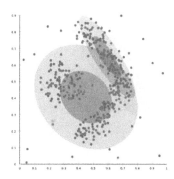

Density-based clusters cannot be modeled using Gaussian distributions

Density-based Clustering

In density-based clustering, clusters are defined as areas of higher density than the remainder of the data set. Objects in these sparse areas - that are required to separate clusters - are usually considered to be noise and border points.

The most popular density based clustering method is DBSCAN. In contrast to many newer methods, it features a well-defined cluster model called "density-reachability".

Similar to linkage based clustering, it is based on connecting points within certain distance thresholds. However, it only connects points that satisfy a density criterion, in the original variant defined as a minimum number of other objects within this radius. A cluster consists of all density-connected objects (which can form a cluster of an arbitrary shape, in contrast to many other methods) plus all objects that are within these objects' range. Another interesting property of DBSCAN is that its complexity is fairly low - it requires a linear number of range queries on the database - and that it will discover essentially the same results (it is deterministic for core and noise points, but not for border points) in each run, therefore there is no need to run it multiple times. OPTICS is a generalization of DBSCAN that removes the need to choose an appropriate value for the range parameter ε, and produces a hierarchical result related to that of linkage clustering. De-Li-Clu, Density-Link-Clustering combines ideas from single-linkage clustering and OPTICS, eliminating the ε parameter entirely and offering performance improvements over OPTICS by using an R-tree index.

The key drawback of DBSCAN and OPTICS is that they expect some kind of density drop to detect cluster borders. Moreover, they cannot detect intrinsic cluster structures which are prevalent in the majority of real life data. A variation of DBSCAN, EnDBSCAN, efficiently detects such kinds of structures. On data sets with, for example, overlapping Gaussian distributions - a common use case in artificial data - the cluster borders produced by these algorithms will often look arbitrary, because the cluster density decreases continuously. On a data set consisting of mixtures of Gaussians, these algorithms are nearly always outperformed by methods such as EM clustering that are able to precisely model this kind of data.

Mean-shift is a clustering approach where each object is moved to the densest area in its vicinity, based on kernel density estimation. Eventually, objects converge to local maxima of density. Similar to k-means clustering, these "density attractors" can serve as representatives for the data set, but mean-shift can detect arbitrary-shaped clusters similar to DBSCAN. Due to the expensive iterative procedure and density estimation, mean-shift is usually slower than DBSCAN or k-Means.

- Density-based clustering examples

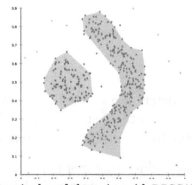

Density-based clustering with DBSCAN.

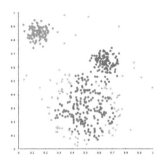

DBSCAN assumes clusters of similar density, and may have problems separating nearby clusters

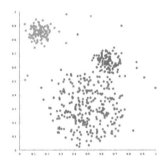

OPTICS is a DBSCAN variant that handles different densities much better

Recent Developments

In recent years considerable effort has been put into improving the performance of existing algorithms. Among them are CLARANS (Ng and Han, 1994), and BIRCH (Zhang et al., 1996). With the recent need to process larger and larger data sets (also known as big data), the willingness to trade semantic meaning of the generated clusters for performance has been increasing. This led to the development of pre-clustering methods such as canopy clustering, which can process huge data sets efficiently, but the resulting "clusters" are merely a rough pre-partitioning of the data set to then analyze the partitions with existing slower methods such as k-means clustering. Various other approaches to clustering have been tried such as seed based clustering.

For high-dimensional data, many of the existing methods fail due to the curse of dimensionality, which renders particular distance functions problematic in high-dimensional spaces. This led to new clustering algorithms for high-dimensional data that focus on subspace clustering (where only some attributes are used, and cluster models include the relevant attributes for the cluster) and correlation clustering that also looks for arbitrary rotated ("correlated") subspace clusters that can be modeled by giving a correlation of their attributes. Examples for such clustering algorithms are CLIQUE and SUBCLU.

Ideas from density-based clustering methods (in particular the DBSCAN/OPTICS family of algorithms) have been adopted to subspace clustering (HiSC, hierarchical subspace clustering and DiSH) and correlation clustering (HiCO, hierarchical correlation clustering, 4C using "correlation connectivity" and ERiC exploring hierarchical density-based correlation clusters).

Several different clustering systems based on mutual information have been proposed. One is Marina Meilă's variation of information metric; another provides hierarchical clustering. Using genetic algorithms, a wide range of different fit-functions can be optimized, including mutual information. Also message passing algorithms, a recent development in Computer Science and Statistical Physics, has led to the creation of new types of clustering algorithms.

Other Methods

- Basic sequential algorithmic scheme (BSAS)

Evaluation and Assessment

Evaluation of clustering results sometimes is referred to as cluster validation.

There have been several suggestions for a measure of similarity between two clusterings. Such a measure can be used to compare how well different data clustering algorithms perform on a set of data. These measures are usually tied to the type of criterion being considered in assessing the quality of a clustering method.

Internal Evaluation

When a clustering result is evaluated based on the data that was clustered itself, this is called internal evaluation. These methods usually assign the best score to the algorithm that produces clusters with high similarity within a cluster and low similarity between clusters. One drawback of using internal criteria in cluster evaluation is that high scores on an internal measure do not necessarily result in effective information retrieval applications. Additionally, this evaluation is biased towards algorithms that use the same cluster model. For example, k-Means clustering naturally optimizes object distances, and a distance-based internal criterion will likely overrate the resulting clustering.

Therefore, the internal evaluation measures are best suited to get some insight into situations where one algorithm performs better than another, but this shall not imply that one algorithm produces more valid results than another. Validity as measured by such an index depends on the claim that this kind of structure exists in the data set. An algorithm designed for some kind of models has no chance if the data set contains a radically different set of models, or if the evaluation measures a radically different criterion. For example, k-means clustering can only find convex clusters, and many evaluation indexes assume convex clusters. On a data set with non-convex clusters neither the use of k-means, nor of an evaluation criterion that assumes convexity, is sound.

The following methods can be used to assess the quality of clustering algorithms based on internal criterion:

- Davies–Bouldin index

  The Davies–Bouldin index can be calculated by the following formula:

  $$DB = \frac{1}{n} \sum_{i=1}^{n} \max_{j \neq i} \left(\frac{\sigma_i + \sigma_j}{d(c_i, c_j)} \right)$$

  where n is the number of clusters, c_x is the centroid of cluster x, σ_x is the average distance of all elements in cluster x to centroid c_x and $d(c_i, c_j)$ is the distance between centroids . Since algorithms that produce clusters with low intra-cluster distances (high intra-cluster similarity) and high inter-cluster distances (low inter-cluster similarity) will have a low Davies–Bouldin index, the clustering algorithm that produces a collection of clusters with the smallest Davies–Bouldin index is considered the best algorithm based on this criterion.

- Dunn index

  The Dunn index aims to identify dense and well-separated clusters. It is defined as the ratio between the minimal inter-cluster distance to maximal intra-cluster distance. For each cluster partition, the Dunn index can be calculated by the following formula:

  $$D = \frac{\min_{1 \leq i < j \leq n} d(i, j)}{\max_{1 \leq k \leq n} d'(k)},$$

  where d(i,j) represents the distance between clusters i and j, and d'(k) measures the intra-cluster distance of cluster k. The inter-cluster distance d(i,j) between two clusters may be any number of distance measures, such as the distance between the centroids of the clusters. Similarly, the intra-cluster distance d'(k) may be measured in a variety ways, such as the maximal distance between any pair of elements in cluster k. Since internal criterion seek clusters with high intra-cluster similarity and low inter-cluster similarity, algorithms that produce clusters with high Dunn index are more desirable.

- Silhouette coefficient

  The silhouette coefficient contrasts the average distance to elements in the same cluster with the average distance to elements in other clusters. Objects with a high silhouette value are considered well clustered, objects with a low value may be outliers. This index works well with k-means clustering, and is also used to determine the optimal number of clusters.

External Evaluation

In external evaluation, clustering results are evaluated based on data that was not used for clustering, such as known class labels and external benchmarks. Such benchmarks consist of a set of pre-classified items, and these sets are often created by (expert) humans. Thus, the benchmark sets can be thought of as a gold standard for evaluation. These types of evaluation methods measure how close the clustering is to the predetermined benchmark classes. However, it has recently been discussed whether this is adequate for real data, or only on synthetic data sets with a factual ground truth, since classes can contain internal structure, the attributes present may not allow separation of clusters or the classes may contain anomalies. Additionally, from a knowledge discovery point of view, the reproduction of known knowledge may not necessarily be the intended result. In the special scenario of constrained clustering, where meta information (such as class labels) is used already in the clustering process, the hold-out of information for evaluation purposes is non-trivial.

A number of measures are adapted from variants used to evaluate classification tasks. In place of counting the number of times a class was correctly assigned to a single data point (known as true positives), such pair counting metrics assess whether each pair of data points that is truly in the same cluster is predicted to be in the same cluster.

Some of the measures of quality of a cluster algorithm using external criterion include:

- Rand measure (William M. Rand 1971)

  The Rand index computes how similar the clusters (returned by the clustering algorithm) are to the benchmark classifications. One can also view the Rand index as a measure of the percentage of correct decisions made by the algorithm. It can be computed using the following formula:

  $$RI = \frac{TP + TN}{TP + FP + FN + TN}$$

  Where TP is the number of true positives, TN is the number of true negatives, FP is the number of false positives, and FN is the number of false negatives. One issue with the Rand index is that false positives and false negatives are equally weighted. This may be an undesirable characteristic for some clustering applications. The F-measure addresses this concern, as does the chance-corrected adjusted Rand index.

- F-measure

  The F-measure can be used to balance the contribution of false negatives by weighting recall through a parameter $\beta \geq 0$. Let precision and recall be defined as follows

  $$P = \frac{TP}{TP + FP}$$

  $$R = \frac{TP}{TP + FN}$$

  where P is the recall rate. We can calculate the F-measure by using the following formula:

$$F_\beta = \frac{(\beta^2 + 1) \cdot P \cdot R}{\beta^2 \cdot P + R}$$

Notice that when $\beta = 0$ $F_0 = P$ In other words, recall has no impact on the F-measure when $\beta = 0$ allocates an increasing amount of weight to recall in the final F-measure.

- Jaccard index

  The Jaccard index is used to quantify the similarity between two datasets. The Jaccard index takes on a value between 0 and 1. An index of 1 means that the two dataset are identical, and an index of 0 indicates that the datasets have no common elements. The Jaccard index is defined by the following formula:

  $$J(A, B) = \frac{|A \cap B|}{|A \cup B|} = \frac{TP}{TP + FP + FN}$$

  This is simply the number of unique elements common to both sets divided by the total number of unique elements in both sets.

- Fowlkes–Mallows index (E. B. Fowlkes & C. L. Mallows 1983)

  The Fowlkes-Mallows index computes the similarity between the clusters returned by the clustering algorithm and the benchmark classifications. The higher the value of the Fowlkes-Mallows index the more similar the clusters and the benchmark classifications are. It can be computed using the following formula:

  $$FM = \sqrt{\frac{TP}{TP + FP} \cdot \frac{TP}{TP + FN}}$$

Where TP is the number of true positives, FP is the number of false positives, and FN is the number of false negatives. The FM index is the geometric mean of the precision and recall P and R while the F-measure is their harmonic mean. Moreover, precision and recall are also known as Wallace's indices B^I and B^{II}

- The Mutual Information is an information theoretic measure of how much information is shared between a clustering and a ground-truth classification that can detect a non-linear similarity between two clusterings. Adjusted mutual information is the corrected-for-chance variant of this that has a reduced bias for varying cluster numbers.

- Confusion matrix

  A confusion matrix can be used to quickly visualize the results of a classification (or clustering) algorithm. It shows how different a cluster is from the gold standard cluster.

Applications

Biology, computational biology and bioinformatics

Plant and animal ecology

cluster analysis is used to describe and to make spatial and temporal comparisons of communities (assemblages) of organisms in heterogeneous environments; it is also used in plant systematics to generate artificial phylogenies or clusters of organisms (individuals) at the species, genus or higher level that share a number of attributes

Transcriptomics

clustering is used to build groups of genes with related expression patterns (also known as coexpressed genes) as in HCS clustering algorithm . Often such groups contain functionally related proteins, such as enzymes for a specific pathway, or genes that are co-regulated. High throughput experiments using expressed sequence tags (ESTs) or DNA microarrays can be a powerful tool for genome annotation, a general aspect of genomics.

Sequence analysis

clustering is used to group homologous sequences into gene families. This is a very important concept in bioinformatics, and evolutionary biology in general.

High-throughput genotyping platforms

clustering algorithms are used to automatically assign genotypes.

Human genetic clustering

The similarity of genetic data is used in clustering to infer population structures.

Medicine

Medical imaging

On PET scans, cluster analysis can be used to differentiate between different types of tissue and blood in a three-dimensional image. In this application, actual position does not matter, but the voxel intensity is considered as a vector, with a dimension for each image that was taken over time. This technique allows, for example, accurate measurement of the rate a radioactive tracer is delivered to the area of interest, without a separate sampling of arterial blood, an intrusive technique that is most common today.

Analysis of antimicrobial activity

Cluster analysis can be used to analyse patterns of antibiotic resistance, to classify antimicrobial compounds according to their mechanism of action, to classify antibiotics according to their antibacterial activity.

IMRT segmentation

Clustering can be used to divide a fluence map into distinct regions for conversion into deliverable fields in MLC-based Radiation Therapy.

Business and marketing

Market research

Cluster analysis is widely used in market research when working with multivariate data from surveys and test panels. Market researchers use cluster analysis to partition the general population of consumers into market segments and to better understand the relationships between different groups of consumers/ potential customers, and for use in market segmentation, Product positioning, New product development and Selecting test markets.

Grouping of shopping items

Clustering can be used to group all the shopping items available on the web into a set of unique products. For example, all the items on eBay can be grouped into unique products. (eBay doesn't have the concept of a SKU)

World wide web

Social network analysis

In the study of social networks, clustering may be used to recognize communities within large groups of people.

Search result grouping

In the process of intelligent grouping of the files and websites, clustering may be used to create a more relevant set of search results compared to normal search engines like Google. There are currently a number of web based clustering tools such as Clusty.

Slippy map optimization

Flickr's map of photos and other map sites use clustering to reduce the number of markers on a map. This makes it both faster and reduces the amount of visual clutter.

Computer science

Software evolution

Clustering is useful in software evolution as it helps to reduce legacy properties in code by reforming functionality that has become dispersed. It is a form of restructuring and hence is a way of direct preventative maintenance.

Image segmentation

Clustering can be used to divide a digital image into distinct regions for border detection or object recognition.

Evolutionary algorithms

Clustering may be used to identify different niches within the population of an evolutionary algorithm so that reproductive opportunity can be distributed more evenly amongst the evolving species or subspecies.

Recommender systems

Recommender systems are designed to recommend new items based on a user's tastes. They sometimes use clustering algorithms to predict a user's preferences based on the preferences of other users in the user's cluster.

Markov chain Monte Carlo methods

Clustering is often utilized to locate and characterize extrema in the target distribution.

Anomaly detection

Anomalies/outliers are typically - be it explicitly or implicitly - defined with respect to clustering structure in data.

Social science

Crime analysis

Cluster analysis can be used to identify areas where there are greater incidences of particular types of crime. By identifying these distinct areas or "hot spots" where a similar crime has happened over a period of time, it is possible to manage law enforcement resources more effectively.

Educational data mining

Cluster analysis is for example used to identify groups of schools or students with similar properties.

Typologies

From poll data, projects such as those undertaken by the Pew Research Center use cluster analysis to discern typologies of opinions, habits, and demographics that may be useful in politics and marketing.

Others

Field robotics

Clustering algorithms are used for robotic situational awareness to track objects and detect outliers in sensor data.

Mathematical chemistry

To find structural similarity, etc., for example, 3000 chemical compounds were clustered in the space of 90 topological indices.

Climatology

To find weather regimes or preferred sea level pressure atmospheric patterns.

Petroleum geology

Cluster analysis is used to reconstruct missing bottom hole core data or missing log curves in order to evaluate reservoir properties.

Physical geography

The clustering of chemical properties in different sample locations.

Software

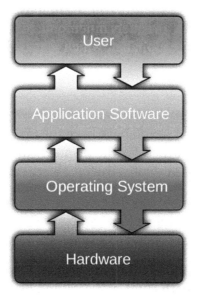

A diagram showing how the user interacts with application software on a typical desktop computer. The application software layer interfaces with the operating system, which in turn communicates with the hardware. The arrows indicate information

Computer software, or simply software, is that part of a computer system that consists of encoded information or computer instructions, in contrast to the physical hardware from which the system is built.

The term "software" was first proposed by Alan Turing and used in this sense by John W. Tukey in 1957. In computer science and software engineering, computer software is all information processed by computer systems, programs and data.

Computer software includes computer programs, libraries and related non-executable data, such as online documentation or digital media. Computer hardware and software require each other and neither can be realistically used on its own.

At the lowest level, executable code consists of machine language instructions specific to an individual processor—typically a central processing unit (CPU). A machine language consists of groups of binary values signifying processor instructions that change the state of the computer from its preceding state. For example, an instruction may change the value stored in a particular storage location in the computer—an effect that is not directly observable to the user. An instruction may also (indirectly) cause something to appear on a display of the computer system—a state change which should be visible to the user. The processor carries out the instructions in the order they are provided, unless it is instructed to "jump" to a different instruction, or interrupted.

The majority of software is written in high-level programming languages that are easier and more efficient for programmers, meaning closer to a natural language. High-level languages are translated into machine language using a compiler or an interpreter or a combination of the two. Software may also be written in a low-level assembly language, essentially, a vaguely mnemonic representation of a machine language using a natural language alphabet, which is translated into machine language using an assembler.

History

An outline (algorithm) for what would have been the first piece of software was written by Ada Lovelace in the 19th century, for the planned Analytical Engine. However, neither the Analytical Engine nor any software for it were ever created

The first theory about software—prior to creation of computers as we know them today—was proposed by Alan Turing in his 1935 essay Computable numbers with an application to the Entscheidungsproblem (decision problem).

This eventually led to the creation of the twin academic fields of computer science and software engineering, which both study software and its creation. Computer science is more theoretical (Turing's essay is an example of computer science), whereas software engineering focuses on more practical concerns.

However, prior to 1946, software as we now understand it—programs stored in the memory of stored-program digital computers—did not yet exist. The very first electronic computing devices were instead rewired in order to "reprogram" them.

Types of Software

On virtually all computer platforms, software can be grouped into a few broad categories.

Purpose, or Domain of Use

Based on the goal, computer software can be divided into:

- Application software, which is software that uses the computer system to perform special functions or provide entertainment functions beyond the basic operation of the computer itself. There are many different types of application software, because the range of tasks that can be performed with a modern computer is so large.

- System software, which is software that directly operates the computer hardware, to provide basic functionality needed by users and other software, and to provide a platform for running application software. System software includes:

    o Operating systems, which are essential collections of software that manage resources and provides common services for other software that runs "on top" of them. Supervisory programs, boot loaders, shells and window systems are core parts of operating systems. In practice, an operating system comes bundled with additional software (including application software) so that a user can potentially do some work with a computer that only has an operating system.

    o Device drivers, which operate or control a particular type of device that is attached to a computer. Each device needs at least one corresponding device driver; because a computer typically has at minimum at least one input device and at least one output device, a computer typically needs more than one device driver.

    o Utilities, which are computer programs designed to assist users in the maintenance and care of their computers.

- Malicious software or malware, which is software that is developed to harm and disrupt computers. As such, malware is undesirable. Malware is closely associated with computer-related crimes, though some malicious programs may have been designed as practical jokes.

Nature or Domain of Execution

- Desktop applications such as web browsers and Microsoft Office, as well as smartphone and tablet applications (called "apps"). (There is a push in some parts of the software industry to merge desktop applications with mobile apps, to some extent. Windows 8, and later Ubuntu Touch, tried to allow the same style of application user interface to be used on desktops, laptops and mobiles.)

- JavaScript scripts are pieces of software traditionally embedded in web pages that are run directly inside the web browser when a web page is loaded without the need for a web browser plugin. Software written in other programming languages can also be run within the web browser if the software is either translated into JavaScript, or if a web browser plugin that supports that language is installed; the most common example of the latter is ActionScript scripts, which are supported by the Adobe Flash plugin.

- Server software, including:

  o Web applications, which usually run on the web server and output dynamically generated web pages to web browsers, using e.g. PHP, Java, ASP.NET, or even JavaScript that runs on the server. In modern times these commonly include some JavaScript to be run in the web browser as well, in which case they typically run partly on the server, partly in the web browser.

- Plugins and extensions are software that extends or modifies the functionality of another piece of software, and require that software be used in order to function;

- Embedded software resides as firmware within embedded systems, devices dedicated to a single use or a few uses such as cars and televisions (although some embedded devices such as wireless chipsets can themselves be part of an ordinary, non-embedded computer system such as a PC or smartphone). In the embedded system context there is sometimes no clear distinction between the system software and the application software. However, some embedded systems run embedded operating systems, and these systems do retain the distinction between system software and application software (although typically there will only be one, fixed, application which is always run).

- Microcode is a special, relatively obscure type of embedded software which tells the processor itself how to execute machine code, so it is actually a lower level than machine code. It is typically proprietary to the processor manufacturer, and any necessary correctional microcode software updates are supplied by them to users (which is much cheaper than shipping replacement processor hardware). Thus an ordinary programmer would not expect to ever have to deal with it.

Programming Tools

Programming tools are also software in the form of programs or applications that software developers (also known as programmers, coders, hackers or software engineers) use to create, debug, maintain (i.e. improve or fix), or otherwise support software. Software is written in one or more programming languages; there are many programming languages in existence, and each has at least one implementation, each of which consists of its own set of programming tools. These tools may be relatively self-contained programs such as compilers, debuggers, interpreters, linkers, and text editors, that can be combined together to accomplish a task; or they may form an integrated development environment (IDE), which combines much or all of the functionality of such self-contained tools. IDEs may do this by either invoking the relevant individual tools or by re-implementing their functionality in a new way. An IDE can make it easier to do specific tasks, such as searching in files in a particular project. Many programming language implementations provide the option of using both individual tools or an IDE.

Software Topics

Architecture

Users often see things differently from programmers. People who use modern general purpose computers (as opposed to embedded systems, analog computers and super-computers) usually see three layers of software performing a variety of tasks: platform, application, and user software.

- Platform software: The Platform includes the firmware, device drivers, an operating system, and typically a graphical user interface which, in total, allow a user to interact with the computer and its peripherals (associated equipment). Platform software often comes bundled with the computer. On a PC one will usually have the ability to change the platform software.

- Application software: Application software or Applications are what most people think of when they think of software. Typical examples include office suites and video games. Application software is often purchased separately from computer hardware. Sometimes applications are bundled with the computer, but that does not change the fact that they run as independent applications. Applications are usually independent programs from the operating system, though they are often tailored for specific platforms. Most users think of compilers, databases, and other "system software" as applications.

- User-written software: End-user development tailors systems to meet users' specific needs. User software include spreadsheet templates and word processor templates. Even email filters are a kind of user software. Users create this software themselves and often overlook how important it is. Depending on how competently the user-written software has been integrated into default application packages, many users may not be aware of the distinction between the original packages, and what has been added by co-workers.

Execution

Computer software has to be "loaded" into the computer's storage (such as the hard drive or memory). Once the software has loaded, the computer is able to execute the software. This involves passing instructions from the application software, through the system software, to the hardware which ultimately receives the instruction as machine code. Each instruction causes the computer to carry out an operation—moving data, carrying out a computation, or altering the control flow of instructions.

Data movement is typically from one place in memory to another. Sometimes it involves moving data between memory and registers which enable high-speed data access in the CPU. Moving data, especially large amounts of it, can be costly. So, this is sometimes avoided by using "pointers" to data instead. Computations include simple operations such as incrementing the value of a variable data element. More complex computations may involve many operations and data elements together.

Quality and Reliability

Software quality is very important, especially for commercial and system software like Microsoft Office, Microsoft Windows and Linux. If software is faulty (buggy), it can delete a person's work, crash the computer and do other unexpected things. Faults and errors are called "bugs" which are often discovered during alpha and beta testing. Software is often also a victim to what is known as software aging, the progressive performance degradation resulting from a combination of unseen bugs.

Many bugs are discovered and eliminated (debugged) through software testing. However, software testing rarely—if ever—eliminates every bug; some programmers say that "every program has at least one more bug" (Lubarsky's Law). In the waterfall method of software development, separate testing teams are typically employed, but in newer approaches, collectively termed agile software development, developers often do all their own testing, and demonstrate the software to users/clients regularly to obtain feedback. Software can be tested through unit testing, regression testing and other methods, which are done manually, or most commonly, automatically, since the amount of code to be tested can be quite large. For instance, NASA has extremely rigorous software testing procedures for many operating systems and communication functions. Many NASA-based operations interact and identify each other through command programs. This enables many people who work at NASA to check and evaluate functional systems overall. Programs containing command software enable hardware engineering and system operations to function much easier together.

License

The software's license gives the user the right to use the software in the licensed environment, and in the case of free software licenses, also grants other rights such as the right to make copies.

Proprietary software can be divided into two types:

- freeware, which includes the category of "free trial" software or "freemium" software (in the past, the term shareware was often used for free trial/freemium software). As the name suggests, freeware can be used for free, although in the case of free trials or freemium software, this is sometimes only true for a limited period of time or with limited functionality.

- software available for a fee, often inaccurately termed "commercial software", which can only be legally used on purchase of a license.

Open source software, on the other hand, comes with a free software license, granting the recipient the rights to modify and redistribute the software.

Patents

Software patents, like other types of patents, are theoretically supposed to give an inventor an exclusive, time-limited license for a detailed idea (e.g. an algorithm) on how to implement a piece of software, or a component of a piece of software. Ideas for useful things that software could do, and user requirements, are not supposed to be patentable, and concrete implementations (i.e. the actual software packages implementing the patent) are not supposed to be patentable either—the latter are already covered by copyright, generally automatically. So software patents are supposed to cover the middle area, between requirements and concrete implementation. In some countries, a requirement for the claimed invention to have an effect on the physical world may also be part of the requirements for a software patent to be held valid—although since all useful software has effects on the physical world, this requirement may be open to debate.

Software patents are controversial in the software industry with many people holding different views about them. One of the sources of controversy is that the aforementioned split between initial ideas and patent does not seem to be honored in practice by patent lawyers—for example the patent for Aspect-Oriented Programming (AOP), which purported to claim rights over any programming tool implementing the idea of AOP, howsoever implemented. Another source of controversy is the effect on innovation, with many distinguished experts and companies arguing that software is such a fast-moving field that software patents merely create vast additional litigation costs and risks, and actually retard innovation. In the case of debates about software patents outside the US, the argument has been made that large American corporations and patent lawyers are likely to be the primary beneficiaries of allowing or continue to allow software patents.

Design and Implementation

Design and implementation of software varies depending on the complexity of the software. For instance, the design and creation of Microsoft Word took much more time than designing and developing Microsoft Notepad because the latter has much more basic functionality.

Software is usually designed and created (a.k.a. coded/written/programmed) in integrated development environments (IDE) like Eclipse, IntelliJ and Microsoft Visual Studio that can simplify the process and compile the software (if applicable). As noted in a different section, software is usually created on top of existing software and the application programming interface (API) that the underlying software provides like GTK+, JavaBeans or Swing. Libraries (APIs) can be categorized by their purpose. For instance, the Spring Framework is used for implementing enterprise applications, the Windows Forms library is used for designing graphical user interface (GUI) applications like Microsoft Word, and Windows Communication Foundation is used for designing web services. When a program is designed, it relies upon the API. For instance, if a user is designing a Microsoft Windows desktop application, he or she might use the .NET Windows Forms library to design the desktop application and call its APIs like Form1.Close() and Form1.Show() to close or open the application, and write the additional operations him/herself that it needs to have. Without these APIs, the programmer needs to write these APIs him/herself. Companies like Oracle and Microsoft provide their own APIs so that many applications are written using their software libraries that usually have numerous APIs in them.

Data structures such as hash tables, arrays, and binary trees, and algorithms such as quicksort, can be useful for creating software.

Computer software has special economic characteristics that make its design, creation, and distribution different from most other economic goods.

A person who creates software is called a programmer, software engineer or software developer, terms that all have a similar meaning. More informal terms for programmer also exist such as "coder" and "hacker" – although use of the latter word may cause confusion, because it is more often used to mean someone who illegally breaks into computer systems.

Industry and Organizations

A great variety of software companies and programmers in the world comprise a software industry. Software can be quite a profitable industry: Bill Gates, the founder of Microsoft was the richest person in the world in 2009, largely due to his ownership of a significant number of shares in Microsoft, the company responsible for Microsoft Windows and Microsoft Office software products.

Non-profit software organizations include the Free Software Foundation, GNU Project and Mozilla Foundation. Software standard organizations like the W3C,

IETF develop recommended software standards such as XML, HTTP and HTML, so that software can interoperate through these standards.

Other well-known large software companies include Oracle, Novell, SAP, Symantec, Adobe Systems, and Corel, while small companies often provide innovation.

Internet

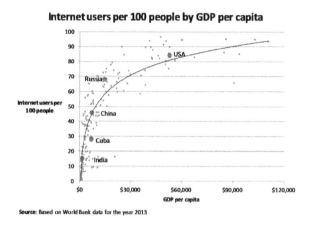

Internet users per 100 people by GDP per capita

Source: Based on World Bank data for the year 2013

Internet users per 100 population members and GDP per capita for selected countries.

The Internet is the global system of interconnected computer networks that use the Internet protocol suite (TCP/IP) to link billions of devices worldwide. It is a network of networks that consists of millions of private, public, academic, business, and government networks of local to global scope, linked by a broad array of electronic, wireless, and optical networking technologies. The Internet carries an extensive range of information resources and services, such as the inter-linked hypertext documents and applications of the World Wide Web (WWW), electronic mail, newsgroups, voice over IP telephony, and peer-to-peer networks for file sharing.

The origins of the Internet date back to research commissioned by the United States federal government in the 1960s to build robust, fault-tolerant communication via computer networks. The primary precursor network, the ARPANET, initially served as a backbone for interconnection of regional academic and military networks in the 1980s. The funding of the National Science Foundation Network as a new backbone in the 1980s, as well as private funding for other commercial extensions, led to worldwide participation in the development of new networking technologies, and the merger of many networks. The linking of commercial networks and enterprises by the early 1990s marks the beginning of the transition to the modern Internet, and generated a sustained exponential growth as generations of institutional, personal, and mobile computers were connected to the network. Although the Internet was widely used by academia since the 1980s, the commercialization incorporated its services and technologies into virtually every aspect of modern life.

Internet use grew rapidly in the West from the mid-1990s and from the late 1990s in the developing world. In the 20 years since 1995, Internet use has grown 100-times, measured for the period of one year, to over one third of the world population. Most traditional communications media, including telephony, radio, television, paper mail and newspapers are being reshaped or redefined by the Internet, giving birth to new services such as email, Internet telephony, Internet television music, digital newspapers, and video streaming websites. Newspaper, book, and other print publishing are adapting to website technology, or are reshaped into blogging, web feeds and online news aggregators (e.g., Google News). The entertainment industry was initially the fastest growing segment on the Internet. The Internet has enabled and accelerated new forms of personal interactions through instant messaging, Internet forums, and social networking. Online shopping has grown exponentially both for major retailers and small businesses and entrepreneurs, as it enables firms to extend their "bricks and mortar" presence to serve a larger market or even sell goods and services entirely online. Business-to-business and financial services on the Internet affect supply chains across entire industries.

The Internet has no centralized governance in either technological implementation or policies for access and usage; each constituent network sets its own policies. Only the overreaching definitions of the two principal name spaces in the Internet, the Internet Protocol address space and the Domain Name System (DNS), are directed by a maintainer organization, the Internet Corporation for Assigned Names and Numbers (ICANN). The technical underpinning and standardization of the core protocols is an activity of the Internet Engineering Task Force (IETF), a non-profit organization of loosely affiliated international participants that anyone may associate with by contributing technical expertise.

Terminology

The Internet Messenger by Buky Schwartz in Holon, Israel.

The term Internet, when used to refer to the specific global system of interconnected Internet Protocol (IP) networks, is a proper noun and may be written with an initial capital letter. In common use and the media, it is often not capitalized, viz. the internet. Some guides specify that the word should be capitalized when used as a noun, but not capitalized when used as an adjective. The Internet is also often referred to as the Net, as a short form of network. Historically, as early as 1849, the word internetted was used uncapitalized as an adjective, meaning interconnected or interwoven. The designers of early computer networks used internet both as a noun and as a verb in shorthand form of internetwork or internetworking, meaning interconnecting computer networks.

The terms Internet and World Wide Web are often used interchangeably in everyday speech; it is common to speak of "going on the Internet" when invoking a web browser to view web pages. However, the World Wide Web or the Web is only one of a large number of Internet services. The Web is a collection of interconnected documents (web pages) and other web resources, linked by hyperlinks and URLs. As another point of comparison, Hypertext Transfer Protocol, or HTTP, is the language used on the Web for information transfer, yet it is just one of many languages or protocols that can be used for communication on the Internet. The term Interweb is a portmanteau of Internet and World Wide Web typically used sarcastically to parody a technically unsavvy user.

History

Research into packet switching started in the early 1960s, and packet switched networks such as the ARPANET, CYCLADES, the Merit Network, NPL network, Tymnet, and Telenet, were developed in the late 1960s and 1970s using a variety of protocols. The ARPANET project led to the development of protocols for internetworking, by which multiple separate networks could be joined into a single network of networks. ARPANET development began with two network nodes which were interconnected between the Network Measurement Center at the University of California, Los Angeles (UCLA) Henry Samueli School of Engineering and Applied Science directed by Leonard Kleinrock, and the NLS system at SRI International (SRI) by Douglas Engelbart in Menlo Park, California, on 29 October 1969. The third site was the Culler-Fried Interactive Mathematics Center at the University of California, Santa Barbara, followed by the University of Utah Graphics Department. In an early sign of future growth, fifteen sites were connected to the young ARPANET by the end of 1971. These early years were documented in the 1972 film Computer Networks: The Heralds of Resource Sharing.

Early international collaborations on the ARPANET were rare. European developers were concerned with developing the X.25 networks. Notable exceptions were the Norwegian Seismic Array (NORSAR) in June 1973, followed in 1973 by Sweden with satellite links to the Tanum Earth Station and Peter T. Kirstein's research group in the United Kingdom, initially at the Institute of Computer Science, University of London and later at University College London. In December 1974, RFC 675 (Specification of Internet Transmission Control Program), by Vinton Cerf, Yogen Dalal, and Carl Sunshine, used the term internet as a shorthand for internetworking and later RFCs repeated this use. Access to the ARPANET was expanded in 1981 when the National Science Foundation (NSF) funded the Computer Science Network (CSNET). In 1982, the Internet Protocol Suite (TCP/IP) was standardized, which permitted worldwide proliferation of interconnected networks.

NSFNET T3 Network 1992

T3 NSFNET Backbone, c. 1992.

TCP/IP network access expanded again in 1986 when the National Science Foundation Network (NSFNet) provided access to supercomputer sites in the United States for researchers, first at speeds of 56 kbit/s and later at 1.5 Mbit/s and 45 Mbit/s. Commercial Internet service providers (ISPs) emerged in the late 1980s and early 1990s. The ARPANET was decommissioned in 1990. By 1995, the Internet was fully commercialized in the U.S. when the NSFNet was decommissioned, removing the last restrictions on use of the Internet to carry commercial traffic. The Internet rapidly expanded in Europe and Australia in the mid to late 1980s and to Asia in the late 1980s and early 1990s. The beginning of dedicated transatlantic communication between the NSFNET and networks in Europe was established with a low-speed satellite relay between Princeton University and Stockholm, Sweden in December 1988. Although other network protocols such as UUCP had global reach well before this time, this marked the beginning of the Internet as an intercontinental network.

Slightly over a year later in March 1990, the first high-speed T1 (1.5 Mbit/s) link between the NSFNET and Europe was installed between Cornell University and CERN, allowing much more robust communications than were capable with satellites. Six months later Tim Berners-Lee would begin writing WorldWideWeb, the first web browser after two years of lobbying CERN management. By Christmas 1990, Berners-Lee had built all the tools necessary for a working Web: the HyperText Transfer Protocol (HTTP) 0.9, the HyperText Markup Language (HTML), the first Web browser (which was also a HTML editor and could access Usenet newsgroups and FTP files), the first HTTP server software (later known as CERN httpd), the first web server (http://info.cern.ch), and the first Web pages that described the project itself. Public commercial use of the Internet began in mid-1989 with the connection of MCI Mail and Compuserve's email capabilities to the 500,000 users of the Internet. Just months later on January 1, 1990, PSI-net launched an alternate Internet backbone for commercial use; one of the networks that would grow into the commercial Internet we know today. In 1991 the Commercial Internet eXchange was founded, allowing PSInet to communicate with the other commercial networks CERFnet and Alternet. Since 1995 the Internet has tremendously impacted culture and commerce, including the rise of near instant communication by email, instant messaging, telephony (Voice over Internet Protocol or VoIP), two-way interactive video calls, and the World Wide Web with its discussion forums, blogs, social networking, and online shopping sites. Increasing amounts of data are transmitted at higher and higher speeds over fiber optic networks operating at 1-Gbit/s, 10-Gbit/s, or more.

Worldwide Internet users			
	2005	2010	2014[a]
World population	6.5 billion	6.9 billion	7.2 billion
Not using the Internet	84%	70%	60%
Using the Internet	16%	30%	40%
Users in the developing world	8%	21%	32%
Users in the developed world	51%	67%	78%
[a] Estimate. Source: International Telecommunications Union.			

The Internet continues to grow, driven by ever greater amounts of online information and knowledge, commerce, entertainment and social networking. During the late 1990s, it was estimated that traffic on the public Internet grew by 100 percent per year, while the mean annual growth in the number of Internet users was thought to be between 20% and 50%. This growth is often attributed to the lack of central administration, which allows organic growth of the network, as well as the non-proprietary nature of the Internet protocols, which encourages vendor interoperability and prevents any one company from exerting too much control over the network. As of 31 March 2011, the estimated total number of Internet users was 2.095 billion (30.2% of world population). It is estimated that in 1993 the Internet carried only 1% of the information flowing through two-way telecommunication, by 2000 this figure had grown to 51%, and by 2007 more than 97% of all telecommunicated information was carried over the Internet.

Governance

The Internet is a global network comprising many voluntarily interconnected autonomous networks. It operates without a central governing body. The technical underpinning and standardization of the core protocols (IPv4 and IPv6) is an activity of the Internet Engineering Task Force (IETF), a non-profit organization of loosely affiliated international participants that anyone may associate with by contributing technical expertise. To maintain interoperability, the principal name spaces of the Internet are administered by the Internet Corporation for Assigned Names and Numbers (ICANN). ICANN is governed by an international board of directors drawn from across the Internet technical, business, academic, and other non-commercial communities. ICANN coordinates the assignment of unique identifiers for use on the Internet, including domain names, Internet Protocol (IP) addresses, application port numbers in the transport protocols, and many other parameters. Globally unified name spaces are essential for maintaining the global reach of the Internet. This role of ICANN distinguishes it as perhaps the only central coordinating body for the global Internet.

ICANN headquarters in the Playa Vista neighborhood of Los Angeles, California, United States.

Regional Internet Registries (RIRs) allocate IP addresses:

- African Network Information Center (AfriNIC) for Africa

- American Registry for Internet Numbers (ARIN) for North America

- Asia-Pacific Network Information Centre (APNIC) for Asia and the Pacific region

- Latin American and Caribbean Internet Addresses Registry (LACNIC) for Latin America and the Caribbean region

- Réseaux IP Européens – Network Coordination Centre (RIPE NCC) for Europe, the Middle East, and Central Asia

The National Telecommunications and Information Administration, an agency of the United States Department of Commerce, continues to have final approval over changes to the DNS root zone. The Internet Society (ISOC) was founded in 1992 with a mission to "assure the open development, evolution and use of the Internet for the benefit of all people throughout the world". Its members include individuals (anyone may join) as well as corporations, organizations, governments, and universities. Among other activities ISOC provides an administrative home for a number of less formally organized groups that are involved in developing and managing the Internet, including: the Internet Engineering Task Force (IETF), Internet Architecture Board (IAB), Internet

Engineering Steering Group (IESG), Internet Research Task Force (IRTF), and Internet Research Steering Group (IRSG). On 16 November 2005, the United Nations-sponsored World Summit on the Information Society in Tunis established the Internet Governance Forum (IGF) to discuss Internet-related issues.

Infrastructure

2007 map showing submarine fiberoptic telecommunication cables around the world.

The communications infrastructure of the Internet consists of its hardware components and a system of software layers that control various aspects of the architecture.

Routing and Service Tiers

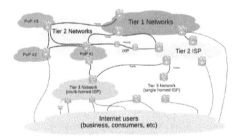

Packet routing across the Internet involves several tiers of Internet service providers.

Internet service providers establish the worldwide connectivity between individual networks at various levels of scope. End-users who only access the Internet when needed to perform a function or obtain information, represent the bottom of the routing hierarchy. At the top of the routing hierarchy are the tier 1 networks, large telecommunication companies that exchange traffic directly with each other via peering agreements. Tier 2 and lower level networks buy Internet transit from other providers to reach at least some parties on the global Internet, though they may also engage in peering. An ISP may use a single upstream provider for connectivity, or implement multihoming to achieve redundancy and load balancing. Internet exchange points are major traffic exchanges with physical connections to multiple ISPs. Large organizations, such as academic institutions, large enterprises, and governments, may perform the same function as ISPs, engaging in peering and purchasing transit on behalf of their internal networks. Research networks tend to interconnect with large subnetworks such as GEANT, GLORIAD, Internet2, and the UK's national research and education network, JANET. Both the Internet IP routing structure and hypertext links of the World Wide Web are examples of scale-free networks. Computers and routers use routing tables in their operating system to direct IP packets to the next-hop router or destination. Routing tables are maintained by manual configuration or automatically by routing protocols. End-nodes typically use a default route that points toward an ISP providing transit, while ISP routers use the Border Gateway Protocol to establish the most efficient routing across the complex connections of the global Internet.

Access

Common methods of Internet access by users include dial-up with a computer modem via telephone circuits, broadband over coaxial cable, fiber optics or copper wires, Wi-Fi, satellite and cellular telephone technology (3G, 4G). The Internet may often be accessed from computers in libraries and Internet cafes. Internet access points exist in many public places such as airport halls and coffee shops. Various terms are used, such as public Internet kiosk, public access terminal, and Web payphone. Many hotels also have public terminals, though these are usually fee-based. These terminals are widely accessed for various usages, such as ticket booking, bank deposit, or online payment. Wi-Fi provides wireless access to the Internet via local computer networks. Hotspots providing such access include Wi-Fi cafes, where users need to bring their own wireless devices such as a laptop or PDA. These services may be free to all, free to customers only, or fee-based.

Grassroots efforts have led to wireless community networks. Commercial Wi-Fi services covering large city areas are in place in New York, London, Vienna, Toronto, San Francisco, Philadelphia, Chicago and Pittsburgh. The Internet can then be accessed from such places as a park bench. Apart from Wi-Fi, there have been experiments with proprietary mobile wireless networks like Ricochet, various high-speed data services over cellular phone networks, and fixed wireless services. High-end mobile phones such as smartphones in general come with Internet access through the phone network. Web browsers such as Opera are available on these advanced handsets, which can also run a wide variety of other Internet software. More mobile phones have Internet access than PCs, though this is not as widely used. An Internet access provider and protocol matrix differentiates the methods used to get online.

Structure

Many computer scientists describe the Internet as a "prime example of a large-scale, highly engineered, yet highly complex system". The structure was found to be highly robust to random failures, yet, very vulnerable to intentional attacks. The Internet structure and its usage characteristics have been studied extensively and the possibility of developing alternative structures has been investigated.

Protocols

While the hardware components in the Internet infrastructure can often be used to support other software systems, it is the design and the standardization process of the software that characterizes the Internet and provides the foundation for its scalability and success. The responsibility for the architectural design of the Internet software systems has been assumed by the Internet Engineering Task Force (IETF). The IETF conducts standard-setting work groups, open to any individual, about the various aspects of Internet architecture. Resulting contributions and standards are published as Request for Comments (RFC) documents on the IETF web site. The principal methods of networking that enable the Internet are contained in specially designated RFCs that constitute the Internet Standards. Other less rigorous documents are simply informative, experimental, or historical, or document the best current practices (BCP) when implementing Internet technologies.

The Internet standards describe a framework known as the Internet protocol suite. This is a model architecture that divides methods into a layered system of protocols, originally documented in RFC 1122 and RFC 1123. The layers correspond to the environment or scope in which their services operate. At the top is the application layer, space for the application-specific networking methods used in software applications. For example, a web browser program uses the client-server application model and a specific protocol of interaction between servers and clients, while many file-sharing systems use a peer-to-peer paradigm. Below this top layer, the transport layer connects applications on different hosts with a logical channel through the network with appropriate data exchange methods.

Underlying these layers are the networking technologies that interconnect networks at their borders and hosts via the physical connections. The Internet layer enables computers to identify and locate each other via Internet Protocol (IP) addresses, and routes their traffic via intermediate (transit) networks. Last, at the bottom of the architecture is the link layer, which provides connectivity between hosts on the same network link, such as a physical connection in the form of a local area network (LAN) or a dial-up connection. The model, also known as TCP/IP, is designed to be independent of the underlying hardware, which the model, therefore, does not concern itself with in any detail. Other models have been developed, such as the OSI model, that attempt to be comprehensive in every aspect of communications. While many similarities exist between the models, they are not compatible in the details of description or implementation; indeed, TCP/IP protocols are usually included in the discussion of OSI networking.

The most prominent component of the Internet model is the Internet Protocol (IP), which provides addressing systems (IP addresses) for computers on the Internet. IP enables internetworking and, in essence, establishes the Internet itself. Internet Protocol Version 4 (IPv4) is the initial version used on the first generation of the Internet and is still in dominant use. It was designed to address up to ~4.3 billion (10^9) Internet hosts. However, the explosive growth of the Internet has led to IPv4 address exhaustion, which entered its final stage in 2011, when the global address allocation pool was exhausted. A new protocol version, IPv6, was developed in the mid-1990s, which provides vastly larger addressing capabilities and more efficient routing of Internet traffic. IPv6 is currently in growing deployment around the world, since Internet address registries (RIRs) began to urge all resource managers to plan rapid adoption and conversion.

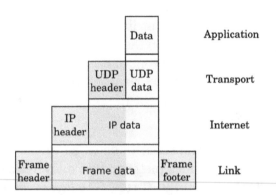

As user data is processed through the protocol stack, each abstraction layer adds encapsulation information at the sending host. Data is transmitted over the wire at the link level between hosts and routers. Encapsulation is removed by the receiving host. Intermediate relays update link encapsulation at each hop, and inspect the IP layer for routing purposes.

IPv6 is not directly interoperable by design with IPv4. In essence, it establishes a parallel version of the Internet not directly accessible with IPv4 software. Thus, translation facilities must exist for internetworking or nodes must have duplicate networking software for both networks. Essentially all modern computer operating systems support both versions of the Internet Protocol. Network infrastructure, however, is still lagging in this development. Aside from the complex array of physical connections that make up its infrastructure, the Internet is facilitated by bi- or multi-lateral commercial contracts, e.g., peering agreements, and by technical specifications or protocols that describe the exchange of data over the network. Indeed, the Internet is defined by its interconnections and routing policies.

Services

The Internet carries many network services, most prominently mobile apps such as social media apps, the World Wide Web, electronic mail, multiplayer online games, Internet telephony, and file sharing services.

World Wide Web

Many people use the terms Internet and World Wide Web, or just the Web, interchangeably, but the two terms are not synonymous. The World Wide Web is the primary application that billions of people use on the Internet, and it has changed their lives immeasurably. However, the Internet provides many other services. The Web is a global set of documents, images and other resources, logically interrelated by hyperlinks and referenced with Uniform Resource Identifiers (URIs). URIs symbolically identify services, servers, and other databases, and the documents and resources that they can provide. Hypertext Transfer Protocol (HTTP) is the main access protocol of the World Wide Web. Web services also use HTTP to allow software systems to communicate in order to share and exchange business logic and data.

This NeXT Computer was used by Tim Berners-Lee at CERN and became the world's first Web server.

World Wide Web browser software, such as Microsoft's Internet Explorer, Mozilla Firefox, Opera, Apple's Safari, and Google Chrome, lets users navigate from one web page to another via hyperlinks embedded in the documents. These documents may also contain any combination of computer data, including graphics, sounds, text, video, multimedia and interactive content that runs while the user is interacting with the page. Client-side software can include animations, games, office applications and scientific demonstrations. Through keyword-driven Internet research using search engines like Yahoo! and Google, users worldwide have easy, instant access to a vast and diverse amount of online information. Compared to printed media, books, encyclopedias and traditional libraries, the World Wide Web has enabled the decentralization of information on a large scale.

The Web has also enabled individuals and organizations to publish ideas and information to a potentially large audience online at greatly reduced expense and time delay. Publishing a web page, a blog, or building a website involves little initial cost and many cost-free services are available. However, publishing and maintaining large, professional web sites with attractive, diverse and up-to-date information is still a difficult and expensive proposition. Many individuals and some companies and groups use web logs or blogs, which are largely used as easily updatable online diaries. Some commercial organizations encourage staff to communicate advice in their areas of specialization in the hope that visitors will be impressed by the expert knowledge and free information, and be attracted to the corporation as a result.

One example of this practice is Microsoft, whose product developers publish their personal blogs in order to pique the public's interest in their work.Collections of personal web pages published by large service providers remain popular and have become increasingly sophisticated. Whereas operations such as Angelfire and GeoCities have existed since the early days of the Web, newer offerings from, for example, Facebook and Twitter currently have large followings. These operations often brand themselves as social network services rather than simply as web page hosts.

Advertising on popular web pages can be lucrative, and e-commerce or the sale of products and services directly via the Web continues to grow. Online advertising is a form of marketing and advertising which uses the Internet to deliver promotional marketing messages to consumers. It includes email marketing, search engine marketing (SEM), social media marketing, many types of display advertising (including web banner advertising), and mobile advertising. In 2011, Internet advertising revenues in the United States surpassed those of cable television and nearly exceeded those of broadcast television.Many common online advertising practices are controversial and increasingly subject to regulation.

When the Web developed in the 1990s, a typical web page was stored in completed form on a web server, formatted in HTML, complete for transmission to a web browser in response to a request. Over time, the process of creating and serving web pages has become dynamic, creating a flexible design, layout, and content. Websites are often created using content management software with, initially, very little content. Contributors to these systems, who may be paid staff, members of an organization or the public, fill underlying databases with content using editing pages designed for that purpose while casual visitors view and read this content in HTML form. There may or may not be editorial, approval and security systems built into the process of taking newly entered content and making it available to the target visitors.

Communication

Email is an important communications service available on the Internet. The concept of sending electronic text messages between parties in a way analogous to mailing letters or memos predates the creation of the Internet. Pictures, documents, and other files are sent as email attachments. Emails can be cc-ed to multiple email addresses.

Internet telephony is another common communications service made possible by the creation of the Internet. VoIP stands for Voice-over-Internet Protocol, referring to the protocol that underlies all Internet communication. The idea began in the early 1990s with walkie-talkie-like voice applications for personal computers. In recent years many VoIP systems have become as easy to use and as convenient as a normal telephone. The benefit is that, as the Internet carries the voice traffic, VoIP can be free or cost much less than a traditional telephone call, especially over long distances and especially for those with always-on Internet connections such as cable or ADSL. VoIP is maturing into a competitive alternative to traditional telephone service. Interoperability between different providers has improved and the ability to call or receive a call from a traditional telephone is available. Simple, inexpensive VoIP network adapters are available that eliminate the need for a personal computer.

Voice quality can still vary from call to call, but is often equal to and can even exceed that of traditional calls. Remaining problems for VoIP include emergency telephone number dialing and reliability. Currently, a few VoIP providers provide an emergency service, but it is not universally available. Older traditional phones with no "extra features" may be line-powered only and operate during a power failure; VoIP can never do so without a backup power source for the phone equipment and the Internet access devices. VoIP has also become increasingly popular for gaming applications, as a form of communication between players. Popular VoIP clients for gaming include Ventrilo and Teamspeak. Modern video game consoles also offer VoIP chat features.

Data Transfer

File sharing is an example of transferring large amounts of data across the Internet. A computer file can be emailed to customers, colleagues and friends as an attachment. It can be uploaded to a website or File Transfer Protocol (FTP) server for easy download by others. It can be put into a "shared location" or onto a file server for instant use by colleagues. The load of bulk downloads to many users can be eased by the use of "mirror" servers or peer-to-peer networks. In any of these cases, access to the file may be controlled by user authentication, the transit of the file over the Internet may be obscured by encryption, and money may change hands for access to the file. The price can be paid by the remote charging of funds from, for example, a credit card whose details are also passed – usually fully encrypted – across the Internet. The origin and authenticity of the file received may be checked by digital signatures or by MD5 or other message digests. These simple features of the Internet, over a worldwide basis, are changing the production, sale, and distribution of anything that can be reduced to a computer file for transmission. This includes all manner of print publications, software products, news, music, film, video, photography, graphics and the other arts. This in turn has caused seismic shifts in each of the existing industries that previously controlled the production and distribution of these products.

Streaming media is the real-time delivery of digital media for the immediate consumption or enjoyment by end users. Many radio and television broadcasters provide Internet feeds of their live audio and video productions. They may also allow time-shift viewing or listening such as Preview, Classic Clips and Listen Again features. These providers have been joined by a range of pure Internet "broadcasters" who never had on-air licenses. This means that an Internet-connected device, such as a computer or something more specific, can be used to access on-line media in much the same way as was previously possible only with a television or radio receiver. The range of available types of content is much wider, from specialized technical webcasts to on-demand popular multimedia services. Podcasting is a variation on this theme, where – usually audio – material is downloaded and played back on a computer or shifted to a portable media player to be listened to on the move. These techniques using simple equipment allow anybody, with little censorship or licensing control, to broadcast audio-visual material worldwide.

Digital media streaming increases the demand for network bandwidth. For example, standard image quality needs 1 Mbit/s link speed for SD 480p, HD 720p quality requires 2.5 Mbit/s, and the top-of-the-line HDX quality needs 4.5 Mbit/s for 1080p.

Webcams are a low-cost extension of this phenomenon. While some webcams can give full-frame-rate video, the picture either is usually small or updates slowly. Internet users can watch animals around an African waterhole, ships in the Panama Canal, traffic at a local roundabout or monitor their own premises, live and in real time. Video chat rooms and video conferencing are also popular with many uses being found for personal webcams, with and without two-way sound. YouTube was founded on 15 February 2005 and is now the leading website for free streaming video with a vast number of users. It uses a flash-based web player to stream and show video files. Registered users may upload an unlimited amount of video and build their own personal profile. YouTube claims that its users watch hundreds of millions, and upload hundreds of thousands of videos daily. Currently, YouTube also uses an HTML5 player.

Social Impact

The Internet has enabled new forms of social interaction, activities, and social associations. This phenomenon has given rise to the scholarly study of the sociology of the Internet.

Users

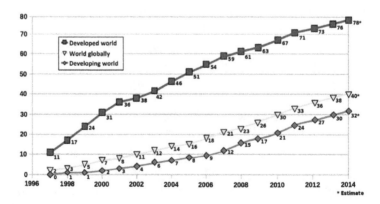

Internet users per 100 inhabitants

Source: International Telecommunications Union.

Internet usage has seen tremendous growth. From 2000 to 2009, the number of Internet users globally rose from 394 million to 1.858 billion. By 2010, 22 percent of the world's population had access to computers with 1 billion Google searches every day, 300 million Internet users reading blogs, and 2 billion videos viewed daily on YouTube. In 2014 the world's Internet users surpassed 3 billion or 43.6 percent of world population, but two-thirds of the users came from richest countries, with 78.0 percent of Europe countries population using the Internet, followed by 57.4 percent of the Americas.

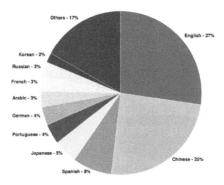

Internet users by language

The prevalent language for communication on the Internet has been English. This may be a result of the origin of the Internet, as well as the language's role as a lingua franca. Early computer systems were limited to the characters in the American Standard Code for Information Interchange (ASCII), a subset of the Latin alphabet.

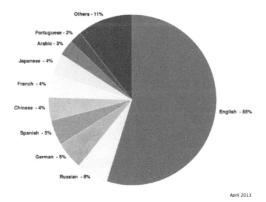

Website content languages

After English (27%), the most requested languages on the World Wide Web are Chinese (25%), Spanish (8%), Japanese (5%), Portuguese and German (4% each), Arabic, French and Russian (3% each), and Korean (2%). By region, 42% of the world's Internet users are based in Asia, 24% in Europe, 14% in North America, 10% in Latin America and the Caribbean taken together, 6% in Africa, 3% in the Middle East and 1% in Australia/Oceania. The Internet's technologies have developed enough in recent years, especially in the use of Unicode, that good facilities are available for development and communication in the world's widely used languages. However, some glitches such as mojibake (incorrect display of some languages' characters) still remain.

In an American study in 2005, the percentage of men using the Internet was very slightly ahead of the percentage of women, although this difference reversed in those under 30.

Men logged on more often, spent more time online, and were more likely to be broadband users, whereas women tended to make more use of opportunities to communicate (such as email). Men were more likely to use the Internet to pay bills, participate in auctions, and for recreation such as downloading music and videos. Men and women were equally likely to use the Internet for shopping and banking. More recent studies indicate that in 2008, women significantly outnumbered men on most social networking sites, such as Facebook and Myspace, although the ratios varied with age. In addition, women watched more streaming content, whereas men downloaded more. In terms of blogs, men were more likely to blog in the first place; among those who blog, men were more likely to have a professional blog, whereas women were more likely to have a personal blog.

According to forecasts by Euromonitor International, 44% of the world's population will be users of the Internet by 2020. Splitting by country, in 2012 Iceland, Norway, Sweden, the Netherlands, and Denmark had the highest Internet penetration by the number of users, with 93% or more of the population with access.

Several neologisms exist that refer to Internet users: Netizen (as in as in "citizen of the net") refers to those actively involved in improving online communities, the Internet in general or surrounding political affairs and rights such as free speech, Internaut refers to operators or technically highly capable users of the Internet, digital citizen refers to a person using the Internet in order to engage in society, politics, and government participation.

Usage

The Internet allows greater flexibility in working hours and location, especially with the spread of unmetered high-speed connections. The Internet can be accessed almost anywhere by numerous means, including through mobile Internet devices. Mobile phones, datacards, handheld game consoles and cellular routers allow users to connect to the Internet wirelessly. Within the limitations imposed by small screens and other limited facilities of such pocket-sized devices, the services of the Internet, including email and the web, may be available. Service providers may restrict the services offered and mobile data charges may be significantly higher than other access methods.

Educational material at all levels from pre-school to post-doctoral is available from websites. Examples range from CBeebies, through school and high-school revision guides and virtual universities, to access to top-end scholarly literature through the likes of Google Scholar. For distance education, help with homework and other assignments, self-guided learning, whiling away spare time, or just looking up more detail on an interesting fact, it has never been easier for people to access educational information at any level from anywhere. The Internet in general and the World Wide Web in particular are important enablers of both formal and informal education. Further, the Internet allows universities, in particular, researchers from the social and behavioral sciences, to conduct research remotely via virtual laboratories, with profound changes in reach and generalizability of findings as well as in communication between scientists and in the publication of results.

The low cost and nearly instantaneous sharing of ideas, knowledge, and skills have made collaborative work dramatically easier, with the help of collaborative software. Not only can a group cheaply communicate and share ideas but the wide reach of the Internet allows such groups more easily to form. An example of this is the free software movement, which has produced, among other things, Linux, Mozilla Firefox, and OpenOffice.org. Internet chat, whether using an IRC chat room, an instant messaging system, or a social networking website, allows colleagues to stay in touch in a very convenient way while working at their computers during the day. Messages can be exchanged even more quickly and conveniently than via email. These systems may allow files to be exchanged, drawings and images to be shared, or voice and video contact between team members.

Content management systems allow collaborating teams to work on shared sets of documents simultaneously without accidentally destroying each other's work. Business and project teams can share calendars as well as documents and other information. Such collaboration occurs in a wide variety of areas including scientific research, software development, conference planning, political activism and creative writing. Social and political collaboration is also becoming more widespread as both Internet access and computer literacy spread.

The Internet allows computer users to remotely access other computers and information stores easily from any access point. Access may be with computer security, i.e. authentication and encryption technologies, depending on the requirements. This is encouraging new ways of working from home, collaboration and information sharing in many industries. An accountant sitting at home can audit the books of a company based in another country, on a server situated in a third country that is remotely maintained by IT specialists in a fourth. These accounts could have been created by home-working bookkeepers, in other remote locations, based on information emailed to them from offices all over the world. Some of these things were possible before the widespread use of the Internet, but the cost of private leased lines would have made many of them infeasible in practice. An office worker away from their desk, perhaps on the other side of the world on a business trip or a holiday, can access their emails, access their data using cloud computing, or open a remote desktop session into their office PC using a secure virtual private network (VPN) connection on the Internet. This can give the worker complete access to all of their normal files and data, including email and other applications, while away from the office. It has been referred to among system administrators as the Virtual Private Nightmare, because it extends the secure perimeter of a corporate network into remote locations and its employees' homes.

Social Networking and Entertainment

Many people use the World Wide Web to access news, weather and sports reports, to plan and book vacations and to pursue their personal interests. People use chat, messaging and email to make and stay in touch with friends worldwide, sometimes in the same way as some previously had pen pals. Social networking websites such as Facebook, Twitter, and Myspace have created new ways to socialize and interact. Users of these sites are able to add a wide variety of information to pages, to pursue common interests, and to connect with others. It is also possible to find existing acquaintances, to allow communication among existing groups of people. Sites like LinkedIn foster commercial and business connections. YouTube and Flickr specialize in users' videos and photographs. While social networking sites were initially for individuals only, today they are widely used by businesses and other organizations to promote their brands, to market to their customers and to encourage posts to "go viral". "Black hat" social media techniques are also employed by some organizations, such as spam accounts and astroturfing.

A risk for both individuals and organizations writing posts (especially public posts) on social networking websites, is that especially foolish or controversial posts occasionally lead to an unexpected and possibly large-scale backlash on social media from other Internet users. This is also a risk in relation to controversial offline behavior, if it is widely made known. The nature of this backlash can range widely from counter-arguments and public mockery, through insults and hate speech, to, in extreme cases, rape and death threats. The online disinhibition effect describes the tendency of many individuals to behave more stridently or offensively online than they would in person. A significant number of feminist women have been the target of various forms of harassment in response to posts they have made on social media, and Twitter in particular has been criticised in the past for not doing enough to aid victims of online abuse.

For organizations, such a backlash can cause overall brand damage, especially if reported by the media. However, this is not always the case, as any brand damage in the eyes of people with an opposing opinion to that presented by the organization could sometimes be outweighed by strengthening the brand in the eyes of others. Furthermore, if an organization or individual gives in to demands that others perceive as wrong-headed, that can then provoke a counter-backlash.

Some websites, such as Reddit, have rules forbidding the posting of personal information of individuals (also known as doxxing), due to concerns about such postings leading to mobs of large numbers of Internet users directing harassment at the specific individuals thereby identified. In particular, the Reddit rule forbidding the posting of personal information is widely understood to imply that all identifying photos and names must be censored in Facebook screenshots posted to Reddit. However, the interpretation of this rule in relation to public Twitter posts is less clear, and in any case, like-minded people online have many other ways they can use to direct each other's attention to public social media posts they disagree with.

Children also face dangers online such as cyberbullying and approaches by sexual predators, who sometimes pose as children themselves. Children may also encounter material which they may find upsetting, or material which their parents consider to be not age-appropriate. Due to naivety, they may also post personal information about themselves online, which could put them or their families at risk unless warned not to do so. Many parents choose to enable Internet filtering, and/or supervise their children's online activities, in an attempt to protect their children from inappropriate material on the Internet. The most popular social networking websites, such as Facebook and Twitter, commonly forbid users under the age of 13. However, these policies are typically trivial to circumvent by registering an account with a false birth date, and a significant number of children aged under 13 join such sites anyway. Social networking sites for younger children, which claim to provide better levels of protection for children, also exist.

The Internet has been a major outlet for leisure activity since its inception, with entertaining social experiments such as MUDs and MOOs being conducted on university servers, and humor-related Usenet groups receiving much traffic. Today, many Internet forums have sections devoted to games and funny videos. Over 6 million people use blogs or message boards as a means of communication and for the sharing of ideas. The Internet pornography and online gambling industries have taken advantage of the World Wide Web, and often provide a significant source of advertising revenue for other websites. Although many governments have attempted to restrict both industries' use of the Internet, in general, this has failed to stop their widespread popularity.

Another area of leisure activity on the Internet is multiplayer gaming. This form of recreation creates communities, where people of all ages and origins enjoy the fast-paced world of multiplayer games. These range from MMORPG to first-person shooters, from role-playing video games to online gambling. While online gaming has been around since the 1970s, modern modes of online gaming began with subscription services such as GameSpy and MPlayer. Non-subscribers were limited to certain types of game play or certain games. Many people use the Internet to access and download music, movies and other works for their enjoyment and relaxation. Free and fee-based services exist for all of these activities, using centralized servers and distributed peer-to-peer technologies. Some of these sources exercise more care with respect to the original artists' copyrights than others.

Internet usage has been correlated to users' loneliness. Lonely people tend to use the Internet as an outlet for their feelings and to share their stories with others, such as in the "I am lonely will anyone speak to me" thread.

Cybersectarianism is a new organizational form which involves: "highly dispersed small groups of practitioners that may remain largely anonymous within the larger social context and operate in relative secrecy, while still linked remotely to a larger network of believers who share a set of practices and texts, and often a common devotion to a particular leader. Overseas supporters provide funding and support; domestic practitioners distribute tracts, participate in acts of resistance, and share information on the internal situation with outsiders. Collectively, members and practitioners of such sects construct viable virtual communities of faith, exchanging personal testimonies and engaging in the collective study via email, on-line chat rooms, and web-based message boards." In particular, the British government has raised concerns about the prospect of young British Muslims being indoctrinated into Islamic extremism by material on the Internet, being persuaded to join terrorist groups such as the so-called "Islamic State", and then potentially committing acts of terrorism on returning to Britain after fighting in Syria or Iraq.

Cyberslacking can become a drain on corporate resources; the average UK employee spent 57 minutes a day surfing the Web while at work, according to a 2003 study by Peninsula Business Services. Internet addiction disorder is excessive computer use that interferes with daily life. Psychologist, Nicolas Carr believe that Internet use has other effects on individuals, for instance improving skills of scan-reading and interfering with the deep thinking that leads to true creativity.

Electronic Business

Electronic business (e-business) encompasses business processes spanning the entire value chain: purchasing, supply chain management, marketing, sales, customer service, and business relationship. E-commerce seeks to add revenue streams using the Internet to build and enhance relationships with clients and partners. According to International Data Corporation, the size of worldwide e-commerce, when global business-to-business and -consumer transactions are combined, equate to $16 trillion for 2013. A report by Oxford Economics adds those two together to estimate the total size of the digital economy at $20.4 trillion, equivalent to roughly 13.8% of global sales.

While much has been written of the economic advantages of Internet-enabled commerce, there is also evidence that some aspects of the Internet such as maps and location-aware services may serve to reinforce economic inequality and the digital divide. Electronic commerce may be responsible for consolidation and the decline of mom-and-pop, brick and mortar businesses resulting in increases in income inequality.

Author Andrew Keen, a long-time critic of the social transformations caused by the Internet, has recently focused on the economic effects of consolidation from Internet businesses. Keen cites a 2013 Institute for Local Self-Reliance report saying brick-and-mortar retailers employ 47 people for every $10 million in sales while Amazon employs only 14. Similarly, the 700-employee room rental start-up Airbnb was valued at $10 billion in 2014, about half as much as Hilton Hotels, which employs 152,000 people. And car-sharing Internet startup Uber employs 1,000 full-time employees and is valued at $18.2 billion, about the same valuation as Avis and Hertz combined, which together employ almost 60,000 people.

Telecommuting

Telecommuting is the performance within a traditional worker and employer relationship when it is facilitated by tools such as groupware, virtual private networks, conference calling, videoconferencing, and voice over IP (VOIP) so that work may be performed from any location, most conveniently the worker's home. It can be efficient and useful for companies as it allows workers to communicate over long distances, saving significant amounts of travel time and cost. As broadband Internet connections become commonplace, more workers have adequate bandwidth at home to use these tools to link their home to their corporate intranet and internal communication networks.

Crowdsourcing

The Internet provides a particularly good venue for crowdsourcing, because individuals tend to be more open in web-based projects where they are not being physically judged or scrutinized and thus can feel more comfortable sharing.

Collaborative Publishing

Wikis have also been used in the academic community for sharing and dissemination of information across institutional and international boundaries. In those settings, they have been found useful for collaboration on grant writing, strategic planning, departmental documentation, and committee work. The United States Patent and Trademark Office uses a wiki to allow the public to collaborate on finding prior art relevant to examination of pending patent applications. Queens, New York has used a wiki to allow citizens to collaborate on the design and planning of a local park. The English Wikipedia has the largest user base among wikis on the World Wide Web and ranks in the top 10 among all Web sites in terms of traffic.

Politics and Political Revolutions

Banner in Bangkok during the 2014 Thai coup d'état, informing the Thai public that 'like' or 'share' activities on social media could result in imprisonment (observed June 30, 2014).

The Internet has achieved new relevance as a political tool. The presidential campaign of Howard Dean in 2004 in the United States was notable for its success in soliciting donation via the Internet. Many political groups use the Internet to achieve a new method of organizing for carrying out their mission, having given rise to Internet activism, most notably practiced by rebels in the Arab Spring. The New York Times suggested that social media websites, such as Facebook and Twitter, helped people organize the political revolutions in Egypt, by helping activists organize protests, communicate grievances, and disseminate information.

The potential of the Internet as a civic tool of communicative power was explored by Simon R. B. Berdal in his 2004 thesis:

As the globally evolving Internet provides ever new access points to virtual discourse forums, it also promotes new civic relations and associations within which communicative power may flow and accumulate. Thus, traditionally ... national-embedded peripheries get entangled into greater, international peripheries, with stronger combined powers... The Internet, as a consequence, changes the topology of the "centre-periphery" model, by stimulating conventional peripheries to interlink into "super-periphery" structures, which enclose and "besiege" several centres at once.

Berdal, therefore, extends the Habermasian notion of the public sphere to the Internet, and underlines the inherent global and civic nature that interwoven Internet technologies provide. To limit the growing civic potential of the Internet, Berdal also notes how "self-protective measures" are put in place by those threatened by it:

If we consider China's attempts to filter "unsuitable material" from the Internet, most of us would agree that this resembles a self-protective measure by the system against the growing civic potentials of the Internet. Nevertheless, both types represent limitations to "peripheral capacities". Thus, the Chinese government tries to prevent communicative power to build up and unleash (as the 1989 Tiananmen Square uprising suggests, the government may find it wise to install "upstream measures"). Even though limited, the Internet is proving to be an empowering tool also to the Chinese periphery: Analysts believe that Internet petitions have influenced policy implementation in favour of the public's online-articulated will ...

Incidents of politically motivated Internet censorship have now been recorded in many countries, including western democracies.

Philanthropy

The spread of low-cost Internet access in developing countries has opened up new possibilities for peer-to-peer charities, which allow individuals to contribute small amounts to charitable projects for other individuals. Websites, such as DonorsChoose and GlobalGiving, allow small-scale donors to direct funds to individual projects of their choice. A popular twist on Internet-based philanthropy is the use of peer-to-peer lending for charitable purposes. Kiva pioneered this concept in 2005, offering the first web-based service to publish individual loan profiles for funding. Kiva raises funds for local intermediary microfinance organizations which post stories and updates on behalf of the borrowers. Lenders can contribute as little as $25 to loans of their choice, and receive their money back as borrowers repay. Kiva falls short of being a pure peer-to-peer charity, in that loans are disbursed before being funded by lenders and borrowers do not communicate with lenders themselves.

However, the recent spread of low-cost Internet access in developing countries has made genuine international person-to-person philanthropy increasingly feasible. In 2009, the US-based nonprofit Zidisha tapped into this trend to offer the first person-to-person microfinance platform to link lenders and borrowers across international borders without intermediaries. Members can fund loans for as little as a dollar, which the borrowers then use to develop business activities that improve their families' incomes while repaying loans to the members with interest. Borrowers access the Internet via public cybercafes, donated laptops in village schools, and even smart phones, then create their own profile pages through which they share photos and information about themselves and their businesses. As they repay their loans, borrowers continue to share updates and dialogue with lenders via their profile pages. This direct web-based connection allows members themselves to take on many of the communication and recording tasks traditionally performed by local organizations, bypassing geographic barriers and dramatically reducing the cost of microfinance services to the entrepreneurs.

Security

Internet resources, hardware, and software components are the target of malicious attempts to gain unauthorized control to cause interruptions or access private information. Such attempts include computer viruses which copy with the help of humans, computer worms which copy themselves automatically, denial of service attacks, ransomware, botnets, and spyware that reports on the activity and typing of users. Usually, these activities constitute cybercrime. Defense theorists have also speculated about the possibilities of cyber warfare using similar methods on a large scale.

Surveillance

The vast majority of computer surveillance involves the monitoring of data and traffic on the Internet. In the United States for example, under the Communications Assistance For Law Enforcement Act, all phone calls and broadband Internet traffic (emails, web traffic, instant messaging, etc.) are required to be available for unimpeded real-time monitoring by Federal law enforcement agencies. Packet capture is the monitoring of data traffic on a computer network. Computers communicate over the Internet by breaking up messages (emails, images, videos, web pages, files, etc.) into small chunks called "packets", which are routed through a network of computers, until they reach their destination, where they are assembled back into a complete "message" again. Packet Capture Appliance intercepts these packets as they are traveling through the network, in order to examine their contents using other programs. A packet capture is an information gathering tool, but not an analysis tool. That is it gathers "messages" but it does not analyze them and figure out what they mean. Other programs are needed to perform traffic analysis and sift through intercepted data looking for important/ useful information. Under the Communications Assistance For Law Enforcement Act all U.S. telecommunications providers are required to install packet sniffing technology to allow Federal law enforcement and intelligence agencies to intercept all of their customers' broadband Internet and voice over Internet protocol (VoIP) traffic.

The large amount of data gathered from packet capturing requires surveillance software that filters and reports relevant information, such as the use of certain words or phrases, the access of certain types of web sites, or communicating via email or chat with certain parties. Agencies, such as the Information Awareness Office, NSA, GCHQ and the FBI, spend billions of dollars per year to develop, purchase, implement, and operate systems for interception and analysis of data. Similar systems are operated by Iranian secret police to identify and suppress dissidents. The required hardware and software was allegedly installed by German Siemens AG and Finnish Nokia.

Censorship

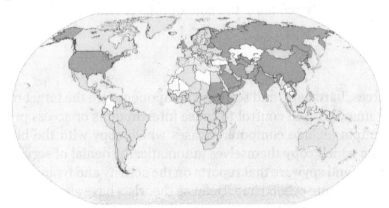

Internet censorship and surveillance by country

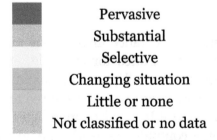

Pervasive
Substantial
Selective
Changing situation
Little or none
Not classified or no data

Some governments, such as those of Burma, Iran, North Korea, the Mainland China, Saudi Arabia and the United Arab Emirates restrict access to content on the Internet within their territories, especially to political and religious content, with domain name and keyword filters.

In Norway, Denmark, Finland, and Sweden, major Internet service providers have voluntarily agreed to restrict access to sites listed by authorities. While this list of forbidden resources is supposed to contain only known child pornography sites, the content of the list is secret. Many countries, including the United States, have enacted laws against the possession or distribution of certain material, such as child pornography, via the Internet, but do not mandate filter software. Many free or commercially available software programs, called content-control software are available to users to block offensive websites on individual computers or networks, in order to limit access by children to pornographic material or depiction of violence.

Performance

As the Internet is a heterogeneous network, the physical characteristics, including for example the data transfer rates of connections, vary widely. It exhibits emergent phenomena that depend on its large-scale organization.

Outages

An Internet blackout or outage can be caused by local signalling interruptions. Disruptions of submarine communications cables may cause blackouts or slowdowns to large areas, such as in the 2008 submarine cable disruption. Less-developed countries are more vulnerable due to a small number of high-capacity links. Land cables are also vulnerable, as in 2011 when a woman digging for scrap metal severed most connectivity for the nation of Armenia. Internet blackouts affecting almost entire countries can be achieved by governments as a form of Internet censorship, as in the blockage of the Internet in Egypt, whereby approximately 93% of networks were without access in 2011 in an attempt to stop mobilization for anti-government protests.

Energy Use

In 2011, researchers estimated the energy used by the Internet to be between 170 and 307 GW, less than two percent of the energy used by humanity. This estimate included the energy needed to build, operate, and periodically replace the estimated 750 million laptops, a billion smart phones and 100 million servers worldwide as well as the energy that routers, cell towers, optical switches, Wi-Fi transmitters and cloud storage devices use when transmitting Internet traffic.

References

- Tufte, Edward (1983). The Visual Display of Quantitative Information. Cheshire, Connecticut: Graphics Press. ISBN 0-9613921-4-2.

- Bailey, Ken (1994). "Numerical Taxonomy and Cluster Analysis". Typologies and Taxonomies. p. 34. ISBN 9780803952591.

- Manning, Christopher D.; Raghavan, Prabhakar; Schütze, Hinrich. Introduction to Information Retrieval. Cambridge University Press. ISBN 978-0-521-86571-5.

- Meilă, Marina (2003). "Comparing Clusterings by the Variation of Information". Learning Theory and Kernel Machines. Lecture Notes in Computer Science. 2777: 173–187. doi:10.1007/978-3-540-45167-9_14. ISBN 978-3-540-40720-1.

- Kim, Byung-Keun (2005). Internationalising the Internet the Co-evolution of Influence and Technology. Edward Elgar. pp. 51–55. ISBN 1845426754.

- Hafner, Katie (1998). Where Wizards Stay Up Late: The Origins Of The Internet. Simon & Schuster. ISBN 0-684-83267-4.

- Mueller, Milton L. (2010). Networks and States: The Global Politics of Internet Governance. MIT Press. p. 61. ISBN 978-0-262-01459-5.

- The Shallows: What the Internet Is Doing to Our Brains, Nicholas Carr, W. W. Norton, 7 June 2010, 276 pp., ISBN 0-393-07222-3, ISBN 978-0-393-07222-8

- MM Wanderley; D Birnbaum; J Malloch (2006). New Interfaces For Musical Expression. IRCAM – Centre Pompidou. p. 180. ISBN 2-84426-314-3.

- Access Controlled: The Shaping of Power, Rights, and Rule in Cyberspace, Ronald J. Deibert, John G. Palfrey, Rafal Rohozinski, and Jonathan Zittrain (eds), MIT Press, April 2010, ISBN 0-262-51435-4, ISBN 978-0-262-51435-4

- Friendly, Michael (2006). "A Brief History of Data Visualization" (PDF). York University. Springer-Verlag. Retrieved 2015-11-22.

- Grandjean, Martin (2015) "Introduction à la visualisation de données, l'analyse de réseau en histoire", Geschichte und Informatik, 18-19, 109-128.

- ICT Facts and Figures 2005, 2010, 2014, Telecommunication Development Bureau, International Telecommunication Union (ITU). Retrieved 24 May 2015.

- "Individuals using the Internet 2005 to 2014", Key ICT indicators for developed and developing countries and the world (totals and penetration rates), International Telecommunication Union (ITU). Retrieved 25 May 2015.

- "Internet users per 100 inhabitants 1997 to 2007", ICT Data and Statistics (IDS), International Telecommunication Union (ITU). Retrieved 25 May 2015.

- "Special Report: The Telecom Consumer in 2020", Pavel Marceux, Euromonitor International, 27 August 2013. Retrieved 7 June 2015.

- Harris, Michael (January 2, 2015). "Book review: 'The Internet Is Not the Answer' by Andrew Keen". Washington Post. Retrieved 25 January 2015.

Information System: An Overview

An information system is an organized system that is mainly used in collecting and storing information. The management of this information is done by the processes laid out by management information systems. The section on information system is an overview of the subject matter incorporating all the major aspects of information system.

Information System

An information system (IS) is any organized system for the collection, organization, storage and communication of information. More specifically, it is the study of complementary networks that people and organizations use to collect, filter, process, create and distribute data.

A computer information system is a system composed of people and computers that processes or interprets information. The term is also sometimes used in more restricted senses to refer to only the software used to run a computerized database or to refer to only a computer system.

Information system is an academic study of systems with a specific reference to information and the complementary networks of hardware and software that people and organizations use to collect, filter, process, create and also distribute data. An emphasis is placed on an Information System having a definitive Boundary, Users, Processors, Stores, Inputs, Outputs and the aforementioned communication networks.

Any specific information system aims to support operations, management and decision-making. An information system is the information and communication technology (ICT) that an organization uses, and also the way in which people interact with this technology in support of business processes.

Some authors make a clear distinction between information systems, computer systems, and business processes. Information systems typically include an ICT component but are not purely concerned with ICT, focusing instead on the end use of information technology. Information systems are also different from business processes. Information systems help to control the performance of business processes.

Alter argues for advantages of viewing an information system as a special type of work system. A work system is a system in which humans or machines perform processes and activities using resources to produce specific products or services for customers. An information system is a work system whose activities are devoted to capturing, transmitting, storing, retrieving, manipulating and displaying information.

As such, information systems inter-relate with data systems on the one hand and activity systems on the other. An information system is a form of communication system in which data represent and are processed as a form of social memory. An information system can also be considered a semi-formal language which supports human decision making and action.

Information systems are the primary focus of study for organizational informatics.

Overview

Silver et al. (1995) provided two views on IS that includes software, hardware, data, people, and procedures. Zheng provided another system view of information system which also adds processes and essential system elements like environment, boundary, purpose, and interactions. The Association for Computing Machinery defines "Information systems specialists [as] focus[ing] on integrating information technology solutions and business processes to meet the information needs of businesses and other enterprises."

There are various types of information systems, for example: transaction processing systems, decision support systems, knowledge management systems, learning management systems, database management systems, and office information systems. Critical to most information systems are information technologies, which are typically designed to enable humans to perform tasks for which the human brain is not well suited, such as: handling large amounts of information, performing complex calculations, and controlling many simultaneous processes.

Information technologies are a very important and malleable resource available to executives. Many companies have created a position of chief information officer (CIO) that sits on the executive board with the chief executive officer (CEO), chief financial officer (CFO), chief operating officer (COO), and chief technical officer (CTO). The CTO may also serve as CIO, and vice versa. The chief information security officer (CISO) focuses on information security management.

The six components that must come together in order to produce an information system are:

1. Hardware: The term hardware refers to machinery. This category includes the computer itself, which is often referred to as the central processing unit (CPU), and all of its support equipments. Among the support equipments are input and output devices, storage devices and communications devices.

2. Software: The term software refers to computer programs and the manuals (if any) that support them. Computer programs are machine-readable instructions

that direct the circuitry within the hardware parts of the system to function in ways that produce useful information from data. Programs are generally stored on some input / output medium, often a disk or tape.

3. Data: Data are facts that are used by programs to produce useful information. Like programs, data are generally stored in machine-readable form on disk or tape until the computer needs them.

4. Procedures: Procedures are the policies that govern the operation of a computer system. "Procedures are to people what software is to hardware" is a common analogy that is used to illustrate the role of procedures in a system.

5. People: Every system needs people if it is to be useful. Often the most over-looked element of the system are the people, probably the component that most influence the success or failure of information systems. This includes "not only the users, but those who operate and service the computers, those who maintain the data, and those who support the network of computers." <Kroenke, D. M. (2015). MIS Essentials. Pearson Education>

6. Feedback: it is another component of the IS, that defines that an IS may be provided with a feedback (Although this component isn't necessary to function).

Data is the bridge between hardware and people. This means that the data we collect is only data, until we involve people. At that point, data is now information.

Types of Information System

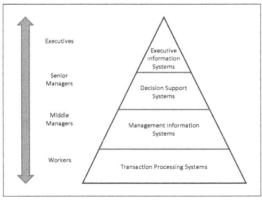

A four level

The "classic" view of Information systems found in the textbooks in the 1980s was of a pyramid of systems that reflected the hierarchy of the organization, usually transaction processing systems at the bottom of the pyramid, followed by management information systems, decision support systems, and ending with executive information systems at the top. Although the pyramid model remains useful, since it was first formulated a number of new technologies have been developed and new categories of information systems have emerged, some of which no longer fit easily into the original pyramid model.

Some examples of such systems are:

- data warehouses

- enterprise resource planning

- enterprise systems

- expert systems

- search engines

- geographic information system

- global information system

- office automation.

A computer(-based) information system is essentially an IS using computer technology to carry out some or all of its planned tasks. The basic components of computer-based information systems are:

- Hardware- these are the devices like the monitor, processor, printer and keyboard, all of which work together to accept, process, show data and information.

- Software- are the programs that allow the hardware to process the data.

- Databases- are the gathering of associated files or tables containing related data.

- Networks- are a connecting system that allows diverse computers to distribute resources.

- Procedures- are the commands for combining the components above to process information and produce the preferred output.

The first four components (hardware, software, database, and network) make up what is known as the information technology platform. Information technology workers could then use these components to create information systems that watch over safety measures, risk and the management of data. These actions are known as information technology services.

Certain information systems support parts of organizations, others support entire organizations, and still others, support groups of organizations. Recall that each department or functional area within an organization has its own collection of application programs, or information systems. These functional area information systems (FAIS) are supporting pillars for more general IS namely, business intelligence systems and dashboards. As the name suggest, each FAIS support a particular function within the organization, e.g.: accounting IS, finance IS, production/operation management (POM) IS, marketing IS, and human resources IS. In finance and accounting, managers use IT systems to forecast revenues and business activity, to determine the best sources and uses of funds, and to perform audits to ensure that the organization is fundamentally sound and that all financial reports and documents are accurate. Other types of organizational information systems are FAIS, Transaction processing systems, enterprise resource planning, office automation system, management information system, decision support system, expert system, executive dashboard, supply chain management system, and electronic commerce system. Dashboards are a special form of IS that support all managers of the organization. They provide rapid access to timely information and direct access to structured information in the form of reports. Expert systems attempt to duplicate the work of human experts by applying reasoning capabilities, knowledge, and expertise within a specific domain.

Information System Development

Information technology departments in larger organizations tend to strongly influence the development, use, and application of information technology in the organizations. A series of methodologies and processes can be used to develop and use an information system. Many developers now use an engineering approach such as the system development life cycle (SDLC), which is a systematic procedure of developing an information system through stages that occur in sequence. Recent research aims at enabling and measuring the ongoing, collective development of such systems within an organization by the entirety of human actors themselves. An information system can be developed in house (within the organization) or outsourced. This can be accomplished by outsourcing certain components or the entire system. A specific case is the geographical distribution of the development team (offshoring, global information system).

A computer-based information system, following a definition of Langefors, is a technologically implemented medium for:

- recording, storing, and disseminating linguistic expressions,

- as well as for drawing conclusions from such expressions.

Geographic information systems, land information systems, and disaster information systems are examples of emerging information systems, but they can be broadly considered as spatial information systems. System development is done in stages which include:

- Problem recognition and specification

- Information gathering

- Requirements specification for the new system

- System design

- System construction

- System implementation

- Review and maintenance.

As an Academic Discipline

The field of study called information systems encompasses a variety of topics including systems analysis and design, computer networking, information security, database management and decision support systems. Information management deals with the practical and theoretical problems of collecting and analyzing information in a business function area including business productivity tools, applications programming and implementation, electronic commerce, digital media production, data mining, and decision support. Communications and networking deals with the telecommunication technologies. Information systems bridges business and computer science using the theoretical foundations of information and computation to study various business models and related algorithmic processes on building the IT systems within a computer science discipline. Computer information system(s) (CIS) is a field studying computers and algorithmic processes, including their principles, their software and hardware designs, their applications, and their impact on society, whereas IS emphasizes functionality over design.

Several IS scholars have debated the nature and foundations of Information Systems which has its roots in other reference disciplines such as Computer Science, Engineering, Mathematics, Management Science, Cybernetics, and others. Information systems also can be defined as a collection of hardware, software, data, people and procedures that work together to produce quality information.

Differentiating IS from Related Disciplines

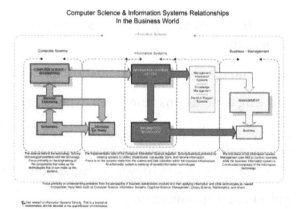

Information Systems relationship to Information Technology, Computer Science, Information Science, and Business.

Similar to computer science, other disciplines can be seen as both related and foundation disciplines of IS. The domain of study of IS involves the study of theories and practices related to the social and technological phenomena, which determine the development, use, and effects of information systems in organization and society. But, while there may be considerable overlap of the disciplines at the boundaries, the disciplines are still differentiated by the focus, purpose, and orientation of their activities.

In a broad scope, the term Information Systems is a scientific field of study that addresses the range of strategic, managerial, and operational activities involved in the gathering, processing, storing, distributing, and use of information and its associated technologies in society and organizations. The term information systems is also used to describe an organizational function that applies IS knowledge in industry, government agencies, and not-for-profit organizations. Information Systems often refers to the interaction between algorithmic processes and technology. This interaction can occur within or across organizational boundaries. An information system is the technology an organization uses and also the way in which the organizations interact with the technology and the way in which the technology works with the organization's business processes. Information systems are distinct from information technology (IT) in that an information system has an information technology component that interacts with the processes' components.

One problem with that approach is that it prevents the IS field from being interested in non-organizational use of ICT, such as in social networking, computer gaming, mobile personal usage, etc. A different way of differentiating the IS field from its neighbours is to ask, "Which aspects of reality are most meaningful in the IS field and other fields?" This approach, based on philosophy, helps to define not just the focus, purpose and orientation, but also the dignity, destiny and responsibility of the field among other fields. International Journal of Information Management, 30, 13-20.

Career Pathways

Information Systems have a number of different areas of work:

- IS strategy
- IS management
- IS development
- IS iteration
- IS organization

There is a wide variety of career paths in the information systems discipline. "Workers with specialized technical knowledge and strong communications skills will have the best prospects. Workers with management skills and an understanding of business practices and principles will have excellent opportunities, as companies are increasingly looking to technology to drive their revenue."

Information technology is important to the operation of contemporary businesses, it offers many employment opportunities. The information systems field includes the people in organizations who design and build information systems, the people who use those systems, and the people responsible for managing those systems. The demand for traditional IT staff such as programmers, business analysts, systems analysts, and designer is significant. Many well-paid jobs exist in areas of Information technology. At the top of the list is the chief information officer (CIO).

The CIO is the executive who is in charge of the IS function. In most organizations, the CIO works with the chief executive officer (CEO), the chief financial officer (CFO), and other senior executives. Therefore, he or she actively participates in the organization's strategic planning process.

Research

Information systems research is generally interdisciplinary concerned with the study of the effects of information systems on the behavior of individuals, groups, and organizations. Hevner et al. (2004) categorized research in IS into two scientific paradigms including behavioral science which is to develop and verify theories that explain or predict human or organizational behavior and design science which extends the boundaries of human and organizational capabilities by creating new and innovative artifacts.

Salvatore March and Gerald Smith proposed a framework for researching different aspects of Information Technology including outputs of the research (research outputs) and activities to carry out this research (research activities). They identified research outputs as follows:

1. Constructs which are concepts that form the vocabulary of a domain. They constitute a conceptualization used to describe problems within the domain and to specify their solutions.

2. A model which is a set of propositions or statements expressing relationships among constructs.

3. A method which is a set of steps (an algorithm or guideline) used to perform a task. Methods are based on a set of underlying constructs and a representation (model) of the solution space.

4. An instantiation is the realization of an artifact in its environment.

Also research activities including:

1. Build an artifact to perform a specific task.

2. Evaluate the artifact to determine if any progress has been achieved.

3. Given an artifact whose performance has been evaluated, it is important to de-

termine why and how the artifact worked or did not work within its environment. Therefore, theorize and justify theories about IT artifacts.

Although Information Systems as a discipline has been evolving for over 30 years now, the core focus or identity of IS research is still subject to debate among scholars. There are two main views around this debate: a narrow view focusing on the IT artifact as the core subject matter of IS research, and a broad view that focuses on the interplay between social and technical aspects of IT that is embedded into a dynamic evolving context. A third view calls on IS scholars to pay balanced attention to both the IT artifact and its context.

Since the study of information systems is an applied field, industry practitioners expect information systems research to generate findings that are immediately applicable in practice. This is not always the case however, as information systems researchers often explore behavioral issues in much more depth than practitioners would expect them to do. This may render information systems research results difficult to understand, and has led to criticism.

In the last ten years the business trend is represented by the considerable increasing of Information Systems Function (ISF) role, especially with regard the enterprise strategies and operations supporting. It became a key-factor to increase productivity and to support new value creation. To study an information system itself, rather than its effects, information systems models are used, such as EATPUT.

The international body of Information Systems researchers, the Association for Information Systems (AIS), and its Senior Scholars Forum Subcommittee on Journals (23 April 2007), proposed a 'basket' of journals that the AIS deems as 'excellent', and nominated: Management Information Systems Quarterly (MISQ), Information Systems Research (ISR), Journal of the Association for Information Systems (JAIS), Journal of Management Information Systems (JMIS), European Journal of Information Systems (EJIS), and Information Systems Journal (ISJ).

A number of annual information systems conferences are run in various parts of the world, the majority of which are peer reviewed. The AIS directly runs the International Conference on Information Systems (ICIS) and the Americas Conference on Information Systems (AMCIS), while AIS affiliated conferences include the Pacific Asia Conference on Information Systems (PACIS), European Conference on Information Systems (ECIS), the Mediterranean Conference on Information Systems (MCIS), the International Conference on Information Resources Management (Conf-IRM) and the Wuhan International Conference on E-Business (WHICEB). AIS chapter conferences include Australasian Conference on Information Systems (ACIS), Information Systems Research Conference in Scandinavia (IRIS), Information Systems International Conference (ISICO), Conference of the Italian Chapter of AIS (itAIS), Annual Mid-Western AIS Conference (MWAIS) and Annual Conference of the Southern AIS (SAIS). EDSIG

[1], which is the special interest group on education of the AITP [2], organizes the Conference on Information Systems and Computing Education [3] and the Conference on Information Systems Applied Research [4] which are both held annually in November.

The impact on Economic Models

- Microeconomic theory model

- Transaction cost theory

- Agency theory

Management Information System

A management information system (MIS) focuses on the management of information systems to provide efficiency and effectiveness of strategic decision making. The concept may include systems termed transaction processing system, decision support system, expert system, or executive information system. The term is often used in the academic study of businesses and has connections with other areas, such as information systems, information technology, informatics, e-commerce and computer science; as a result, the term is used interchangeably with some of these areas.

Management information systems (plural) as an academic discipline studies people, technology, organizations, and the relationships among them. This definition relates specifically to "MIS" as a course of study in business schools. Many business schools (or colleges of business administration within universities) have an MIS department, alongside departments of accounting, finance, management, marketing, and may award degrees (at undergraduate, master, and doctoral levels) in Management Information Systems.

MIS professionals help organizations to maximize the benefit from investments in personnel, equipment, and business processes.

Management

There are different areas of concentration with different duties and responsibilities in information system managers starting from the Chief information officer (CIOs), Chief technology officer (CTOs), IT directors and IT security managers. Chief information officers (CIOs) are responsible for the overall technology strategy of their organizations. Basically, they are more of the decision makers and action takers when it comes down to determining the technology or information goals of an organization and making sure the necessary planning to implement those goals is being met.

Chief technology officers (CTOs) are responsible for evaluating how new technology can help their organization. They usually recommend technological solutions to support the policies issued by the CIO.

IT directors including MIS directors are in charge of both their organization's Information technology departments and the supervision of thereof. They are also in charge of implementing the policies chosen by the other top branches (CIOs, CTOs). It is their role to ensure the availability of data and network services by coordinating IT activities.

IT Security Managers oversee the network and security data as the title implies. They develop programs to offer information and awareness to their employees about security threats. This team is very important because they must keep up-to-date on IT security measures in order to be successful within their organization. Any security violations need to be investigated and supervised by this specific team.

History

Kenneth and Aldrich Estel identify six eras of Management Information System evolution corresponding to the five phases in the development of computing technology:

1. mainframe and minicomputer computing,

2. personal computers,

3. client/server networks,

4. enterprise computing, and

5. cloud computing.

The first era (mainframe and minicomputer) was ruled by IBM and their mainframe computers; these computers would often take up whole rooms and require teams to run them—IBM supplied the hardware and the software. As technology advanced, these computers were able to handle greater capacities and therefore reduce their cost. Smaller, more affordable minicomputers allowed larger businesses to run their own computing centers in-house / on-site / on-premises.

The second era (personal computer) began in 1965 as microprocessors started to compete with mainframes and minicomputers and accelerated the process of decentralizing computing power from large data centers to smaller offices. In the late 1970s, minicomputer technology gave way to personal computers and relatively low-cost computers were becoming mass market commodities, allowing businesses to provide their employees access to computing power that ten years before would have cost tens of thousands of dollars. This proliferation of computers created a ready market for interconnecting networks and the popularization of the Internet. (NOTE that the first microprocessor — a four-bit device intended for a programmable calculator — was introduced in 1971 and microprocessor-based systems were not readily available for several years. The MITS Altair 8800 was the first commonly known microprocessor-based system, followed closely by the Apple I and II. It is arguable that the microprocessor-based system did not make significant inroads into minicomputer use until 1979, when Visi-Calc prompted record sales of the Apple II on which it ran. The IBM PC introduced in 1981 was more broadly palatable to business, but its limitations gated its ability to challenge minicomputer systems until perhaps the late 1980s to early 1990s.)

As technological complexity increased and costs decreased, the need to share information within an enterprise also grew—giving rise to the third era (client/server), in which computers on a common network access shared information on a server. This lets thousands and even millions of people access data simultaneously. The fourth era (enterprise) enabled by high speed networks, tied all aspects of the business enterprise together offering rich information access encompassing the complete management structure. Every computer is utilized.

The fifth era (cloud computing) is the latest and employs networking technology to deliver applications as well as data storage independent of the configuration, location or nature of the hardware. This, along with high speed cellphone and Wi-Fi networks, has led to new levels of mobility in which managers may access the MIS remotely with laptops, tablet computers and smartphones.

Types and Terminology

The terms management information system (MIS), information system, enterprise resource planning (ERP), and information technology management (IT) are often confused. Information systems and MIS are broader categories that include ERP. Information technology management concerns the operation and company of information technology resources independent of their purpose.

- Management information systems, produce fixed, regularly scheduled reports based on data extracted and summarized from the firm's underlying transaction processing systems to middle and operational level managers to identify and inform semi-structured decision problems.

- Decision support systems (DSS) are computer program applications used by middle and higher management to compile information from a wide range of sources to support problem solving and decision making. A DSS is used mostly for semi-structured and unstructured decision problems.

- Executive information systems (EIS) is a reporting tool that provides quick access to summarized reports coming from all company levels and departments such as accounting, human resources and operations.

- Marketing Information Systems are Management Information Systems designed specifically for managing the marketing aspects of the business

- Accounting information systems are focused accounting functions.

- Human resource management systems are used for personnel aspects.

- Office automation systems (OAS) support communication and productivity in the enterprise by automating workflow and eliminating bottlenecks. OAS may be implemented at any and all levels of management.

- School Information Management Systems (SIMS) cover school administration, and often including teaching and learning materials.

- Enterprise resource planning facilitates the flow of information between all business functions inside the boundaries of the organization and manage the connections to outside stakeholders.

Advantages

The following are some of the benefits that can be attained using MISs.

- Companies are able to identify their strengths and weaknesses due to the presence of revenue reports, employees' performance record etc. Identifying these aspects can help a company improve its business processes and operations.

- Giving an overall picture of the company.

- Acting as a communication and planning tool.

- The availability of customer data and feedback can help the company to align its business processes according to the needs of its customers. The effective management of customer data can help the company to perform direct marketing and promotion activities.

- MIS can help a company gain a competitive advantage. Competitive advantage is a firm's ability to do something better, faster, cheaper, or uniquely, when compared with rival firms in the market.

- MIS report help to take decision and action on certain object with quick time.

Enterprise Applications

- Enterprise systems—also known as enterprise resource planning (ERP) systems—provide integrated software modules and a unified database that personnel use to plan, manage, and control core business processes across multiple locations. Modules of ERP systems may include finance, accounting, marketing, human resources, production, inventory management, and distribution.

- Supply chain management (SCM) systems enable more efficient management of the supply chain by integrating the links in a supply chain. This may include suppliers, manufacturers, wholesalers, retailers, and final customers.

- Customer relationship management (CRM) systems help businesses manage relationships with potential and current customers and business partners across marketing, sales, and service.

- Knowledge management system (KMS) helps organizations facilitate the collection, recording, organization, retrieval, and dissemination of knowledge. This may include documents, accounting records, unrecorded procedures, practices, and skills. Knowledge management (KM) as a system covers the process of knowledge creation and acquisition from internal processes and the external world. The collected knowledge is incorporated in organizational policies and procedures, and then disseminated to the stakeholders.

Development

"The actions that are taken to create an information system that solves an organizational problem are called system development". These include system analysis, system design, computer programming/implementation, testing, conversion, production and finally maintenance.

Conversion is the process of changing or converting the old system into the new. This can be done in three basic ways:

- Direct cut – The new system replaces the old at an appointed time.

- Parallel implementation - both old and new systems run at the same time until developers are certain the new system is operating correctly.

- Pilot study - Introducing the new system to a small portion of the operation to see how it fares. If results are good then the new system expands to the rest of the company.

References

- Simison, Graeme. C. & Witt, Graham. C. (2005).Data Modeling Essentials.3rd Edition. Morgan Kauffman Publishers. ISBN 0-12-644551-6

- Whitten, Jeffrey L.; Lonnie D. Bentley, Kevin C. Dittman. (2004). Systems Analysis and Design Methods. 6th edition. ISBN 0-256-19906-X.

- Len Silverston, W.H.Inmon, Kent Graziano (2007). The Data Model Resource Book. Wiley, 1997. ISBN 0-471-15364-8. Reviewed by Van Scott on tdan.com. Accessed November 1, 2008.

- Joshi, Girdhar (2013). Management Information Systems. New Delhi: Oxford University Press. p. 328. ISBN 9780198080992.

- Costa, A; Ferreira, C.; Bento, E.; Aparicio, F. (2016). "Enterprise resource planning adoption and satisfaction determinants". Computers in Human Behavior. 63: 659–671. doi:10.1016/j.chb.2016.05.090.

- Taylor, Victoria. "Supply Chain Management: The Next Big Thing?". Sept. 12, 2011. Business Week. Retrieved 5 March 2014.

- Laudon, K.,&Laudon, J. (2010). Management information systems: Managing the digital firm. (11th ed.). Upper Saddle River, NJ: Pearson Prentice Hall.

Permissions

All chapters in this book are published with permission under the Creative Commons Attribution Share Alike License or equivalent. Every chapter published in this book has been scrutinized by our experts. Their significance has been extensively debated. The topics covered herein carry significant information for a comprehensive understanding. They may even be implemented as practical applications or may be referred to as a beginning point for further studies.

We would like to thank the editorial team for lending their expertise to make the book truly unique. They have played a crucial role in the development of this book. Without their invaluable contributions this book wouldn't have been possible. They have made vital efforts to compile up to date information on the varied aspects of this subject to make this book a valuable addition to the collection of many professionals and students.

This book was conceptualized with the vision of imparting up-to-date and integrated information in this field. To ensure the same, a matchless editorial board was set up. Every individual on the board went through rigorous rounds of assessment to prove their worth. After which they invested a large part of their time researching and compiling the most relevant data for our readers.

The editorial board has been involved in producing this book since its inception. They have spent rigorous hours researching and exploring the diverse topics which have resulted in the successful publishing of this book. They have passed on their knowledge of decades through this book. To expedite this challenging task, the publisher supported the team at every step. A small team of assistant editors was also appointed to further simplify the editing procedure and attain best results for the readers.

Apart from the editorial board, the designing team has also invested a significant amount of their time in understanding the subject and creating the most relevant covers. They scrutinized every image to scout for the most suitable representation of the subject and create an appropriate cover for the book.

The publishing team has been an ardent support to the editorial, designing and production team. Their endless efforts to recruit the best for this project, has resulted in the accomplishment of this book. They are a veteran in the field of academics and their pool of knowledge is as vast as their experience in printing. Their expertise and guidance has proved useful at every step. Their uncompromising quality standards have made this book an exceptional effort. Their encouragement from time to time has been an inspiration for everyone.

The publisher and the editorial board hope that this book will prove to be a valuable piece of knowledge for students, practitioners and scholars across the globe.

Index

A

Algorithms And Data Structures, 12, 14, 178

Applied Computer Science, 15

Artificial Intelligence, 10, 12-13, 15, 54-56, 104, 116-117, 202, 204

Automatic Data Processing, 177

C

Centralized Governance, 164, 230

Centroid-based Clustering, 209

Cluster Analysis, 55-56, 63, 158, 179, 205-206, 208, 218-221, 253

Collaborative Information Seeking, 45-47, 49-51, 54, 84

Commercial Data Processing, 177

Computational Science, 12, 17

Computer Data Storage, 71, 86, 105, 107, 110

Computer Networks, 1, 17, 20, 115, 171, 173, 229, 231, 236

Computer Science, 7-9, 11-19, 25-26, 40-41, 54, 56, 59, 80, 116-118, 129, 178-179, 199, 202, 204, 214, 219, 222, 231-232, 254, 260, 264

Computer Technology, 2, 5, 9, 17, 56, 169, 258

Content Management, 162-165, 188, 240, 245

Core Competence, 145

Corporate Data Quality Management, 186

Cybernetics, 15, 202, 260

D

Data Analysis, 11, 55-56, 63, 121, 177-178, 187, 190-191, 194-195, 201, 205

Data Architecture, 180, 182-187

Data Management, 54, 60, 86-87, 123, 184-189

Data Manipulation, 4

Data Mining, 5, 15, 27, 54-65, 84, 185, 188, 205 206, 208, 220, 260

Data Modeling, 86, 97-98, 100, 102-104, 187, 268

Data Modeling Process, 100

Data Presentation Architecture, 199-200

Data Processing, 3, 26, 56, 86, 176-178, 182-185

Data Retrieval, 4, 184

Data Storage, 3, 27, 70-72, 75-77, 86, 105, 107, 110-111, 113-114, 186, 266

Data Storage Device, 27, 70

Data Transfer, 83-84, 241, 253

Data Transmission, 4, 14, 27, 79-83

Data Visualization, 190-191, 194-196, 199-201, 254

Database, 3-4, 13, 17, 27-28, 37, 49-50, 54-56, 60, 62, 67, 93-98, 100-102, 106, 110, 115, 164, 178, 180, 183-185, 187, 212, 255-256, 258, 260, 267

Databases, 3-4, 6, 11, 17, 44, 55-56, 59-60, 90, 94 98, 104, 125, 129, 132, 183, 225, 239-240, 258

Density-based Clustering, 211-212, 214

Distribution-based Clustering, 210-211

Domain Ontology, 119-120

E

Electronic Data Processing, 177

Elements Of Data Architecture, 183

F

Fast Path" Databases, 95

Federated Governance, 164

Full Function" Databases, 94

G

Generic Data Modeling, 103

H

Hybrid Ontology, 120

I

Ibm Information Management System, 86, 93

Information Access, 42, 179, 266

Information And Coding Theory, 13

Information And Communications Technology, 1, 19-20

Information Architect, 181

Information Architecture, 116, 179-182, 201

Information Extraction, 65-70, 84, 120, 123

Information Management, 1, 3, 40-41, 64, 86-93, 95, 97, 99, 101, 103, 105, 107, 109, 111, 113, 115, 117, 119, 121, 123, 125, 127, 129, 131, 133, 135, 137, 139, 141, 143, 145, 147, 149, 151, 153, 155, 157, 159, 161, 163, 165, 167, 169-171, 173, 175,

177, 189, 260-261, 267

Information Retrieval, 27-28, 30-31, 34-46, 53, 66, 84-85, 131, 179, 181, 205, 214, 253

Information Retrieval Facility, 27, 39-40

Information Seeking, 43-47, 49-52, 54, 84

Information Society, 23, 25-26, 165-175, 235

Information System, 91, 97, 102, 128, 182-184, 255 261, 263-269

Information System Development, 259

Integrated Data Management, 189

Internet And Information Availability, 151

K

Knowledge Organization, 129, 175

L

Localized Governance, 164

Logic Of Information, 202

M

Management Information System, 259, 264-266

Manual Data Processing, 176

Mean Average Precision, 31, 34

N

Network Connectivity, 115

O

Off-line Storage, 110-114

Ontology (information Science), 116

Operationalising Information Management, 92

P

Philosophy Of Information, 202-203

Physical Data Architecture, 183

Portable Methods, 72-74

Primary Storage, 107-109, 111-115

Programming Language Theory, 7, 14

Programming Tools, 225

R

Robotic Storage, 115-116

Routing And Service Tiers, 235

S

Scientific Goals, 41

Secondary Storage, 108-110, 112

Semantic Data Modeling, 104

Semantic Supercomputing, 42

Semi-portable Methods, 73-74

Software, 1, 5, 10, 12-15, 18, 20-21, 40, 53-54, 62 65, 69-70, 81, 91, 96-97, 102, 104, 116, 120, 122 124, 155, 159, 162-164, 175, 178-180, 182, 184, 186, 188, 195, 204, 219, 221-229, 232, 235-241, 245, 251-253, 255-258, 260, 265, 267

Software Engineering, 12-14, 18, 40, 53, 97, 102, 116, 124, 204, 222

Strategic Management, 89, 133-139, 143, 149, 154, 156-157, 159

Strategic Planning, 134, 136-139, 142, 146-147, 154, 249, 262

Strategic Thinking, 134, 146-147, 156, 158-159

T

Technological Capacity, 21, 72, 166-167

Telecommuting, 248

Tertiary Storage, 108-111, 115

Theoretical Computer Science, 12-13, 15, 178

Theory Of Computation, 7, 12-13

U

Upper Ontology, 119-120, 125-127

V

Value Chain, 91, 138, 145, 150, 161, 248

W

World Wide Web Applications, 68